More Praise for *The Art* ⟨

M000286798

"If you could have only one book in your library that presents the latest research on training, choose this one. It is a veritable tour de force that cleverly combines the perspectives of art and science. With wonderful insights including learning theory, technology, enhanced delivery, and the latest research on transfer, this is destined to be the bible of treatises on learning and development."

—Jack Zenger, CEO, Zenger Folkman, Bestselling Author, The Extraordinary Leader

"Elaine Biech has captured several key validations for me within the same chapter: 'learners do better when they are solving a problem' and a 'moderate amount of stress helps in the learning process.' Now I know why as a lifelong complex problem solver, I love being in the mix of learning from these challenges!"

—Rear Admiral (ret) Gib Godwin, Managing Director, PricewaterhouseCoopers

"Training and development and teaching professionals in all types of organizations have long needed practical but sound advice on how best to approach the baffling task of helping others learn. Elaine Biech's book and its intuitive and easy-to-access structure fill the bill to a T."

—Robert O. Brinkerhoff, Professor Emeritus, Western Michigan University

"*The Art and Science of Training* provides the perfect balance between scientific fact and the artistic elements that, when combined, make training impactful, meaningful, and engaging. I strongly recommend this book for practitioners who want to raise the bar on their training design and for academics who want to complement their scientific teachings with real-world examples and application."

—Karl Kapp, Professor of Instructional Technology, Bloomsburg University,
Author, The Gamification of Learning and Instruction

"Elaine Biech nailed it from the title to the last page—training truly is an art and science. But how many trainers can say they've mastered the art or truly understand the brain science? Whether you've been in the industry for days or decades, *The Art and Science of Training* is a go-to guide for your professional library. The Bob Pike Group pioneered instructor-led, participant-centered training 40 years ago, and this book earns our stamp of approval."

—Becky Pike Pluth, CEO, The Bob Pike Group

"I've always believed that the longest distance in training is the 15 inches from a participant's head to his or her heart. When attempting to provide the transformational experience for the learner, the trainer must connect with both (and understand why). In *The Art and Science of Training*, you'll examine the 'how' and the 'why' for making this a part of every session you lead. Through this rich and timely behind-the-curtain look, Elaine Biech shows you how to consistently lead sessions in which your learners hear, see, and feel what you're saying—and do something with it."

—Jim "Mr. Energy" Smith Jr., Author, Speaker, Trainer, Coach,
President and CEO, Jim Smith Jr. International

"In the search for understanding learners better, Elaine Biech has simplified a vast, complex topic by presenting practical information supported by research and experience. In *The Art and Science of Training*, you'll discover countless gems connecting the science of training with the art of facilitation. This is a must-read for anyone who wants to better connect with today's learners and be a more effective facilitator."

—Julie Straw, Vice President of Assessment Solutions, John Wiley & Sons

"Practical, credible, insightful, useful, immediately relevant, research-based—*The Art and Science of Training* is the most valuable guide I've read in a long time. Elaine Biech takes us on a journey through the scientific foundation of learning and the artistic application of principles. Have you ever wondered how the research of Gagné and Knowles are best applied in today's world of virtual and social learning? Look no further. Elaine has done all the research for you!"

—Jenn Labin, Principal, TERP associates, Author, Real World Training Design

"Elaine Biech extols us to see training as both an art and a science. When you infuse objective research and scientific foundations with creativity and flexibility tailored to the learners' needs and your own style, the results can be epic. Don't let your training be stagnant— check out the many ideas, tips, and actionable insights in this book to become a master in our profession."

—Halelly Azulay, Author, Employee Development on a Shoestring, *Host,*
The TalentGrow Show podcast

"You really need to read this book, especially if you're a trainer or facilitator. The whole point of training is to improve the performance of the learner. As Elaine Biech masterfully shows, effective trainers need to deliver research-based content (science) in creative and imaginative ways (art). Read this book and you'll be a better trainer. Period."

—Bill Treasurer, Author, Leaders Open Doors

"Elaine Biech has put the entire 'system' of training together, explaining clearly the process and passion for our work in learning and development. She starts by clarifying the learners and the needs and then continues all the way through how to change performance when the learners get back to their workplace. These are big questions for us in our profession and questions we very often ignore. This book will have a place on my desk and be required reading for my team."

—*Lou Russell, Queen/CEO, Russell Martin & Associates*

"Trainers and instructional designers are truly engaged in work that demands creativity shaped by research evidence of methods that support learning. In this book, you will find a rare synthesis of how evidence-based research principles can be implemented in creative ways. It's a must-read practical and grounded guide for talent development professionals."

—*Ruth Colvin Clark, Author*, Evidence-Based Training Methods

"In *The Art and Science of Training*, we have a way to explain the science behind the magic we weave. If you are just starting out in the training field, no one can give you a better foundation than Elaine Biech. A self-taught trainer, she summarizes her years of experience into practical 'how-to' steps that make the science work for you while you use the artist within to encourage learning and create an environment conducive to the same. For those with more experience, she does a masterful job of cutting through all the 'neuroscience noise' that is all the rage, as she demonstrates chapter by chapter how the early cognitive science of training we have used for decades is still relevant. This is my new favorite go-to book to share with staff and colleagues, whether they are artists or scientists—or a little of both!"

—*Kathy Shurte, Performance and Training Manager, Florida Department of Transportation*

"Do you need to know the state of the training and development field today? If so, you want this book. It provides a concise, easy-to-read description of how the field has evolved. I strongly recommend it."

—*William J. Rothwell, President, Rothwell & Associates, Inc., Professor, Workforce, Education & Development, The Pennsylvania State University*

"*The Art and Science of Training* is a master class in instructional design and delivery. It includes decades of the best research on what makes training world class. And it's beautifully organized and accessible. Like a master teacher, the book is ready to inspire on every page to propel you beyond your current level of expertise. When you put what you read into action, your participants will produce workplace outcomes beyond expectation."

—*Calhoun Wick, Founder, Fort Hill Company*

"*The Art and Science of Training* enthusiastically celebrates reality—you can't have one without the other! Embedded in every chapter are crucial training tools to ensure trainers have a balanced game plan for learning. Elaine Biech has done it again—this book is a great guide for a relevant learning strategy that works!"

—*Pamela J. Schmidt, Executive Director, ISA—The Association of Learning Providers*

"Regardless of your knowledge or experience, this book must be in the library of every talent development and human resources professional. Elaine Biech eloquently summarizes extensive scientific background in familiar terms. Her thought-provoking questions make you think and apply a step-by-step approach to delivery as an art form that guarantees success."

—*Norma Dávila and Wanda Piña-Ramírez, Partners, The Human Factor Consulting Group, Authors,* Cutting Through the Noise *and* Passing the Torch

"If you're a training professional who wants to ensure success for your learners, then Elaine Biech's new book, *The Art and Science of Training*, is for you. She shares training secrets from both the science (data) point of view as well as the art (creative) point of view. Both sides are important, both sides are needed, and you will appreciate how skillfully she weaves them together. You'll gain clarity on the reasons why certain activities are a hit in your classes and gain confidence in creating new exercises to achieve results."

—*Cindy Huggett, Author,* The Virtual Training Guidebook

"Most people think of training as soft skills and not related to hard skills such as science or the creative skill of art. Who better to help us understand this relationship than training guru Elaine Biech? I fell in love with her recipe analogy. In a delicious recipe, there is science to the ingredient proportions but there is also the art of knowing when you need to improvise to make it delicious. The same is true with your training. I highly recommend *The Art and Science of Training* for both seasoned and new learning and development professionals."

—*Deborah Covin Wilson, Director, Organizational Development and Consulting Services, Georgia State University*

"*The Art and Science of Training* is a masterful look at the profession of adult learning and talent development. Elaine Biech captures the essence of what it really takes to design and deliver effective learning and development programs. She reminds us that 'it's all about the learner,' while at the same time emphasizes the importance of the facilitator's role to balance technique and style to bring it all together for the learner."

—*Maureen Orey, Founder, Workplace Learning & Performance Group*

The Art and Science of Training

Elaine Biech

PRESS

ATD Press is an internationally renowned source of insightful and practical information on talent development, workplace learning, and professional development.

ATD Press
1640 King Street
Alexandria, VA 22314 USA

Ordering information: Books published by ATD Press can be purchased by visiting ATD's website at www.td.org/books or by calling 800.628.2783 or 703.683.8100.

Library of Congress Control Number: 2016957823

ISBN-10: 1-60728-094-9
ISBN-13: 978-1-60728-094-1
e-ISBN: 978-1-60728-095-8

ATD Press Editorial Staff
Director: Kristine Luecker
Manager: Christian Green
Senior Associate Editor: Melissa Jones
Associate Director, Communities of Practice: Justin Brusino
Text Design: Iris Sanchez
Cover Design: Emily Weigel, Faceout Studio

Printed by Versa Press, Inc., East Peoria, IL

For Shane and Thad
who taught me the value of asking questions
and the wisdom of replying creatively.

Contents

Acknowledgments

Those of you who know me know how important ASTD and now ATD have been in my life. It has given me a lifetime of learning and development. It has provided an enthusiastic laboratory for me to try out my own scientific hypotheses. It has offered me many blank canvases for dabbling in my art to create books, conference presentations, and certificate programs. I value every staff member with whom I've interacted, every committee I've supported, and every opportunity I've had to lend an ear or a hand when I could. ATD is responsible for my professional happiness in finding the work I love.

Thank you, Justin Brusino, for inviting me to write this book. "Art and Science" immediately excited me, then confused me, then terrified me! The topic is so vast; science so precise; art so innovative. Could I do it? After weeks and weeks of investigating the research, clarifying the creative, and stacking the results in piles around my office, I decided I was ready. Then I read a quote from one of my just-for-fun authors that said, "But even Picasso had classical training. You have to know what the rules are before you break them." At that point I became energized and couldn't wait to start. It's been another fantastic learning experience. Thank you.

As I write in the book, all trainers owe a great deal to those learning leaders who came before us. A partial list includes Malcolm Knowles, Robert Gagné, Robert Mager, Howard Gardner, Kurt Lewin, Benjamin Bloom, B.F. Skinner, Jerome Bruner, Albert Bandura, Abraham Maslow, David Kolb, Walter Dick, Lou Carey, M. David Merrill, Hermann Ebbinghaus, Michael Lombardo, and

Robert Eichinger. And, yes, there are certainly others who deserve to be on this list.

Again, thank you to Justin Brusino, the man who imagines exciting projects that provide benefit to ATD members. Thanks for inviting me to be a part of this one. Thank you to Christian Green, editor extraordinaire, who ferreted out my funky phrases and presented better ways to say what I actually meant. Thanks to everyone at ATD Press who help make all of us authors look good and to everyone in the marketing department who help make our products look even better. And of course, thank you to Tony Bingham for once again leading the way for those of us in the talent development profession.

Introduction

Writing *The Art and Science of Training* is a once-in-a-lifetime opportunity. The name is one of those titles that exudes both intelligence and passion. But what does it mean? A quick search on Amazon led me to these books: *The Art and Science of Negotiation, The Art and Science of Low Carbohydrate Living, The Art and Science of Cytopathology, The Art and Science of Getting What You Want, The Art and Science of Leadership, The Art and Science of Hand Reading, The Art and Science of Java. The Art and . . .* well, you get the idea. I assumed these titles would offer some insight into the "art and science" framework.

- Art: The creative, imaginative, artistic, free-wheeling perspective.
- Science: The logical, data, research, testing numbers perspective.

Unfortunately, they didn't and I realized that these authors were not treating art and science as two different topics.

What does "art and science" mean? Do the paths of art and science cross? Do similarities exist? What is the relationship between science and art? Do scientists find value in art? Do artists find value in science? Do scientists stay in their logical, data-driven lane? Do artists maintain their innovative, unique mystique? Let's view a couple of examples.

Leonardo da Vinci is best known as an artist, but his works were informed by his scientific investigation. He studied physiology and anatomy to create accurate images of people. Claude Monet, Edgar Degas, and Vincent van Gogh all studied the physiological, psychological, and phenomenal effects of color and light before they created their masterpieces (Eskridge n.d.)

Albert Einstein, one of the world's greatest physicists, was also a great pianist and violinist. He believed that "all great achievements of science must start from intuitive knowledge" (Calaprice 2000). He stated in no uncertain terms that the Theory of Relativity was a "musical thought that came to him intuitively." It seems that the artistic qualities of music would guide him in new and creative directions.

Another scientist, Jonas Salk, strongly believed that art and science go hand-in-hand. The institute that bears Salk's name is recognized by scientists around the world for research in neurobiology and stem cells, but it also plays host to symphonies and artists such as glass sculptor Dale Chihuly.

"I am enough of an artist to draw freely upon my imagination. Imagination is more important than knowledge."

—Albert Einstein

Although it would seem that data-driven science and emotion-driven art are different, there are more similarities than differences between how artists and scientists work. Both ask many questions. Both search for answers. Both are dedicated to achieving the "best" outcome, whatever that might be. DaVinci said, "Art is the queen of all sciences communicating knowledge to all the generations of the world."

Whether the result is from the world of science or the world of art, it seems that science is the basis. Picasso, for example, succeeded at Cubism after becoming an accomplished representational painter. The science of the skill is the foundation, but the passionate use of art creates spectacular results.

Could it be that the connection between art and science goes back as far as the Egyptian pyramids? Certainly someone had an artistic vision of a beautiful potential structure. Perhaps another possessed the mathematical and scientific knowledge of how the vision could become a reality. Combining the artistic vision and scientific methods produced one of the Seven Wonders of the Ancient World.

Art and Science in Training

Although development strategies should clearly be based on sound science and research, knowing when to use them and with whom is more of an art. This book's title was selected to convey that effective training is both art and science. It is an art in the sense that effective trainers are as varied as their effective techniques. It is a science in the sense that there are effective learning strategies supported by research. These strategies are tools in a trainer's toolbox. All trainers use these tools in different ways and at different times. Research will never be able to define a one-way-works-best approach. Excellent trainers will continue to create approaches that fit between the lines. And we are all thankful that they do.

The Art and Science of Training is like a recipe. It's about understanding the science behind best practices (for example, what proportions of butter to flour to milk to sugar make the best cake) and where a little spicing up will make it taste better (for example, adding cocoa, cinnamon, or salt). A professional baker is astute enough to know when something will work "by the book" and when it needs pecans or chocolate chips to make it even better. As a trainer you know when the addition of novelty is required to get the desired results.

Art and science have always been interconnected and they naturally overlap. Whether you think of your training role more like a scientist who is discovering or an artist who is originating, both require dedication and an innate, intrinsic desire to develop others.

It's all about looking for the right blend to support the needs of your learners and the organization. You have various techniques from which you can select: live classroom sessions, online instructor-led sessions, games, informal learning opportunities, on-the-job experiences, reading, social learning, performance support, self-paced asynchronous courses, MOOCs, coaching, and mentoring, to name a few. You have an opportunity to try these different approaches and determine the right mix of blended learning. When you have the science within you, adding your artistic touches will only make your training better.

Both science and art help trainers define the qualities that make them great facilitators. Both science and art help them deliver what their learners need. Know the science and apply your art to facilitate others' learning.

Chapter Design

In the chapters that follow, I present both an artistic and a scientific strategy. Each chapter has a common design: The title of each chapter is a question. That question is answered at the end of the chapter after both the scientific data and the artistic ideas are presented to you.

Although I have not separated the science from the art exclusively, I do emphasize that the smart people who laid the foundation for the training profession knew what they were doing. The experts who conducted research, evaluated results, and documented valid conclusions still guide learning practices, ensuring that training is done correctly. Therefore the content of each chapter is summarized with a list of the scientific facts: "What We Know for Sure." You will find facts that guide how we design, deliver, and evaluate learning options.

"The Art Part" presents ideas that you can use immediately to implement some of the concepts in each chapter. You can enjoy putting your own artistic spin on each and using them with your team or your learners.

Finally, any good research that looks into the future should produce more questions than answers. And so it is with this book. View the questions in "Art and Science Questions You Might Ask" as a challenge for you to create your own mini-hypotheses.

Know the science; apply your art.

"There are only two ways to live your life. One is as though nothing is a miracle. The other is as though everything is a miracle."

—Albert Einstein

Resources

Calaprice, A., ed. 2000. *The Expanded Quotable Einstein*. Princeton, NJ: Princeton University Press.

Eskridge, R. n.d. "The Enduring Relationship of Science and Art." The Art Institute of Chicago, Science, Art, and Technology Program. www.artic.edu/aic/education/sciarttech/2a1.html.

What Is the Science and Art of Training?

The Greek philosopher Aristotle once declared that "Teaching is the highest form of understanding," meaning that one who teaches has the deepest understanding of the topic. That's still true today. I'm no Greek philosopher, but I'd like to suggest that another way to view learning is that "Understanding is the highest form of teaching."

It seems that to truly facilitate learning for others, trainers must understand them first; learning comes after that. Trying to impart knowledge without thoroughly understanding the learner is like venturing into enemy territory without first doing reconnaissance. Success happens because you understand others; it's not from understanding the content.

This book examines this point through science and artistic perspectives. Let's establish a few definitions to make sure we both have the same foundation and are using the same language. Are you a facilitator, trainer, talent development professional, teacher, instructor, designer, or something else? What distinguishes learners, participants, trainees, and students? How about the difference between training, educating, and instructing? And finally, what's the difference between learning, knowledge, skills, and performance?

Who's Who?

Our profession has debated for years about what to call ourselves. This book does not attempt to resolve that issue. Instead it will help you find the best way to help others learn and develop. What you do is much more important than what you call yourself. So what's in a name? Here are my thoughts:

- *Facilitators* make sure learners take an active role in their learning; the term is sometimes interchangeable with trainers.
- *Trainers* are the learning catalysts that help adults learn new skills and obtain knowledge; their role is interchangeable with facilitators.
- *Talent developer* is the newest name bestowed upon us.
- *Presenters* deliver speeches at conferences or to larger groups; there is a minimal amount of emphasis on two-way communication.
- *Instructors* are teachers typically found in academia. They may also teach a specific skill set, such as tennis instructors or flight instructors.
- *Teachers* instruct children and focus on pedagogy.

What about the terms for individuals who receive training?

- *Learner* is a neutral term that can be used for anyone gaining information.
- *Participant* is a general term used by facilitators and trainers to refer to anyone in a learning or training session; that is, a learner.
- *Trainee* is synonymous with *participant*; the term has most recently been replaced by *learners* or *participants*. It may not project professionalism, especially when the learners are employed beyond entry-level jobs.
- *Student* is used for young children—again, pedagogical.

You will find that I use *facilitator, trainer,* and *talent development professional*. I also prefer *learner* or *participant*. These words send a message that says this is adult learning for adults.

What's What?

The activity that occurs between the facilitator and the learner in the preceding section may be called any of these:

- *Facilitating* may be interchanged with the term *training*. It usually refers to taking less of a leading role and being more of a catalyst of learning.
- *Training* is the activity conducted by adults who are learning new skills. Knowledge is generally put to immediate use; hands-on practice is included.
- *Instructing* allows participants to generalize beyond what has been taught. It involves minimal hands-on practice, but sounds too much like a college class to me.
- *Teaching* and *educating* generally impart knowledge in a broader context with delayed implementation. Historically there is little hands-on practice and both suggest pedagogical learning.

I prefer *facilitating* because it implies that you are enabling learners; pulling it out of them rather than pushing learning toward them.

The Results?

So what do learners take away from the activities? Each of the following, when training is done correctly:

- *Learning* is gaining knowledge and skills to make change.
- *Knowledge* is gaining cognitive competence and information assimilation.
- *Skill development* is gaining psychomotor competence and the ability to perform better or in a new way.
- *Attitude* is the willingness to change based on new knowledge.
- *Performance* is the ability to implement the knowledge and skills that have been learned.

You may find other labels for these roles and what occurs; as the profession grows and changes you're likely to find even more. What you call yourself is not nearly as important as the significant work you accomplish: Helping adults learn so they can improve their performance.

Does label choice make a difference? In their groundbreaking research, neuroscientist Andrew Newberg and Loyola professor Mark Waldman discovered a valuable communication strategy that includes the power of words. They write: "a single word has the power to influence the expression of genes that regulate physical and emotional stress" (Newberg and Waldman 2012). They found that the use of words, both positive and negative, can be recorded on an fMRI scan. You can see an increase of activity in the amygdala and the release of dozens of hormones and neurotransmitters when we listen to someone speak. Single words have the ability to support or interrupt the normal functions of the brain, such as those involved with logic, reason, language processing, and communication.

Adults may have negative memories of school, which they could bring with them to your training. Why use words such as *teacher*, *lesson plan*, or *student* if they may generate negative memories—especially if you don't need to. If science tells you words can make a difference, be artful and use terms and labels that have a more positive connotation. For example, use *learner* instead of *student* or *project* instead of *homework*.

A Final Note

As training professionals, our role has been changing and expanding for some time. If you've coached managers about how to develop their people; if you've mentored senior leaders about how to best implement change; if you've led an initiative to build a department team; or if you've acted as a consultant to illustrate how social media can extend learning, you've experienced a trainer's changing role. We'll address these changes further in chapter 13.

Defining Science

This book is about the *art* and *science* of training, so it's important to define what that means. Remember coming up with a hypothesis for your science project back in sixth grade? "If (I do this) then (this) will happen." Remember studying the scientific method in high school?

The word *science* probably conjures up a variety of images: your biology textbook, white lab coats, microscopes, telescopes, Einstein's equations scribbled on a chalkboard, the space shuttle launch, bubbling beakers. These images reflect an aspect of science, but none provides a complete picture because science has so many facets.

Science is both a body of knowledge and a process. You might remember studying the Mohs scale, the laws of motion, the periodic table of elements, or differential calculus. Equally important to all the facts is the process of discovery that allows you to link isolated facts into a comprehensive understanding of the natural world. This process is the scientific method. It is the process of asking scientific questions and conducting experiments. The steps of the scientific method are:

1. Ask a question.
2. Do background research.
3. Construct a hypothesis.
4. Test your hypothesis by conducting an experiment.
5. Analyze your data and draw a conclusion.
6. Communicate your results.

So what, you might ask. Well, the science part of this book ferrets out the facts and processes that create a foundation of understanding and the body of knowledge that trainers call their profession. The science of training provides a way to discover what's new and what works. Knowledge generated by science is powerful and reliable. It can be used to develop new training techniques or address current problems. It's exciting that science will continue to expand our knowledge of the profession.

Most of what we do as trainers is based on scientific research conducted by Gagné, Bloom, Skinner, and a host of others. These researchers conducted studies, evaluated the results, and presented valid conclusions about what really works—separating fact from fiction. But it isn't all facts and logic. Training is also dynamic and creative, so we'll also look at the "art" of training.

Defining Art

When you hear the word *art*, what comes to mind? Perhaps you think about paintings, art galleries, sculptures, a ballet, or a concert. Like science, art has many facets; though presented from a different perspective.

Art is the expression or application of a diverse range of human creative skills and imagination. It is typically presented in visual form, but can also be auditory or performing works intended to be appreciated for their beauty or emotional power.

Again, you might be thinking, so what? Well everything doesn't always occur the way science says it should. There will always be exceptions to the rule: the unwilling learner, the uninformed supervisor, the inappropriate delivery medium, mismatched content, or the unmanageable performance challenge. When you come upon these—and I am sure you have—you need to think on your feet and become an artist of sorts. You need to paint a new plan and sculpt a successful learning experience for all of your learners.

As stated in the previous section, this book provides the science for learning and development, but it's important to recognize that success is all about Plan B: what you do when things don't follow the rules of science. There will be plenty of opportunities to put on your artist's beret and create Plan B for your learners. I've been in many "what's-Plan-B" scenarios, so I can speak of successes, mistakes, and experiences. That's the art.

The refrain throughout this book is, "It's all about the learner." It's important to make everything come together to ensure that your learners gain the knowledge and skills to improve their performance. You work in an exciting profession. You develop others through the art and science of training. When you put the learner first you ensure that "understanding is the highest form of teaching."

"The aim of art is to represent not the outward appearance of things, but their inward significance."

—Aristotle

Adults and Learning

There are a couple of points to make about the fundamentals of training. You're an adult and you are learning all the time. Think back over the past two months. What did you learn and why did you learn it? List two or three on a piece of paper or enter them on your tablet. Remember to list *what* you learned and *why* you learned it. You can use this format:

I learned _____, because _____.
          (what?)   (why?)

What did you learn? When your car had a flat tire, did you *need* to learn how to change it? When your supervisor asked you to prepare a plan for how your department could use mobile learning, did you *need* to conduct research to learn more? Do your friends golf, so you also *want* to learn? Does your neighbor bake delicious bread, so you *want* to learn her secrets? These examples illustrate that almost all of what you learn as an adult is steeped in your desires. You either *need* to learn something to solve a problem or you *want* to learn something to satisfy yourself.

Review your examples again. What did you discover about why you learn? Generally you will find that you learned something because you need to learn it or want to learn it. This is somewhat different from children who learn something in school to prepare to learn something at the next stage of their lives. For example, you learned to count to 10 as a child so that when you reached school you could learn to add. You learned to add so that you could learn to subtract and multiply. Later you used this knowledge so that you could learn algebra, trigonometry, and calculus.

Adult Learning Theory—Not Just for Adults

Adult learning theory is not only for adults. It is also a great way for children to learn. Many U.S. schools have started to implement concepts similar to adult learning strategies, such as learning in teams, respecting learners, and helping learners relate the content to their real world. I have always been a proponent that learning should be fun and relevant for everyone!

It's All About the Learner

Carl Rogers first introduced the concept of "learner-centered learning." In their book, *Telling Ain't Training*, Harold Stolovitch and Erica Keeps support Rogers' concept. They admonish us to remember their mantra, "learner centered . . . performance based . . . learner centered . . . performance based." Why? They want their readers to remember that these are the keys to transforming learners.

They have found that most trainers begin any quest to train by looking at the content. However, they argue that trainers should first focus on the learners' needs, concerns, desires, fears, frustrations, and characteristics. I couldn't agree more. Focus on the learner. It's not about covering content. It's about helping the learner do something better, faster, easier. It's about transformation.

Sure, easy for me to write that. But you've got a real program with pages of material supported by dozens of PowerPoint slides. You will be evaluated on how well you complete all the activities. You are measured on how thoroughly you deliver your material. In addition, the three-hour classroom has been cut to a 90-minute virtual training session. This is when you tap into the art of training. Here are a few ideas to start your thinking. There will be more in the upcoming chapters.

- Mind the time basics. Start your session on time. Start on time after every break, even if it means you might start without some participants. Use timekeepers for activities.

- Organize your materials and yourself. Use the most efficient method for distributing materials—perhaps set them up on the tables ahead of time.
- Prepare to run out of time: Know what content can be shortened, mentioned as a reference, or even be skipped completely.
- Manage large group discussions. Time can get away from you during group discussions. If everyone isn't interested and involved, you could be frittering away valuable minutes.
- In a virtual session, the biggest time waster can be at the start: too much time spent on introductions, logistics, or how to use the tools. It's not that these aren't important; simply find the most efficient way to handle them, including prior to the event.
- Use pre- and post-training strategies: video introductions; pre-reading; participant- and supervisor-guided discussions; learning what's most important to participants and their supervisors; or developing checklists, job aids, and tip sheets that make the learning go faster and can be used after the training event.

Yes, the content is important, but what is the best way to help your participants learn to improve their performance? What's the best use of their time? It's all about the learner.

Tapping Into the Early Science of the Profession

Many people have contributed to the foundation of the training profession. It is less important to be able to repeat their theories, but it is critical that you know how to implement their theories for training and development. And it's important to understand their value. Let's begin by looking at Instructional Systems Design (ISD), Bloom's Taxonomy, and Gagné's Conditions of Learning.

"He who loves practice without theory is like the sailor who boards a ship without a rudder and compass and never knows where he may cast."

—Leonardo da Vinci

The Training Cycle

The training cycle, commonly called Instructional Systems Design (ISD), is the first thing trainers think about when designing or developing training programs. ISD models have been around since the 1950s. ADDIE is the most familiar and was developed initially by the U.S. military to effectively create training programs. The acronym ADDIE represents the five steps required to design, deliver, and continue to improve the delivery of training:

- analyze
- design
- develop
- implement
- evaluate.

It's important to picture these steps in a circular model to serve as a reminder that training needs to be continually improved. The model was originally developed by Florida State University and was presented as a linear model in 1981 by Russell Watson, chief of the staff and faculty training division at Fort Huachuca, Arizona.

Figure 1-1: The Training Cycle

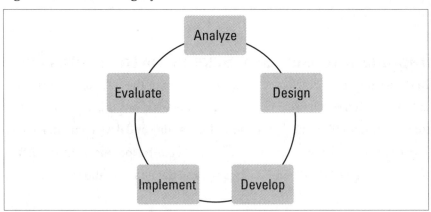

The training cycle starts with an analysis. Evaluate is the final step of the cycle, but once you move around it the first time you'll use what you learn during evaluation as input to analyze the results and determine if it is the best it can be. This training cycle is used whether you are designing from scratch or just tailoring a training program you purchased from a vendor.

Analyze

The first stage of the training cycle is called analysis in the ADDIE acronym. Generally, you need to conduct an assessment and analyze the data to identify specific needs. There are two main reasons for completing an assessment and analysis.

First, you want to make sure there is a reason to conduct training. You may discover after conducting the analysis that the relevant issue can be addressed by something other than training. For example, you may be able to do on-the-job coaching; or online content may exist that could be delivered either asynchronously or synchronously; or you may believe an article in the company newsletter alerts employees to the information needed. Or you may find that the issue isn't the learners' performance at all. Perhaps it is a process or equipment or another issue unrelated to your learners.

Second, if you do determine that training is necessary, the analysis tells you exactly what should be taught in the training session. It also helps determine your training objectives.

There are many ways to conduct assessments. You can use a formal instrument that measures a person's skill or knowledge, or one that simply measures a person's preference. You can also use written questionnaires or personal interviews with employees or supervisors. If you use interviews, you can meet with individuals one-on-one or conduct small focus groups. Another way to assess a need is to observe an employee working or to take a work sample. Or you can obtain records or reports that already exist.

Your goal in collecting the data is to determine the gap between a job requirement and an individual's actual skill or knowledge. The bottom line is to determine what is preventing the desired performance. You will need this information for the next stage of the training cycle.

Design

After you have determined that there is a legitimate training requirement, your next step is to state exactly what you want the training to accomplish. You do this by writing objectives. Two kinds of objectives from two perspectives are used in training.

The Learning or Performance Objective

This is a statement of the desired performance (knowledge or skill) after the training has been conducted. It doesn't matter whether you call them learning or performance objectives, as long as you understand that the purpose is to demonstrate what your participants have learned and can perform. What behavior changes did they make? Learning objectives should be based on the information you discovered during the analysis step. For example, at the end of this training session, "Participants will be able to design participant-focused learning activities."

The Training Objective

This is a statement of what the instructor hopes to accomplish during the training session. This may be an outcome, or it may be a description of what the instructor plans to do to accomplish the learning objectives. For example, "This session will create a positive learning climate that encourages participants to get involved and ask questions."

Some trainers include both learning and training objectives in their design. Learning objectives are a required step in every good training design. Training objectives help the trainer to focus on designing and delivering a first-class training program by setting targets for the trainer to achieve.

Learners are informed of the learning objectives at the beginning of a training session, and it's preferable that they are also told about the training content at the same time.

Develop

After you determine the objectives, you can begin to develop the program. This is the stage of the training cycle that I like best. You decide exactly what you're going to do to accomplish the objectives you set. There are many things to consider in designing a training program.

If you haven't already, you will decide which type of delivery will achieve the best results based on your analysis: on-site classroom, virtual classroom, self-paced e-learning, performance support tools, self-study, or a combination of these and others in a blended learning solution. These questions will help determine the type and location of the training program:

- How many participants need new knowledge or skills?
- What performance is required?
- Where are participants located?
- How much time is required?
- How much consistency is needed?
- When is training required?
- How many participants will be in each class?
- What level of trainer expertise will be required?

You may also decide whether you even need to develop the content. Given the availability of thousands of off-the-shelf products, you may decide to purchase predesigned content and customize it. In addition to ensuring that learning objectives are met, consider the following:

- your audience
- the best training techniques
- how to provide opportunities to practice
- what will be meaningful
- how they will implement learning in the real world
- how it will improve performance
- how to add creativity to the program.

You should also build in methods to ensure that the learning is applied back on the job, as well as a process to evaluate the program's effectiveness.

If you design the training, it will be a big task to develop the materials. What participant materials do the learners need? What audiovisual materials and equipment will you use? If it is an online course, what technical support will you require? Will your learners require job aids—either paper or electronic? While this stage can be exciting, it can also be exhausting.

Implement

This is the training cycle stage during which you actually conduct the training program. There is a huge amount of preparation before the program. And even after taking the time to prepare, there is no guarantee that it will go off without a hitch. That's why some trainers pilot a program with a group of pseudolearners who provide feedback before the session is ready.

Trainers use presentation and facilitation skills in both the traditional and virtual classroom.

- Presenters provide more information. If much of the information is new or technical, trainers may need to present. The preferred role, however, is as a facilitator.
- Facilitators are catalysts who are tasked with ensuring learners' participation. A good trainer is often synonymous with the term *facilitator*.

Excellent delivery skills are required whether you're facilitating a virtual or traditional classroom. While conducting the training, you want to constantly read your audience to find out whether you're meeting their needs. If you see that an approach isn't working, stop and try another. Don't be afraid to stray from the agenda if it will be more helpful to the learners. This is the stage during which platform experience and good facilitation skills are required.

Evaluate

When it's over, it's not actually over. The evaluation stage is an important part of the training cycle for three reasons:

- First, the evaluation tells you whether the objectives were accomplished.
- Second, information from the evaluation stage should be fed into the analyze stage. It is used to improve the training program should it be conducted again. This is why this model is circular.

- Finally, evaluation information serves as the basis for determining needs for future programs or other changes an organization may need to make.

The stages and the science behind them will be addressed in more depth starting in chapter 3, "How Do You Design So Others Can Learn?" ADDIE presents a good ISD basis, and organizations often adapt or combine concepts to create their own customized model.

Is ADDIE Too Old and Cumbersome?

I'm sure you've heard the battle to "leave ADDIE" for SAM because ADDIE is too old, too cumbersome, too rigid, and has outlived its usefulness. Maybe it's the training profession. Maybe it's a need to be a guru. Maybe it's just human nature to sensationalize when possible. Rather than adapt a good thing, the training profession often wants to get rid of it and create something new. This is confusing to new trainers who are trying to understand the elements of the profession, the acronyms, and the jargon! If you've heard the battle of ADDIE vs. Agile vs. SAM, I suggest that you stick with ADDIE.

Here's the rest of the story. Because ADDIE has been around since the 1970s, it is believed to be outdated and too rigid for practical use. I'm a self-taught trainer and I have used ADDIE all my life. No one told me that it was rigid, so I used common sense and made it my tool, increasing agility when needed.

The perceived advantage of Agile is that the model allows you to share your mockups, prototypes, and early suggestions with the customer, allowing you to adjust along the way. No one ever told me that I was not allowed to do that with ADDIE, so I do work with my customers right from the start. It's just common sense. Feel free to explore other options, but I recommend that you use ADDIE and add what works for you. This is a great example of making the science work for you using your creative side.

Is ADDIE outdated? The U.S. Armed Forces doesn't think so. They have been using it quite successfully in today's VUCA (volatile, uncertain, complex, and ambiguous) environment. In case you are unaware, the U.S. military invented the term *VUCA*.

Bloom's Taxonomy

In the early 1950s, Benjamin Bloom and a university committee identified three learning domains: cognitive, psychomotor, and affective. Because the project was completed by academics, the terms may seem a bit abstract. Trainers typically use knowledge (cognitive), skills (psychomotor), and attitude (affective)—frequently referred to as KSAs—to describe the three categories of learning. You may think of these as the ultimate goal of the training process—what your learner acquires as a result of training.

Bloom's group further expanded on the domains, creating a hierarchical ordering of the cognitive and affective learning outcomes. Their work subdivided each domain, starting from the simplest behavior to the most complex: knowledge, comprehension, application, analysis, synthesis, and evaluation (Table 1-1). Each level builds on the earlier one. For example, knowledge must occur prior to comprehension; comprehension must occur before application. Each level of learning identifies a desired specific, observable, and measurable result.

Table 1-1: Bloom's Taxonomy

Behavioral Level	Skills	Examples
Knowledge	Define, list, name, recall, or repeat knowledge or information.	Name six levels of Bloom's Taxonomy.
Comprehension	Translate, describe, or explain information in your own words.	Explain Bloom's six levels.
Application	Apply, demonstrate, or use knowledge in new situations.	Apply Bloom's theory to write learning objectives.
Analysis	Analyze, compare, question, or break knowledge into parts.	Compare and contrast aspects of Bloom's model.
Synthesis	Arrange, create, plan, or prepare a new whole from parts.	Design a new learning model.
Evaluation	Appraise, assess, judge, or score information based on knowledge.	Evaluate and defend the benefits of Bloom's Taxonomy.

This work is known as Bloom's Taxonomy, and the research will help you in the design and the delivery phases of training (Bloom et al. 1956). The learning categories are not absolute, and other systems and hierarchies have been developed since then. Bloom's Taxonomy, however, is easily understood and may be the most widely applied to learning objectives.

Gagné's Conditions of Learning

Robert Gagné and his Conditions of Learning provide the third body of knowledge that forms foundational concepts for you as a trainer. Learning theories attempt to describe what is happening when people learn. A learning theory leads to learning strategies, tactics, and experiences that support the theory.

"Learning theories try to provide conceptual structures involved in the process of taking in information and getting it transformed so that it is stored in long-term memory and later recalled as an observable human performance."
—Robert Gagné

Gagné identified nine instructional events. Applying these events to your training is helpful and ensures that learning will occur. Here are Gagné's Instructional Events:

- Gain the learners' attention.
- Share the objectives of the session.
- Ask learners to recall prior learning.
- Deliver the content.
- Use methods to enhance understanding; for example, case studies, examples, graphs.
- Provide an opportunity to practice.
- Provide feedback.
- Assess performance.
- Provide job aids or references to ensure transfer to the job.

If you've been around the training field for a while, you know that these events are commonplace and are assumed to be a part of any effective training program. If you are new to the training field, add these to your list of steps required to ensure effective training.

We'll refer to these three theories—The Training Cycle, Bloom's Taxonomy, and Gagné's Conditions of Learning—in the next chapter, "How Do You Learn?"

What We Know for Sure

Science tells us that we can rely on several proven facts:

- Words matter. Choose yours carefully.
- Adults learn because they want to or need to.
- Training is all about the learner.
- Using an ISD model ensures an efficient and effective process.
- The ADDIE ISD model is effective.
- Bloom's Taxonomy is an excellent resource for setting objectives.
- A wealth of practical advice is embedded in Gagné's Conditions of Learning.

The Art Part

Your success will depend upon how well you adapt to the situation and your learners' needs. Tap into some of these ideas to help your learners grow, to develop yourself, and to add your personal creative touch.

Make ADDIE work for you. When people complain that the ADDIE model takes too long, I ask what they are doing to shorten the time. I work iteratively between the design and development stages. To me they are one step. That way I don't get too far along with making a decision that "officially" falls into the design phase before moving to the development phase and learning that I have too little time or not enough variety in my activities. This is much more efficient than working in a linear fashion—doing all design first before you start development. I also build evaluation into every ADDIE step to ensure I'm planning with the end in mind.

Partner with your client. If you use ADDIE, connect with your client or customer early and often. Share your learning objectives and preliminary plan to create a dialogue. Don't worry if it is not perfect and pretty. You are in a partnership and both of you want the best for the learners and the best for the organization.

 ## Art and Science Questions You Might Ask

These questions provide you with potential challenges for your personal growth and development:

- What foundational content can you develop and improve?
- How well do you learn about your learners?
- How likely are you to start with the basics of a theory and creatively mold it to meet your learners' needs?
- How do you rate regarding keeping your learners' needs and desires at the forefront? What could you do better?

What Is the Science and Art of Training?

Well, that's the question, isn't it? This book presents the scientific angle, addressing humans, society, and the laws of existence. Science is expected to be free of subjectivity and is guided by a high level of consciousness. Science offers learners competence.

This book also presents the artistic angle, addressing the message that is grounded in emotion and intuition. Art is expected to affect emotions and create pleasure. Art offers learners confidence and commitment.

What is science and art? Imagine that science helps to explain *why* and art demonstrates *how*.

Resources

Barrow, J. 1991. *Theories of Everything.* Oxford, UK: Oxford University Press.

Biech, E. 2009. *10 Steps to Successful Training.* Alexandria, VA: ASTD Press.

———, ed. 2014. *ASTD Handbook: The Definitive Reference for Training and Development.* 2nd ed. Alexandria, VA: ASTD Press.

———. 2015. *Training Is the Answer: Making Learning and Development Work in China.* Fairfax, VA: Trainers Publishing House.

Bloom, B. 1968. *Learning for Mastery.* Los Angeles: The Center for the Study of Evaluation of Instructional Programs, University of California.

Bloom, B.S., M.D. Engelhart, E.J. Furst, W.H. Hill, and D.R. Krathwohl. 1956. *Taxonomy of Educational Objectives.* New York: Longman.

Gagné, R.M., W. Wager, K. Golas, and J. Keller. 2005. *Principles of Instructional Design.* 5th ed. Belmont, CA: Thomson/Wadsworth.

Newberg, A., and M.R. Waldman. 2012. *Words Can Change Your Brain: 12 Conversation Strategies to Build Trust, Resolve Conflict, and Increase Intimacy.* New York: Hudson Street Press.

Stolovitch, H., and E. Keeps. 2011. *Telling Ain't Training.* 2nd ed. Alexandria, VA: ASTD Press.

Watson, R. October 1981. *Instructional System Development.* Paper presented to the International Congress for Individualized Instruction. EDRS publication ED 209 239.

How Do You Learn?

What do you know about learning? Have you ever thought about it? You've been learning since you were born. In fact you can learn a great deal by observing how a baby learns. Volumes and volumes have been written about how people learn. In this chapter I only have space to scratch the surface. This chapter introduces you to key theories that provide solid grounding for how people learn.

Training is a method to enhance performance. Whenever a person's ability to perform a job is limited by a lack of knowledge or skill, there's an opportunity to bridge the gap by providing the required instruction.

Sounds simple, doesn't it? Not really. The problem begins with the fact that learning something you don't already know requires another person (a trainer) or medium (a book, smartphone, or computer) to provide it. Trainers need to think about not only what, but *how* they are covering the topic, making sure they do not prevent the learner from uncovering it themselves. This only happens by virtue of the learner's own activity. Ultimately, you—or a book or a computer—cannot do the work for the learner.

Ensuring that learning occurs requires knowledge of how adults learn and all the techniques available to you as a trainer. Most often the key to effective training is how the learning activities are designed and delivered—the participants should acquire the knowledge and skills rather than merely receive them.

Trainers do not deliver knowledge and skills; they facilitate learners to acquire them.

There is so much more to training than "show and tell." Learning is not an automatic consequence of pouring information into another's head. It requires the learner's own mental involvement and participation. Lecturing and demonstrating, by themselves, will not lead to real, lasting learning. Only trainers who facilitate participants to take control of their own needs will ensure learning lasts.

"Orville Wright didn't have a pilot's license."

—Richard Tate

What Happens When Learning Occurs?

As mentioned in chapter 1, there are four learning theories that attempt to describe what is happening when we learn:

- **Constructivism** focuses on knowledge acquisition through experiences and interactions with the environment. When you learn you use previous knowledge to "construct" new understanding.
- **Behaviorism** focuses on observable behavior and the reasons that learning occurs when strengthening or weakening associations between stimuli and responses. Learning designs would include chunking and creating objectives.
- **Cognitivism** is based on the idea that learning occurs when you store information in long-term memory. Learning is based on how content is processed, stored, and retrieved, relying on Gagné's nine conditions of learning.
- **Connectivism** explains how Internet technology has created new opportunities for learning by using networks to access information you need, when you need it.

So which theory is correct? All of the above. It appears that cognitivism replaced behaviorism in the 1960s as the dominant paradigm, but if you want to be practical, all four theories have strengths depending upon what the learner needs to learn. According to Darryl Sink (2014), good designers select the best practice from all four theories based on the desired results.

Let's build on these learning theories and examine other areas that help define how you learn best: adult learning principles, cognitive science, and the 70-20-10 framework.

Adult Learning Principles

Malcolm Knowles is considered the father of adult learning theory in the United States. He took the topic of adult learning from theory to practice with his adult learning theory assumptions and principles. He popularized the word *andragogy* to describe the growing body of knowledge about how adults learn. His easy-to-read book *The Adult Learner: A Neglected Species*, published in 1973, took the topic from theoretical to practical.

So, what's so special about these principles? They have deep and foundational meaning to trainers. When training adults, Knowles believed that:

1. **They need to know why something is important.** Adults have a need to know why they should learn something before they'll invest time in a learning event. As trainers, we must ensure that the learners know the purpose for training as early as possible. Participants need to know how this information or content is going to affect them, why they should care, and how it will make a difference.

2. **They have a self-concept of who they are.** Adults enter any learning situation seeing themselves as self-directing, responsible grown-ups and don't like taking directions from others. Therefore, trainers must help adults identify their needs and direct their own learning experience. They will establish their own goals.

3. **They bring life experiences and want to be recognized.** Adults come to a learning opportunity with a wealth of experience and a great deal to contribute. Trainers will be more successful if they identify ways to build on and make use of adults' hard-earned experience and knowledge.

4. **They prefer relevance.** Adults have a strong readiness to learn those things that will help them cope with daily life effectively. Training that relates directly to situations adults face will be viewed as more relevant.

5. **They are practical.** Adults are willing to devote energy to learning those things that they believe will help them perform better or solve problems. Trainers who determine needs and interests and develop content in response to those needs will be most helpful to adult learners.

6. **They are internally motivated.** Adults are more responsive to internal motivators, such as increased self-esteem, than they are to external motivators, such as higher salaries. Trainers can ensure that this internal motivation is not blocked by barriers, such as a poor self-concept or time constraints, by creating a safe learning climate.

Learner Questions

Knowles's assumptions highlighted questions participants ask themselves when entering a training session. As adults we wonder:

- Why do I need to know this?
- Will I be able to make some decisions or are you going to re-create my grade-school memories of having to obey the teacher?
- Why am I here? How do I fit? What do they think they can teach me?
- How is this going to simplify my life? How will this make my job easier?

- Do I want to learn this? How will it help me?
- Why would I want to learn this? Does this motivate me? Am I open to this information?

Apply Adult Learning Theory

Theory and principles are great, but it is not enough to simply know adult learning principles. You must be able to apply them. They should become part of your basic makeup as a trainer. Think about how to incorporate each of Knowles's principles in your future designs and in your delivery. Think about what you could do to address your participant's concerns. We'll review these as they relate to design in chapter 3 and delivery in chapter 7.

Cognitive Science

Cognitive science helps you understand how knowledge is held together in a "mental model," how you process it, and how you remember it. It is all related to the input, short- and long-term memory, and how these three stages work together. Trainers need to ensure that the content is relevant, and remember that short-term memory can only handle two to four chunks of information at a time. This means that to be successful as a trainer you should draw on personal memory, use questions to help structure a mental model, work with multiple senses to grab attention quickly, and structure information in short chunks.

So how does the brain work? John Medina (2008), author of *Brain Rules*, says, "We have no idea. We are still in the very beginning stages of understanding the basics." The brain is made up of between 50 and 100 billion neurons that transmit chemical and electrical signals to form networks (Jensen 2008). Stimuli cause signals to be sent from one neuron to another across a synapse (tiny gap). Thousands of neurons connect using trillions of synaptic connections. We've known for more than 30 years how important it is to strengthen and build these neuron bridges to teach a skill or change behavior.

Memories are not held in one part of the brain, but are scattered throughout different regions. Retention is achieved by repeatedly drawing them all together (sometimes with different results). Cognitive scientists study learning to determine how the brain reacts to different stimuli in different environments. They help us understand how social, environmental, and physiological changes affect learning (Halls 2014).

This is not about quick fixes, but about understanding our learners better.

What Can We Learn From the Study of Neuroscience?

In her ATD Science of Learning blog post, "What Do You Know About Brain Science and Adult Learning," Patti Shank (2016) tells us that we have learned little from neuroscience and that many of the things being attributed to neuroscience are really cognitive science. But we hear something attributed to "neuro" almost daily. It seems that most of what is related to our profession is actually from cognitive science. However, using terms such as *neuroscience* or *brain science* are more appealing than cognitive science, and marketing departments have co-opted both terms!

Disappointed? Don't be. Neuroscience has made understanding what's known about cognition and adult learning cool again. Ultimately, it's good that people are seeking out scientific approaches, but they may have a foundational misunderstanding about where those findings come from.

What's the difference between neuroscience and cognitive science? Neuroscientists are proficient in methods of scientific inquiry and neuroimaging. They offer a descriptive approach. Cognitive scientists actually offer prescriptive approaches and suggestions for how we can support learning. Unfortunately, neuromyths abound (Corballis 1999). For example, humans only use 10 percent of our brains; we have different learning styles; we use different sides of our brains for different tasks; and novices and experts think the same way.

I'm amused at some of the statements attributed to neuroscience: physiology affects learning; people learn better in a safe environment; learners respond best when they are solving real problems; trainers should use visual aids to enhance learning. Isn't that what Malcolm Knowles professed in the last century? Bringing these important basic adult learning principles to light is positive. No matter which science gets the credit, it is important. It's up to you to take these scientific facts and artfully build them into your training design or delivery.

What Is Neuroscience?

Neuroscience is an interdisciplinary science that looks at thought, emotion, and behavior using sophisticated technology such as brain-scanning devices. Its popularity is due to a form of brain imaging called functional magnetic resonance imaging (fMRI), which measures brain activity and translates it into the colorful pictures you've seen in news sources and journals for every profession. Unfortunately, neuroscience is not responsible for as many things as you may have heard.

Why the fascination? Well, first it's about people! It's about your brain and my brain, and it's captivating to learn what makes everyone tick. (I'm sure you've taken one of those quick 10-question quizzes to learn how you rate on your career, IQ, personality, saving habits, or another facet of who you are and how you think.) Your brain is the most complex structure known to mankind. And now neuroscience promises that you can understand it better in colored pictures.

Neuroscience has been linked to finding answers in politics, marketing, addiction, mental illness, hiring, and even in training and learning. As Sally Satel and Scott Lilienfeld (2013) state in their book, *Brainwashed: The Seductive Appeal of Mindless Neuroscience*, "To regard research findings as settled wisdom is folly . . . from a technology that is still poorly understood." A great deal of information is available, but the snags lie in the interpretations. Scientists can't just look inside your brain to find answers—maybe someday, but not today.

Fact or Fiction?

So how can you separate any scientific fact from fiction? Stella Collins (2015) suggests that there are six questions you should ask about any scientific fact:

1. Who did the research?
2. What's on their agenda?
3. Where was it published first?

4. When was it published?

5. How was the science conducted?

6. What does the result really say?

The bottom line is that you need to be wary of what you read and even more wary of what you hear. Anyone who says they have the magic elixir based on neuro-anything probably doesn't have anything you need or want.

THINKING OUTSIDE THE BRAIN BOX

It would be interesting and helpful if neuroscience could answer all "brainy questions." But be careful what you ask for. Although none of the following questions can be answered today, it is likely that there will be answers in the future. Imagine that neuroscience could explain one or more of these:

- Why do you need to sleep? Can't you just absorb energy from the sun?
- If you must sleep, what are dreams? How can you harness dreaming to learn while you sleep?
- How do you really store and access information? Is it possible to facilitate learning easier and faster?
- What is consciousness and perception? How does your self-direction create your thoughts, opinions, feelings, and preferences? And how can you relate that to design experiences that are more helpful to learners?
- How does the brain affect your personality? We've heard of the famous "twin studies" where twins separated at birth grow up to have identical jobs, personalities, and preferences. But if the brain is constantly absorbing and reconciling more information, how does that affect who we become?

Yes, there are still many questions to answer about the brain. Sam Harris, a neuroscientist and bestselling author, believes that eventually studying the brain will explain the mind as well as human values (2010). This goes way beyond how we learn and it is exciting.

The Reality of 70-20-10

In the 1980s colleagues who worked at the Center for Creative Leadership (CCL) in North Carolina set out to conduct research about how leaders learned the craft of leadership. The team included Morgan McCall Jr., Michael Lombardo, and Ann Morrison. Their research concluded that 70 percent was learned as hands-on experience on the job and directed by the individual's manager;

20 percent was learned through developmental interactions that some now call social learning; and 10 percent was learned through formal learning that consisted of classes, workshops, or reading (Lombardo and Eichinger 2011). The research came to be known as the 70-20-10 framework—perhaps one of the most well-known sets of numbers in our profession.

The framework continues to serve as a valuable guideline for using a wide variety of developmental options. As talent development professionals we are experts in the 10 percent category—delivering training or programs—but are still creating a place for ourselves in the other two. Lombardo and Robert Eichinger adapted the research that led to the current 70-20-10 framework. Today 70-20-10 is often used as a talent development strategy aimed at improving workplace performance. Chapter 4 is dedicated to the 70-20-10 framework, so all we'll note here are a few bullet points about its relationship to how we learn:

- The purpose of 70-20-10 was always meant to serve as a rough guide to help think about how people develop.
- The numbers project a solution that isn't as simple as it first appears.
- The numbers will never be exact and an organization should use them as a guide not an absolute.
- Three essential ingredients to learning must accompany the framework: challenging tasks, support from others (which includes feedback), and a supply of new content.
- The 70-20-10 framework is a powerful holistic approach.
- The guidelines are more relevant today than ever before.
- Although formal learning is only 10 percent or so, it is critical to gain new information and learning.
- The best learning strategy is one that draws upon elements of all three categories.

And the Winner Is

You may have heard about the formal versus informal battle. Which is better? Well it turns out neither is better. We need both to learn, grow, and develop.

Most of us in this profession, however, need to learn more about how we can support and encourage more of the informal elements. We need to uncover, discover, or perhaps even create a new role for ourselves and our organizations that support managers and employees to be thoughtful about implementing more learning on the job and through social connections.

Adult learning principles, cognitive science, neuroscience, how we learn—is your head spinning yet? Let's begin to think about how you can use this information as a trainer.

How Trainers Create Successful Learning Experiences

Combining what you know from adult learning theory, cognitive science, and the 70-20-10 framework allows you to create effective learning experiences for your participants.

For people to learn something well, they must hear it, see it, question it, discuss it, and do it. They may even teach it to someone else to solidify their understanding of the information or skill. An active approach to training requires a variety of strategies that promote all six processes—hearing, seeing, questioning, discussing, doing, and teaching. Take time to consider more fully how each of these learning experiences emanates from the science of learning. Determine how you can add to them so they work for you.

Involve Multiple Senses

You probably know that participants retain less when listening to a lecture and more when what they hear is paired with a visual; they retain even more when they practice by doing. There are several reasons why most adults tend to forget what they hear. One of the most interesting has to do with the rate at which a trainer speaks and the rate at which participants listen.

Most trainers speak at about 180 words per minute. But how many of these words do participants hear? It depends on how they are listening. If the participants are really concentrating, they might be able to listen attentively to about half of what a trainer is saying. That's because participants are thinking while they are listening. Even if the material is interesting, it's hard to concentrate for a sustained period of time. Participants probably hear at the rate of 400 to 500 words per minute. When they are listening for a sustained period of time to a trainer who is talking more slowly at 180 words per minute, they are likely to get bored and their minds will wander. A steady diet of lecture is problematic, because the lecturer and the listener are often not in sync.

To alleviate the audio bombardment of lecturing, master trainer Becky Pluth Pike (2016), CEO of The Bob Pike Group, recommends that participants should be given a chance every eight minutes to internalize what they have been hearing before it's simply supplanted by the next wave of information. Ruth Clark (2014) points out that still visuals are helpful to learning, and generally impose less mental load than animated visuals. Still visuals have been shown to be more effective for teaching general content (animated visuals are better for procedures). That could be true because between 80 to 90 percent of all information that is absorbed by the brain is visual (Jensen 2008).

When teaching has both an auditory and a visual dimension, the message is reinforced by two delivery systems. It helps to not only use presentation slides along with meaningful words, but several other sources of visual information too, such as objects, documents, or vivid stories. Some people prefer one mode of delivery over the other. By using both you have a greater chance of meeting the preferences of more participants.

Ask Questions

The adult brain does not function like an audio or video recorder—it doesn't just receive information; it processes it. The brain is suffused with a vast number of networks through which it sorts all incoming information. Information already stored influences how and what you understand and eventually learn. Through these mental models a learner's brain tries to make connections.

If adults discuss information with others and if they are invited to ask questions about it, their brains can do a better job of connecting with information they've already stored. The brain starts the work of learning because it has a question about information it is obtaining from the senses (hearing, sight, touch, taste, smell) that feed it. If the brain could talk, it would ask questions such as: Where does this information fit? Does it confirm what I already know? Does it disagree with what I already know?

If the brain isn't curious about incoming information, however, it takes the path of least resistance and attends to something else. Therefore, getting participants to ask questions puts them in a seeking mode rather than a passive mode. Their brains are activated to obtain answers rather than merely "logging in." If participants are asked to listen to a lecture or view presentation slides with few or no questions, their brains treat the information superficially. If they are trying to find out something, their brains will treat the information with more consideration. Better yet, if adults can discuss the information with their peers, they can obtain feedback about how well they understand it.

As a trainer you can help by asking questions and facilitating discussion. Learning is enhanced if you ask participants to:

- Volunteer information in their own words.
- Provide examples of it.
- Reflect on the information.
- Look for connections between it and other facts or ideas.
- Practice higher-order thinking, such as analysis, synthesis, and evaluation.
- Apply it to case situations.

Increase Involvement

Even better than simply asking questions is giving your participants an opportunity to do something with the information. Research conducted at Stanford University suggests that the optimal environment for learning allows people at different times to be partners, teammates, and teachers (Levin 1996). In a training context, this occurs best when learning teams are organized to engage in "action learning" tasks, in which they challenge participants to solve problems and apply what they know to real work situations. Furthermore, giving participants the opportunity to learn information or a skill and then teach it to peers allows them to discover that teaching, coaching, and mentoring others can be a great way to learn.

In many ways, the brain is like a computer and people are its users. A computer needs to be "on" to work. The brain needs to be on as well. When learning is passive, the brain isn't on. A computer needs the right software to interpret the data that are entered. The brain needs to link what's being taught with what is already known and how you think. When learning is passive, the brain doesn't make these linkages to the software of our mind. Finally, a computer cannot retain information that it has processed without "saving it." The brain needs to test the information, recapitulate it, or explain it to someone else to store it in its memory bank. When learning is passive, the brain doesn't save what has been presented.

What occurs when trainers inundate participants with their own thoughts (however insightful and well organized they may be) or when they rely too often on "let me show you how" demonstrations and explanations? Pouring facts and concepts into participants' heads and masterfully performing skills and procedures actually interfere with learning. The presentation may make an immediate impression on the brain, but without a photographic memory, participants simply cannot retain very much for any period of time, even though they think they will never forget it. As Eric Jensen (2008), author of *Brain-Based Learning*, explains, "the traditional stand and delivery approach is brain antagonistic. The brain is not very good at absorbing countless bits of semantic (factual) information."

Improve Spacing

Learning is not a one-shot event; it comes in waves. The "spacing effect" was first reported by Hermann Ebbinghaus in 1885. "Spacing" means that when practice opportunities are distributed over time, learning is better. Learning requires several exposures to material for true understanding. It also takes different kinds of exposures, not just a repetition of input. For example, a software application can be taught with manuals, through classroom exercises, and through an asynchronous online class. Each way shapes the participants' understanding. Even more important is the way in which the exposure happens. If it happens to the learner, there will be little mental engagement by the learner. As Ruth Clark, author of *Evidence-Based Training Methods*, states, "Even though the spacing effect has been reported and consistently demonstrated for more than 100 years, this important principle is rarely applied."

Real learning is not memorization. Most of what we memorize is lost in hours. To retain what has been taught, participants must chew on it. Learning can't be swallowed whole. A trainer can't do the mental work for participants because they must put together what they hear and see to form a meaningful whole. Without the opportunity to discuss, ask questions, do, and perhaps even teach someone else, real learning will not occur.

Introduce Moderate Stress

The stress response curve illustrated here represents the Yerkes-Dodson law, a relationship between stress and performance. Originally developed in 1908 by psychologists Robert Yerkes and John Dodson, the law states that performance increases with mental stress, but only up to a point. As Figure 2.1 shows, stress and performance are related in an "inverted U curve." When levels of stress become too high, performance decreases (Yerkes 1908).

Figure 2-1: Stress Response Curve

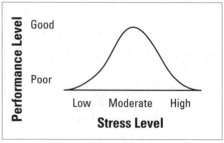

Stimulation to learn requires a moderate amount of stress (measured in the level of cortisol). A low degree of stress is associated with low performance, as is high stress, which can set the system into fight-or-flight mode, causing less brain activity in the cortical areas where higher-level learning happens. Moderate levels of cortisol correlate with the highest performance. Moderate stress is beneficial for learning, while mild and extreme stress are both detrimental to it.

The shape of the curve will depend on the situation and the individual. Four influencers can affect how much pressure people feel: skill, personality, trait anxiety, and task complexity.

THE ART OF STRESS: NOT TOO MUCH, NOT TOO LITTLE

What should you consider when introducing the "right amount" of stress? You want to stretch your learners, but not too much. Consider the four influencers of stress:

- **Skill level:** Your learners' skill level directly influences how well they perform. Ensure that they receive enough time to practice to build competence and confidence. When put under pressure, they are less able to think methodically or flexibly. If the task is required for high-pressure situations, they will need more practice so that the task feels natural.
- **Personality:** There is some correlation between the level of stress and whether learners are extroverts or introverts. As you might expect, extroverts are more likely to perform under higher levels of stress (Posella 2010; Ryan and Connell 1989; Bosworth et al. 2001).
- **Trait anxiety:** Self-confidence helps learners stay focused under higher levels of pressure. Self-confident people appear to manage their self-talk to ensure they can concentrate completely on the situation. Positive thinking can often lower anxiety about learning new tasks.
- **Task complexity:** Initially, more complex tasks require calm, low-pressure environments. Simpler tasks can be completed under more pressure.

These are only influencers, and you should be aware of them when training new tasks. Aim for balance so that optimum learning occurs. And, yes, everyone will react differently. Remember that your learners may experience pressure from other places, such as home or the job, when they are involved in training. A better way to think about stress is to ask how far you can stretch your learners.

Encourage Practice

Quite a few studies have compared learning outcomes among individuals playing a game with individuals assigned to a more traditional instructional method, such as lectures or computer tutorials. In these studies the same content is presented in a game version and in a traditional version and learning is measured with a test. In *Evidence-Based Training Methods* Ruth Clark

(2015) reports that while the results aren't clear cut, in one study simulation games resulted in learning gains 9 to 14 percent higher than comparison groups. However, the comparison groups learned more than the game groups when taught with active instructional methods. The game groups learned more than the comparison groups when the comparison groups were taught with passive instructional methods. Clark states, "My conclusion from the review is that active engagement leads to learning and any method that incorporates relevant active engagement (with feedback) will lead to better learning than a method that relies primarily on a passive learning environment such as lectures or reading."

This is supported by research conducted at the University of Wisconsin that demonstrated the educational and social benefits of digital games—even those that are not specifically geared toward education bring together ways of knowing and doing (Shaffer, Squire, Halverson, and Gee 2005).

Make It Social

We all face a world of exploding knowledge, rapid change, and uncertainty. As a result, participants may be anxious and defensive when they show up for training. Abraham Maslow taught us that humans have within them two sets of forces or needs—one that strives for growth and one that clings to safety. A person who must choose between these two needs will choose safety over growth. The need to feel secure has to be met before the need to reach out, take risks, and explore the unfamiliar can be entertained. Growth takes place in little steps. According to Maslow (2014), "each step forward is made possible by the feeling of being safe, of operating out into the unknown from a safe home port."

One of the key ways people feel safe and secure is when they feel connected to other people and are included in a group. This feeling of belonging enables participants to face the challenges set before them. When they are learning with others rather than alone, they have the emotional and intellectual support that allows them to go beyond their present level of knowledge and skill.

Maslow's concepts underlie the development of the small-group learning methods that are popular in training circles. Placing participants in teams and giving them tasks in which they depend upon one another to complete the work is a way to capitalize on their social needs. They tend to get more engaged in learning because they are doing it with their peers. Once they have become involved, they also have a need to talk with others about what they are experiencing, which leads to further connections.

Collaborative learning activities help drive active training. Although independent study and large group instruction also stimulate active learning, the ability to teach through small-group cooperative activities will enable you to promote active learning in a special way. Remember that what participants discuss with others and what they teach others enables them to acquire understanding and master learning. The best collaborative learning methods meet these requirements. Giving different assignments to different participants prompts them not only to learn together, but also to teach each other.

David Rock's Model: AGES

When learning is passive, learners come to the encounter without curiosity, without questions, and without interest in the outcome. When learning is active, learners are seeking something. They want an answer to a question, need information to solve a problem, or are searching for a better way to do a job. David Rock, director of the NeuroLeadership Institute and author of *Your Brain at Work*, uses an AGES model that identifies four requirements to embed ideas:

- **A**ttention must be very high; multitasking dramatically reduces recall. The chemical processes to encode memory is activated when we are very focused.
- **G**enerate a mental map around the new ideas; participants can't just watch or listen. Remember that everyone has a different mental model.
- **E**motions need to be high; people only remember things they feel strongly about.
- **S**pacing learning is critical.

A high AGES score is required for participants to recall ideas. Attention, generation, emotion, and spacing form the AGES model. Practicing in the form of small group work, gamification, contests, or team teaching can all increase a learning event's AGES score (2009).

Apply Brain-Based Techniques to Your Training

Scientific theories are always helpful, but what really matters is how you apply what you learn. Jonathan Halls says that trainers "are in the business of making things easy to understand and remember" (2014). Whether you are designing or delivering in a classroom or virtually, plan to make it easy for your learners' brains to absorb the content. What can you modify to enhance the learning experience?

We will cover various brain-based principles in more depth throughout the book. However, just in case you don't get past this chapter, here are a dozen ways you can apply the research to engage your learners' brains and increase your chances of success:

1. **Create patterns.** Patterns form the way we think, so the brain looks for patterns and uses prior experiences to fill in the blanks. You can use this to your advantage to accelerate learning. Know what your learners already know.

2. **Preclude mindsets.** Prior experience noted in the first bullet is good, except when the experience exhibits itself as a stubborn mindset that resists change. The learner's mindset may have a different pattern that the brain cannot reconcile with the new information and this can interfere with learning. How can you get around this? Provide context, engage emotions, incorporate novelty, and provide time for reflection and practice.

3. **Grab attention immediately.** Then hold onto it with novel ways of presenting content, and encouraging learners to ask questions and discover their own answers. Be sure to model what your participants can expect at the start. Don't start with the boring "housekeeping!"

4. **Involve learners.** Prevent your learners from being bored.

Your learners come from a world of constant stimulus and interruptions. Build in activities that allow for socialization and movement to increase oxygen flow to the brain. Ask questions. Writing, talking, or even teaching keeps the brain involved.

5. **Plan breaks.** Face it, your learners will not be fully engaged all the time. We used to blame it on mental mini-vacations, but now smartphones, email, Facebook, and other distractions can interfere with learners' attention. Plan for plenty of breaks so learners can address the rest of their world and maintain focus during your session. In addition, from the brain's perspective, memories are strengthened during periods of rest. Spacing between chunks of content is valuable. Breaks help your learners retain information.

6. **Practice.** To move content to long-term memory, build in plenty of time to rehearse new skills—especially those that are critical.

7. **Balance stress.** Find ways to stretch your learners. Keep them excited about learning but don't overdo it; creating too much stress will shut learning down. Align the design to match the learner's needs. Keep activities relatively risk free early in your sessions.

8. **Know your learners.** You need to invest time before the session to understand your participants and their needs. Be ready to cut something that is less important to meet your learners' needs.

9. **Engage emotions.** Use stories, interactions, experiences, visuals, or other stimuli to improve memory.

10. **Build rapport.** Create rapport with your learners, but also build learner-to-learner rapport. Start with an icebreaker that introduces everyone. The social aspect helps to decrease feelings of threat from strangers or of learning something new.

11. **Plan for follow up.** We'd all like to be reassured that our learners will remember everything that happened in the session, but that isn't going to be true. Plan for continued spacing such as implementing peer practice groups, meeting with supervisors, emailing tips, or texting reminders.

12. **Finally remember, all learners' brains are distinctly their own.** We all have our own mental models and preferred methods of learning and thinking. Plan for a broad variety of styles. In addition, be aware of how your own preferences influence you as a trainer. It is critical that you are flexible and adept at facilitating to appeal to all the brains in your session.

"If I had my life to live over again, I would have made a rule to read some poetry and listen to some music at least once every week."

—Charles Darwin

Is Learning to Learn the Answer?

Did anyone teach you effective ways to take notes? Or to read efficiently? Your answer is probably "no." Learning is something we all do from the moment of birth, so most of us likely take this complex process for granted. Although most of us have a general sense of what it means to learn, you may have many assumptions. Few of us were taught how to learn in school.

Learning to learn has its own set of steps: diagnosing one's need for learning, establishing goals, identifying essential information, determining patterns, and seeking help when needed (Petrie 2015). It also means using efficient memory tactics and spacing intake of information. These aren't the kinds of skills that we either seek or learn naturally. We need to be introduced to the concept.

 ## What We Know for Sure

Science tells us that we can rely on several proven facts:

- Learning theories provide models to design better learning events.
- Adult learning principles establish a foundation for understanding how adults learn.

- Cognitive science explains how knowledge is held together in a mental model, how we process it, and how we remember it.
- Neuroscience is the study of how the brain works; at this time, we understand very little about it.
- The 70-20-10 framework defines the circumstances surrounding how and where we learn.
- Learning is enhanced when learners:
  - involve multiple senses
  - respond to and discuss questions and concepts
  - are involved in learning
  - have an opportunity to space learning
  - experience moderate stress
  - have an opportunity to practice skills
  - collaborate socially during and after the learning event.

The Art Part

Your success will depend upon how well you adapt to the situation and your learners' needs. Tap into some of these ideas to help your learners grow, to develop yourself, and to add your personal creative touch.

Knowles and you. List Malcolm Knowles's principles of adult learning on a page. Think about the last time you attended a training session, either face-to-face or virtually. Write the questions you were asking yourself when you first arrived. How similar or different were your questions from those used as examples? Why do you think that was? How do you compare yourself to what this chapter presented? Next, look at your training from your learners' perspectives. What do you see? What do you need to change?

Rock with AGES. David Rock's AGES model is easy to remember and use. If you are short on time, use it to review your training event. It will provide you with enough information to ensure that you are attending to the necessary elements of learning.

Art and Science Questions You Might Ask

These questions provide potential challenges for your personal growth and development:

- How can you incorporate all adult learning principles into your work?
- How would implementing adult learning principles improve your delivery or design?
- What effect do Malcolm Knowles's principles have on your learners?
- How is your philosophy similar to Knowles's assumptions? How is your philosophy different?
- Which ideas under the brain-based learning strategies do you need to incorporate in your learning events?
- What creative ways can you involve your learners' multiple senses in your next learning event?
- What thought-provoking questions will lead to better performance?
- How can you increase involvement in a meaningful way in your next learning event?
- Where can you use the 70-20-10 framework to improve spacing of the learning? How?
- How well do you stretch your participants in your design and delivery?
- How can you focus on encouraging practice in the most critical parts of your learning event?
- How can you make it social?
- If you understood more about how adults learn, how would you use this information?

How Do You Learn?

Science sometimes confirms what you've always known intuitively. And it's good to know that science endorses what all the experts such as Thiagi,

Silberman, Pike, Clark, and others you've relied on have been telling us for years. We learn best when:

- The design organizes content in a meaningful process; chunks information into small bites; allows time for reflection and practice; builds on what participants know; and is designed around images.
- Your delivery creates a safe and welcoming environment; involves multiple senses; encourages participation; communicates what's in it for the learner; and encourages social involvement.

And don't forget to take breaks and serve food!

Resources

Biech, E. 2014. *ASTD Handbook: The Definitive Reference for Training and Development.* 2nd ed. Alexandria, VA: ASTD Press.

———. 2015. *Training and Development for Dummies.* Hoboken, NJ: John Wiley & Sons.

Bosworth, H., J. Feaganes, P. Vitaliano, D. Mark, and I. Siegler. 2001. "Personality and Coping With a Common Stressor." *Journal of Behavioral Medicine* 24:17-31.

Clark, R. 2015. *Evidence-Based Training Methods: A Guide for Training Professionals.* 2nd ed. Alexandria, VA: ATD Press.

Collins, S. 2015. "Neuroscience Under Scrutiny." *Training Journal*, June.

Corballis, M.C. 1999. "Are We in Our Right Minds?" In *Mind Myths: Exploring Popular Assumptions About the Mind and Brain*, edited by S. Della Sala, 25-41. New York: John Wiley & Sons.

Ebbinghaus, H. 1964. *Memory: A Contribution to Experimental Psychology.* New York: Dover. (Originally published, 1885).

Halls, J. 2014. "Memory and Cognition in Learning." *Infoline.* Alexandria, VA: ASTD Press.

Harris, S. 2010. *The Moral Landscape: How Science Can Determine Human Values.* New York: Simon and Schuster.

Huggett, C. 2013. *The Virtual Training Guidebook: How to Design, Deliver, and Implement Live Online Learning.* Alexandria, VA: ASTD Press.

Jensen, E. 2008. *Brain-Based Learning.* Thousand Oaks, CA: Corwin Press.

Knowles, M.S. III, E. Holton, and R. Swanson. 2015. *The Adult Learner: The Definitive Classic in Adult Education and Human Resource Development.* 8th ed. Burlington, MA: Elsevier/Butterworth-Heinemann.

Levin, H. 1996. *Innovations in Learning: New Environments for Education.* Mahwah, NJ: Lawrence Erlbaum Associates.

Lombardo, M., and R. Eichinger. 2011. *The Leadership Machine: Architecture to Develop Leaders for Any Future.* Minneapolis: Lominger International: A Korn/Ferry Company.

Maslow, A. 2014. *Toward a Psychology of Being.* 3rd ed. Floyd, VA: Sublime Books.

Medina, J. 2008. *Brain Rules: 12 Principles for Surviving and Thriving at Work, Home, and School.* Seattle: Pear Press.

Petrie, N. 2015. *The How-To of Vertical Leadership Development—Part 2.* Greensboro, NC: Center for Creative Leadership.

Pluth, B. 2016. *Creative Training: A Train-the-Trainer Field Guide.* Eden Prairie, MN: Creative Training Productions.

Posella, D. 2010. "Coping Styles Used by Introverts and Extroverts in Varying Stress Situations." Allegany, NY: St. Bonaventure University.

Rock, D. 2009. *Your Brain at Work: Strategies for Overcoming Distraction, Regaining Focus, and Working Smarter All Day Long.* New York: HarperCollins.

Ryan, R.M., and J.P. Connell. 1989. "Perceived Locus of Causality and Internalization: Examining Reasons for Acting in Two Domains." *Journal of Personality and Social Psychology* 57:749-761.

Satel, S., and S. Lilienfield. 2013. *Brainwashed: The Seductive Appeal of Mindless Neuroscience.* New York: Basic Books.

Shaffer, D., K. Squire, R. Halverson, and J. Gee. 2005. "Video Games and the Future of Learning." *The Phi Delta Kappan* 87(2):104-111.

Shank, P. 2016. "What Do You Know About Brain Science and Adult Learning." Science of Learning Blog, April 14. www.td.org/Publications/Blogs/Science-of-Learning-Blog/2016/04/What-Do-You-Know-About-Brain-Science-and-Adult-Learning

Sink, D. 2014. "Design Models and Learning Theories for Adults." In *ASTD Handbook: The Definitive Reference for Training and Development*, 2nd ed., edited by E. Biech, 181-199. Alexandria, VA: ASTD Press.

Yerkes, R., and J. Dodson. 1908. "The Relation of Strength of Stimulus to Rapidity of Habit-Formation." *Journal of Comparative Neurology and Psychology* 18:459-482.

How Do You Design So Others Can Learn?

Chapter 2 laid out research and theories about how you learn. This chapter builds on that foundation of research. I will also address several other learning concepts and show you how to use all of them to design an effective training program. First, let's take a look at designing participant materials and learning activities.

Designing Materials

This section presents considerations for designing materials you will use. We'll discuss learning objectives, visuals, and learning styles.

Are Learning Objectives Necessary?

Learning objectives are written to specify the performance (knowledge or skill) that is desired after the training has been completed. I think you will be surprised about the "science" I present about learning objectives. I include it here because learning objectives are valuable. What purpose do learning objectives serve? They:

- Ensure clarity between designer and customer.
- Clearly communicate purpose to learners.

- Keep you focused on designing for requirements and eliminating anything that is just nice to include.
- Ensure that your course balances independence with guidance (Eberly 2008).
- Connect content and assessment to learning.
- Guide the selection of learning activities that will best achieve objectives.
- Give learners a clear picture of what to expect and what's expected of them.
- Form a basis for evaluating trainer, learner, and curriculum effectiveness.

What Constitutes a Good Learning Objective?

Learning objectives are written to specify the desired performance (knowledge or skill) of the learner once training has been completed. You should use the information gathered during the assessment stage to write learning objectives. An objective should meet several criteria:

- **Specific:** It should be specific so that there is no question about what you mean, and it should use words that can be observed or heard.
- **Measurable:** It should be measurable, which means you can either count it or determine that it was or was not completed.
- **Attainable:** It should be attainable. It should not be too difficult, yet it should not be too easy.
- **Relevant:** It should be relevant to the organization and to the change that is desired.
- **Timely:** It should be time bound; that is, it should have a limit that states when the participant is expected to achieve the objective.

The first letter of each of these spells SMART. Objectives should be SMART. An objective can easily be written by filling in the blank to this easy-to-remember question:

Who will do what, by when, and how well?

For example, "You will be able to write effective learning objectives by the end of this module 100 percent of the time." This addresses Robert Mager's (1997) "Three Parts of a Performance-Based Objective": a performance or action, conditions under which the learner must perform, and criteria (by which the performance is evaluated by another; or, in other words, how well the action must be completed).

Remember Bloom?

In chapter 1, you read about Bloom's Taxonomy, the hierarchy of learning outcomes. This is the point in the training cycle during which Bloom's Taxonomy comes in handy: specifying exactly what the learner will know or be able to do at the end of the training experience. Bloom's Taxonomy is useful for writing learning objectives.

Bloom's Taxonomy divides the way people learn into three domains: cognitive, psychomotor, and affective (Bloom 1968). Each is presented in a hierarchical order in which the skill requires more complex skills. The cognitive domain, which emphasizes intellectual outcomes, is presented in Table 3-1. This domain is further divided into categories or levels. The key words used and the type of questions asked may aid in the establishment and encouragement of critical thinking, especially in the higher levels.

Table 3-1: Bloom's Cognitive Domain

Knowledge	Comprehension	Application	Analysis	Synthesis	Evaluation
Copy a model or pattern behavior	Follow direction	Perfect original work	Separate into parts	Form new, bring together parts	Judge based on criteria
Arrange	Complete	Demonstrate	Adjust	Build	Assess
Copy	Compute	Devise	Calibrate	Combine	Criticize
Define	Describe	Drive	Compare	Compose	Critique
Duplicate	Explain	Modify	Coordinate	Create	Defend
Imitate	Match	Operate	Detect	Design	Evaluate
List	Model	Organize	Diagram	Initiate	Estimate
Recall	Move	Perfect	Draw	Invent	Judge
Repeat	Paraphrase	Refine	Experiment	Originate	Justify
Select	Respond	Repair	Organize	Support	Rate
State	Reproduce	Solve	Plan	Write	Validate

Skills in the cognitive domain revolve around knowledge, comprehension, and critical thinking on a particular topic. Traditional education tends to emphasize the skills in this domain, particularly the lower-order objectives.

Using Bloom's various domains can assist you to find the most descriptive verb to write your objective.

Another Perspective on Objectives

Will Thalheimer, a consultant who uses research-based insights to help organizations improve performance, presents another perspective on learning objectives. In a short video he presents the idea that it is more important to select nouns that help learners focus than worrying about the right verb. He also reminds us that Robert Mager's original work with objectives was focused on developing objectives for designers and facilitators.

Because learners have a limited working memory capacity it is critical that designers select very specific words—both verbs and nouns—when writing objectives to help learners focus their attention on the correct items (Britton et al. 1985; Rothkopf and Koether 1978). Select words that learners will connect to the most important content.

Thalheimer makes several excellent points; the most important is that trainers have forgotten some of the excellent foundational research that supports what we do. For example, he differentiates between learning objectives and design objectives. When I started in the training profession trainers were expected to write both kinds of objectives. Up until about 10 years ago, I always had two formally written lists of objectives. Now, my clients rarely want to see the design objectives, so I keep them in my personal notes. What's the difference? Learner objectives are those that you are most familiar with: performance, content, and motivation. Design objectives focus on organizational objectives, evaluation, design issues, and at times the transitional situation. I encourage you to view Thalheimer's video at www.work-learning.com/2015/01/video-on-lobjs.html.

A CHECKLIST FOR EFFECTIVE OBJECTIVES

Whether you are a new or experienced designer, whether you've written a few objectives or hundreds, you can use these reminders about what to consider before writing objectives for your next training program.

- Be brief and to the point; include only one major item in each objective.
- Although some research will tell you that it is less important to select the right verb, it is beneficial to use an observable action verb to describe the expected result. You can see (or hear) "list," "demonstrate," and "calculate." You cannot see someone "remember," "believe," or "learn."
- Based on the research mentioned, also select a very specific noun.
- Specify a timeframe or target date of completion; generally, this occurs at the end of the training session.
- Specify resource limitations (money, personnel, equipment) as appropriate.
- Describe the participants' expected performance.
- Specify results to be achieved in measurable or observable terms.
- Choose areas over which you have direct influence or control; don't write objectives for which your training program has no accountability.
- Make objectives realistic in terms of what can actually be accomplished in the training as well as in terms of resources you have available to you.
- Include enough challenge in the objective to make it worth formulating.
- Indicate the minimum level of acceptable performance.
- Specify the conditions (if any) under which the action must be performed.
- Specify degree of success if less than 100 percent is acceptable.
- Select objectives that are supportive and consistent with overall organizational missions and goals.

Selecting and Planning to Use Visuals

You have numerous visual choices available—everything from computer displays to paper. Visuals support your training session and make it easier for the learner to acquire the skills or knowledge intended. Visuals also improve retention (Clark 2015). If you are conducting a virtual instructor-led training, you may be limited in your options. On the other hand, if you are conducting a video conference, all the options could be used.

Creating and planning how you will use visuals is a lot of work! Is it really worth it? The benefits of visuals to you and your participants are clear. Your participants learn through their five senses. Tap into them. Many people prefer to learn in a certain way, which means that adding visual support to your verbal message is a major benefit to your participants. By using visuals in your training sessions, participants grasp the information faster, understand it better, and retain it longer.

Ruth Clark, author of *Evidence-Based Training Methods* (2015), states that with regard to visuals, evidence demonstrates that trainers should heed these four lessons based on experimental evidence accumulated over the past 15 years:

- Use relevant visuals to illustrate your content, especially for learners who are new to the content.
- Keep visuals simple depending on your goal. Simple line drawings often result in the best learning. Match the details to the level of detail you are imparting.
- Explain complex visuals with brief audio narration—either your voice or a recorded message, depending on the type of learning event.
- Avoid seductive visuals. They are distracting to the learners even if they are related to the topic.

Remember that our brains love pictures and visuals enhance learning retention in many ways. They also help us make sense of complex, abstract, or unusual content. At least 50 percent of the cortex is used for visual processing and only around 10 percent for auditory processing (Snowden, Thompson, and Troscianko 2012).

"Design is not solely about making things aesthetically pleasing, although this is part of it. Design, at its core, is about solving problems. And whatever that problem is—from squeezing oranges to running faster to communicating effectively—designers strive to help users solve their dilemma in the most convenient, simple, and elegant way."

—Nancy Duarte

Ensure That the Visual Adds to the Learning

You are a professional. Using visuals can enhance your image and increase the confidence participants have in you. On the other hand, if you don't have professionally designed visuals, if you haven't practiced, and if you don't know the best way to use them, your participants may lose all confidence in you. Visuals are only effective when:

- They are relevant to the subject.
- They are visible and understandable to the participants.

That may seem like common sense, but sometimes we just don't think about all the details required. These additional guides will make your visuals the best they can be:

- **Orient the visuals for your learners.** Imagine that you are one of the participants and are seeing the visuals for the first time. Tell learners what they are looking at: "Here are four criteria for listening actively." A good visual may not need words to describe it.
- **Be well practiced.** It should be comfortable and natural to use your visuals. That comes with practice.
- **Ensure that your visuals enhance your performance rather than replace it.** Your visuals should not take center stage, but they should help to explain or clarify the concepts you are presenting. This is what Ruth Clark means when she refers to avoiding "seductive" visuals!
- **Prepare for an emergency.** Emergencies that occur during the presentation don't have to be a complete disaster. Being prepared if you can't use your slides or your handouts aren't delivered reduces the effect on your participants.
- **Select a visual theme.** Your audience has probably seen every template available from PowerPoint. Go online to find other PowerPoint designs or create your own. Use color to enhance your theme, but use it judiciously. A light background with dark lettering is generally better.

- **Add interest.** Use bullets, graphics, and a layout that is attractive. Even changing your bullets to triangles adds a new twist. Remember, pictures say it best and graphs explain numbers best. On the other hand, avoid too much moving text or graphics. It may look like fun, but overdone it can be distracting and annoying to some members of your group. Use it when appropriate or to help make your point.
- **Check for accuracy.** Give your slides to someone else to proof. Make sure that all information is complete, correct, and current.

And finally, in the words of that famous trainer, Anonymous: "Keep it simple, keep it simple, keep it simple."

What's Available?

PowerPoint presentations have become ubiquitous in the training world. They are easy and fast to create. The tools to design them reside inside everyone's laptop. They can be changed or updated on the spot. They add color automatically and may include animation and sound effects, or video clips.

However, they may also be boring and overused. If you aren't careful they can be less effective than other forms of media and visuals that are available. To guard against this, I like what Becky Pluth (2016) says: "I prefer to view my PowerPoint slide as a billboard. As you drive past a billboard, at a glance, do you get the main point?" Think of your visuals as support to help your learners stay focused and to keep you on track. The following are just a few of the media and visuals available to you:

- **Videos.** Use them to demonstrate a skill, illustrate behavior, or to have an expert deliver content in a way that you could not.
- **Participants' devices.** Tap into the many resources your participants bring: laptops, iPads or other tablets, phones and watches that connect to the Internet, wearable devices, pens that record action, and many other tools.
- **Flipcharts.** Flipcharts can create visuals in the moment or compile learners' ideas. They work well for creating on-the-spot lists, capturing ideas generated by the group, and creating real-time plans.

There is a sense of immediacy and spontaneity to the information presented. Flipcharts are helpful when you're asked to do spur-of-the-moment facilitating.

- **Blackboards, whiteboards, magnetic boards, felt boards, electronic whiteboards.** All of these are useful for small group recording of ideas.
- **Props.** Props usually don't plug in, turn on, make sounds, show animation, or have glitches. They may include samples, models, demonstrations, or any article that a trainer holds to drive a point home.

After reviewing a number of studies about media and technology, Ruth Clark advises us to select a mix of media, such as pairing video clips with slides or demonstrations with flipcharts, that supports core human psychological learning processes (2015).

The Learning Style Concept Is a Neuromyth

A *neuromyth* is a word used to describe the inaccuracies and fallacies we are discovering about how our brain functions. One of the most commonly held myths is that we all have specific learning styles. Numerous researchers have weighed in on learning styles—including Allcock and Hulme (2010); Choi, Lee, and Kang (2009); Kappe et al. (2009); Kozub (2010); Martin (2010); Sankey, Birch, and Gardiner (2011); and Zacharis (2011)—but none are more adamant than Ruth Clark. She's reviewed the studies and states that there is no evidence for the validity of learning styles. There is no evidence that knowing or diagnosing your participants' learning styles will lead to optimal learning, if you do not know that piece of data. Experts on the topic such as Harold Pashler and Doug Rohrer (2008) state that any minimal existing data is weak and there is virtually no evidence to support using assessments to identify learning styles. That's the science half.

The art half is more exciting. Consider that you have many different people in your learning events. Your learners are all visual learners; they are all auditory learners; they are all kinesthetic learners. They all bring with them their own preferences. Wouldn't it seem logical to try to provide techniques and tools that support all of these learning modes and preferences? Be careful that your training preference doesn't interfere. If you truly believe it's all about the learner, then you have an obligation to tailor your training style to address your learners. Learning and how our brain processes information is much more complex than you may have considered.

In addition, the most effective way for us to learn is based not on our individual preferences but on the nature of the material we're being taught. The existence of learning styles can't be proven from the science perspective. On the other hand, from an artist's perspective, it is important to design training that taps into all senses: visual, auditory, and of course hands-on whenever we can.

Designing Activities

This section presents considerations for designing activities. It includes discussions about how to apply Knowles's adult learning principles, practice guidelines, chunking, and taking time for invisible learning.

Applying Adult Learning Theory

Let's begin by reviewing Knowles's assumptions. Knowles's andragogical theory is based on four assumptions that differ from those of pedagogy: changes in self-concept, the role of experience, readiness to learn, and orientation to learning. Theory and principles are great, but it is more important to know how to apply the information. It is not enough to just know adult learning principles. You must be able to apply them unconsciously. They should become a part of your basic makeup as a trainer. If you recall, Knowles's assumptions lead to questions participants ask themselves when entering a training session. How can we respond to the following six questions during the design?

1. "Why do I need to know this?" Adults have a need to know why they should learn something before investing time in a learning event.

Share the purpose. You could incorporate these into your design:

- Plan time at the beginning of the course to address the purpose of the session.
- Build in time to respond to questions about the need to know.
- Be prepared to respond to questions about the organization's "ulterior" motives.
- Ensure the objectives are clear and directed at what the participants will learn.
- Decide if a listing of expectations is required for the session.
- Create a self-evaluation.

2. "Will I be able to make some decisions or are you going to re-create my grade school memories?" Adults enter any learning situation with a self-concept of themselves as self-directing, responsible gown-ups.

    Maintain self-concept. You could incorporate these into your design:

    - If a self-assessment has been designed, be sure to allow time for participants to process their results by themselves or in pairs.
    - Avoid words in materials that hearken of "school." For example, do not use words—such as students, teachers, workbooks, lessons, education, report card, grade, test, or desk—that remind participants of their school experience.
    - Design a bright ideas board in which participants can post names of books or ideas that can help other participants with their unique concerns.

3. "Why am I here? How do I fit? What do they think they can teach me?" Adults come to a learning opportunity with a wealth of experience and a great deal to contribute.

    Acknowledge experience. You could incorporate these into your design:

- Interview participants prior to designing the session to identify typical participant expertise and experience.
- If something has changed, identify ways to allow participants to "let go" of the old and welcome the new. Sometimes journaling or self-guided questions address this concern.
- Build in time for discussion.
- Design an icebreaker that allows participants to get to know each other and what they have to contribute.

4. "How is this going to simplify my life? How will this make my job easier?" Adults have a strong readiness to learn those things that will help them cope with daily life effectively.

   Make it relevant. You could incorporate these into your design:
   - Address issues participants face on the job.
   - Develop case studies, critical incidents, and role plays that focus on real daily work issues.
   - Interview participants before designing to obtain specific examples.

5. "Do I want to learn this? Do I need to learn this?" Adults are willing to devote energy to learning those things that they believe will help them perform a task or solve a problem.

   Deliver solutions. You could incorporate these into your design:
   - Build in a problem-solving clinic in which participants bring up their own problems that need solving.
   - Allow time in the design for self-reflection so participants can revise their thought process or adapt the material to their own situations.
   - Design experiential learning scenarios that link the material to why a participant might either want to or need to invest the time to learn the content.

6. "Why would I want to learn this? Does this motivate me? Am I open to this information and if not, why not?" Adults are more

responsive to internal motivators such as increased self-esteem, than to external motivators such as higher salaries.

Respect self-motivation. You could incorporate these into your design:

- Plan activities that help participants explore their own motivation—journaling or small group discussions may be useful.
- Participants can be intrinsically motivated if they know how they fit into the bigger plan, organizationally.
- Write materials in a conversational manner using first and second person and polite phrases. A study completed by Moreno and Mayer (2000) found that using first- and second-person language resulted in greater learning.
- Design certificates.
- Design ways for participants to explore their personal growth and development needs.

Plan how you will incorporate Knowles's principles into your future designs.

Practice Guidelines

Practice is essential to learning new skills, but all practice is not equal (Ericsson, Krampe, and Tesch-Romer 1993). What are the inequalities? As you build it into your design, you will want to consider three features of practice: type of practice, amount of practice, and the spacing of practice.

Type of Practice

It is usually best to practice realistic events and apply actions rather than simply repeat content. If you anticipate different responses to different categories of problems you will want to mix practice options.

Amount of Practice

The amount will depend entirely on the topic. Ruth Clark (2015) suggests that you base the amount on these elements:

- More practice if the consequences of error are serious.
- Less practice if using a job aid is acceptable.
- More practice if the work is complex, to ensure automation.

Spacing Practice

When you distribute practice throughout your session rather than cramming it all in at once, you give participants a better chance of absorbing the information. For example, you could start with a discussion of the topic in which learners uncover problems they have, incorporate the information in an activity, and later in the day combine several topics in a practice role play.

Giving Feedback

Follow practice with feedback. Ruth Clark has assembled evidence that suggests that giving feedback may be more complex than we originally thought. For example, giving feedback immediately and including not just an evaluation, but an explanation about what was wrong usually results in positive results. However, there are a few learners who actually get more depressed by the feedback due to how it is given, the timing, and their personality type (Butler et al. 2007). And when giving feedback we should elaborate on whether the task was completed correctly or incorrectly. Clark also tells us that it isn't always necessarily important to provide feedback immediately. For example, if the task has a number of steps, it is sometimes better to wait until everything has been completed because the individual learns from mistakes. And you thought guidelines for giving feedback were clear!

Do you create activities in which participants provide feedback to other participants? Clark and others recommend that you are clear about the feedback other participants should give—not just on the outcomes, but also on techniques and processes. Feedback can be one of the most potent learning factors (Butler, Karpicke, and Roedige 2008; Paschler et al. 2005).

Be sure you allow enough time for practice and that the practice is experiential. In addition, be sure to allow time for processing the activities, and practice with questions such as "What?" "So what?" "Now what?"

Learn From Mistakes

Asking learners to identify mistakes can be powerful in making substantial progress in learning (Butler, Karpicke, and Roedige 2008). For example you could perform a task incorrectly. A study by McLaren et al. (2012) gave the same content to two groups—one group was given correct information to discuss, and the second group was given incorrect information and asked to find what was wrong. Follow-up tests showed that both groups raised their individual scores by about the same amount. However, a second follow-up test given six days later demonstrated that the group that reviewed the incorrect information scored 12 percent higher. They increased their personal scores even more! The other group scored about the same as they did for the original post-test. This is exciting research. Imagine what you can do with it. It tells us that learning from mistakes is better for the long term. By the way, I love the name of this study, "To Err Is Human; To Explain and Correct Is Divine."

Chunk Away

Chunking is a strategy of breaking down content into bite-sized pieces so the brain can digest it more readily. This is necessary because the brain's working memory holds a limited amount of information at a time. The concept was articulated by George Miller in 1956 when he stated that working memory could hold seven (plus or minus two) chunks of information (1956). Cognitive scientists know that the capacity actually depends on the kind of information and the ability of the individual. In addition, scientists now think that the number may be smaller than seven. How can you chunk information as you design a training program? Try the following tips:

- Start at the highest level. You can start with large portions of content and divide them as modules—much like a chapter in a book.
- Divide the modules into smaller related chunks, which become lessons and break the content down one more time to become topics and content or activities within the topics.

- Throughout the process, think in terms of working memory. How much information do you really need? Can you eliminate some of the content?

As a final check, review the program design. If the learners need to retain more than a few things in their memory at the same time, you may need to break it down again.

Take Time

Incorporate enough time for all the invisible learning. It's probably not something that you've considered as a topic for designing training. It's important to make sure we heed the research that informs us of the value of reflection, discussion, building rapport, and yes, even breaks. Edgar Schein (1983), MIT Sloan Fellows professor of management emeritus, who researches organizational culture, learning, and change, states that reflection is a key factor in adult learning.

"We do not learn from experience . . . we learn from reflecting on experience."

—John Dewey

Plan Individual Reflection Time

A study in the journal of *Psychological Science* reported that some of the most important scientific breakthroughs by people such as Einstein occurred when they allowed their minds to wander (Baird et al. 2012). Engaging in simple external tasks promotes creative problem solving. I like to add a "reflection" page at the end of each module to encourage learners to think about what they have learned and to process it.

Schedule Discussions

If you want your learners to discuss a topic, you will need to build it into your schedule. Be sure to plan questions that lead to a healthy give and take. You should also allow time for involvement from all who wish to be part of the discussion.

Build Rapport

Plan to create rapport with your learners, but also be a catalyst to build learner-to-learner rapport to facilitate shared ideas, networking, and social collaboration by designing small group exercises and competition.

Honor Breaks

Sometimes you will fall behind, so feel free to skip over content. More content is not always better. It's just more. Besides, cognitive science tells us that breaks can be valuable spacing times. Breaks help your learners retain information.

How Much Time Does Design Require?

I've mentioned several times that you need to allow enough time for design. So how much time is enough? As you can imagine there are different opinions—even with research to back up the figures. Bryan Chapman (2010) of Brandon Hall found these average design times to create one hour of training content:

- 33:1 for PowerPoint to e-learning conversion.
- 34:1 for instructor-led training (ILT), including design, lesson plans, handouts, and PowerPoint slides.
- 220:1 for standard e-learning, which includes the presentation, audio, some video, test questions, and 20 percent interactivity.
- 345:1 for third-party courseware—the time it takes for online learning publishers to design, create, test, and package third-party courseware.
- 750:1 for simulations from scratch—creating highly interactive content (Chapman 2006).

The eLearning Guild states that approximate development times to create one hour of e-learning for each type of delivery can vary:

- Simple asynchronous (static HTML pages with text and graphics): 117 hours.
- Simple synchronous (static HTML pages with text and graphics): 86 hours.

- Average asynchronous (above plus Flash, JavaScript, animated GIFs): 191 hours.

- Average synchronous (above plus Flash, JavaScript, animated GIFs): 147 hours.

- Complex asynchronous (above plus audio, video, interactive simulations): 276 hours.

- Complex synchronous (above plus audio, video, interactive simulations): 222 hours.

Karl Kapp (2009) begins one of his blog posts by saying, "Designing training is as much of an art as it is a science." He goes on to say that it is still important to try to figure out approximately how much time design requires. He conducted research and provides a "low" and a "high" number of hours to give you the range provided in Table 3-2. For more about his research, you can check out the link to his blog, which is listed in the resources.

Table 3-2: Number of Hours Required for Design

Type of Training per 1 Hour	Low Hours per Hour of Instruction	High Hours per Hour of Instruction
Stand-up training (classroom)	43	185
Self-instructional print	40	93
Instructor-led, web-based training delivery (using software such as Centra, Adobe Connect, or WebEx-two-way live audio with PowerPoint)	49	89
E-learning Developed Without a Template		
Text-only; limited interactivity; no animations	93	152
Moderate interactivity; limited animations	122	186
High interactivity; multiple animations	154	243
E-learning Developed Within a Template		
Limited interactivity; no animations (using software such as Lectora, Captivate, ToolBook, TrainerSoft)	118	365
Moderate interactivity; limited animations (using software such as Lectora, Captivate, ToolBook, TrainerSoft)	90	240
High interactivity; multiple animations (using software such as Lectora, Captivate, ToolBook, TrainerSoft)	136	324
Limited interactivity; no animations (using software such as Articulate)	73	116

E-learning Developed Within a Template		
Moderate interactivity; limited animations (using software such as Articulate)	97	154
High interactivity; multiple animations (using software such as Articulate)	132	214
Simulations		
Equipment or hardware (equipment emulation)	949	1743
Softskills (sales, leadership, ethics, diversity, etc.)	320	731

You can see that investment in course design can add up to a great deal of time. Part of the reason is that there are so many elements to consider as you design the participant materials and learning activities.

What We Know for Sure

Science tells us that we can rely on several proven facts:

- There is little research around learning objectives, but it would be inane to think that they are not useful when designing training.
- We need to use the research completed by Bloom when writing objectives to help us focus on the accurate result.
- Visuals are valuable and we can ensure they are optimal if we follow a few evidence-based guidelines.
- Research does not support learning styles; however, that does not mean you should treat everyone the same. We are all different. The key is to include enough variation in your designs to appeal to everyone.
- Incorporating Malcolm Knowles's adult learning principles into your training will actually lead to some exciting and practical activities.
- Practice is critical.
- Giving feedback and learning from mistakes are both important in how we learn.
- Chunking is a strategy to break down content into bite-sized pieces so the brain can more easily digest them.
- Ensure that you have enough time for invisible learning to occur.
- "Down time" is a key to learning.

 **The Art Part**

Your success will depend upon how well you adapt to the situation and your learners' needs. Tap into some of these ideas to help your learners grow, to develop yourself, and to add your personal creative touch.

Props are a surprising treat. Props include a diverse assortment of three-dimensional items that participants use to discuss or practice with. They may be used as practical, hands-on support to:

- Display samples of product, errors, and so on for participants to examine.
- Introduce models of actual equipment, locations, and buildings.
- Practice skills using actual tools, equipment, or materials.
- Demonstrate a correct process or procedure.
- Use as a metaphor to make a point visually.
- Make a closing statement.

Skype the CEO. Have your organization's president or CEO welcome learners to a class in real time.

Creative objectives. Instead of presenting learning objectives, create a game quiz. Based on their performance, learners determine their gaps and write their own objectives.

Art and Science Questions You Might Ask

These questions provide potential challenges for your personal growth and development:

- What design skills do you need to ensure learners effectively interact with new knowledge?
- How can you chunk content into digestible bites?
- Do you build in enough time for reflection and practice?
- What techniques can you use to review content?
- What job aids or checklists can you design for continued learning on the job?

- How can you use physical movement to engage learners?
- What can you do during the design that enhances your relationship with the learners?
- What questions can you ask that will inspire, influence, and encourage dialogue?
- How could you use incorrect information to train?

How Do We Design So Others Can Learn?

A huge amount of research has been conducted about the best way to design training. As long as you are logical and don't do anything that is inaccurate, I doubt that you can do any harm. And of course your learners will tell you whether you hit the mark during your first delivery. I suggest that you start your design and then go back to check some of the research and compare how you did. You can always make changes before you deliver the class.

Finally, take all the advice and read all the research. You will find research that contradicts other research, which is not surprising. All learners are unique (Jensen 2008), they all have different brains, and they all learn differently. You will be successful if you use your common sense.

Resources

Allcock, S., and J. Hulme. 2010. "Learning Styles in the Classroom: Educational Benefit or Planning Exercise?" *Psychology Teaching Review* 16:2.

Baird, B., et al. 2012. "Inspired by Distraction: Mind Wandering Facilitates Creative Incubation" *Psychological Science* 23(10): 1117-1122.

Biech, E. 2007. *90 World-Class Activities by 90 World-Class Trainers*. Hoboken, NJ: John Wiley & Sons.

——. 2011. *The Book of Road-Tested Activities*. Hoboken, NJ: John Wiley & Sons.

——. 2014. *ASTD Handbook: The Definitive Reference for Training and Development*. 2nd ed. Alexandria, VA: ASTD Press.

———. 2015. *101 More Ways to Make Training Active*. Hoboken, NJ: John Wiley & Sons.

———. 2015. *Training and Development for Dummies*. Hoboken, NJ: John Wiley & Sons.

Bloom, B. 1968. *Learning for Mastery*. Los Angeles: The Center for the Study of Evaluation of Instructional Programs, University of California.

Britton, B., S. Glynn, K. Muth, and M.J. Penland. 1985. "Instructional Objectives in Text: Managing the Reader's Attention." *Journal of Reading Behavior* XVII(2):101-113.

Butler, A.C., J. Karpicke, and H.L. Roedige III. 2007. "The Effect of Type and Timing of Feedback on Learning From Multiple-Choice Tests." *Journal of Experimental Psychology: Applied* 13(4):273-281.

———. 2008. "Correcting a Metacognitive Error: Feedback Increases Retention of Low-Confidence Correct Responses." *Journal of Experimental Psychology: Learning, Memory, and Cognition* 34(4):918-928.

Chapman, B. 2010. *How Long Does It Take to Create Learning?* Chapman Alliance, September. http://www.chapmanalliance.com/howlong/.

Choi, I., S.J. Lee, and J. Kang. 2009. "Implementing a Case-Based E-Learning Environment in a Lecture-Oriented Anesthesiology Class: Do Learning Styles Matter in Complex Problem Solving Over Time?" *British Journal of Educational Technology* 40(5):933-947.

Clark, R. 2015. *Evidence-Based Training Methods: A Guide for Training Professionals*. 2nd ed. Alexandria, VA: ATD Press.

Dirksen, J. 2012. *Design for How People Learn*. Berkeley, CA: New Riders Publishing.

Duarte, N. 2008. *Slide:ology: The Art and Science of Creating Great Presentations*. Sebastopol, CA: O'Reilly Media.

Eberly Center for Teaching Excellence. 2008. "The Educational Value of Course-Level Learning Objectives/Outcomes. Carnegie Mellon Unversity. www.cmu.edu/teaching/resources/Teaching/CourseDesign/Objectives/CourseLearningObjectivesValue.pdf.

eLearning Guild. 2002. "The e-Learning Development Time Ratio Survey." The eLearning Development www.elearningguild.com/pdf/1/time%20to%20 develop%20Survey.pdf.

Ericson, K., R. Krampe, and C. Tesch-Romer. 1993. "The Role of Deliberate Practice in the Acquisition of Expert Performance." *Psychological Review* 100(3):363-406.

Jensen, E. 2008. *Brain-Based Learning: The New Paradigm of Teaching.* Thousand Oaks, CA: Corwin Press.

Kapp, K., and R. Defelice. 2009. "Time to Develop One Hour of Training." *Learning Circuits,* August 31. www.td.org/Publications/Newsletters/ Learning-Circuits/Learning-Circuits-Archives/2009/08/Time-to-Develop-One-Hour-of-Training.

Kappe, F.R., L. Boekholt, C. den Rooyen, and H. Van der Flier. 2009. "A Predictive Validity Study of the Learning Style Questionnaire (LSQ) Using Multiple, Specific Learning Criteria." *Learning & Individual Differences.* 19(4):464-467. doi: 10.1016/j.lindif.2009.04.001.

Kozub, R.M. 2010. "An ANOVA Analysis of the Relationships Between Business Students' Learning Styles and Effectiveness of Web Based Instruction." *American Journal of Business Education* 3(3):89-98.

Mager, R.F. 1997. *Preparing Instructional Objectives: A Critical Tool in the Development of Effective Instruction.* 3rd ed. Atlanta: The Center for Effective Performance.

Martin, S. 2010. "Teachers Using Learning Styles: Torn Between Research and Accountability?" *Teaching and Teacher Education* 26(8):1583-1591.

McLaren, B.M., et al. 2012. "To Err Is Human, to Explain and Correct Is Divine: A Study of Interactive Erroneous Examples." In *21st Century Learning for 21st Century Skills,* edited by A. Ravenscroft, 222-235. Berlin: Springer.

Medina, J. 2008. *Brain Rules: 12 Principles for Surviving and Thriving at Work, Home, and School.* Seattle: Pear Press.

Miller, G.A. 1956. "The Magical Number Seven, Plus or Minus Two: Some Limits on Our Capacity for Processing Information." *Psychological Review* 63(2):81-97.

Moreno, R., and R.E. Mayer. 2000. "Engaging Students in Active Learning: The Case for Personalized Multimedia Messages." *Journal of Educational Psychology* 93:724-733.

Pashler, H., M. McDaniel, D. Rohrer, and R. Bjork. 2008. "Learning Styles Concepts and Evidence." *Psychological Science in the Public Interest* 9:105-119.

Pashler, H., N. Cepeda, J. Wixted, and D. Rohrer. 2005. "When Does Feedback Facilitate Learning of Words?" *Journal of Experimental Psychology: Learning, Memory, and Cognition* 31:3-8.

Pluth, B. 2016. *Creative Training: A Train-the-Trainer Field Guide*. Eden Prairie, MN: Creative Training Productions.

Rothkopf, E.Z., and M.E. Koether. 1978. "Instructional Effects of Discrepancies in Content and Organization Between Study Goals and Information Sources." *Journal of Educational Psychology* 70:67-71.

Rothkopf, E.Z., and R. Kaplan. 1972. "An Exploration of the Effect of Density and Specificity of Instructional Objectives on Learning From Text." *Journal of Educational Psychology* 63:295-302.

Sankey, M.D., D. Birch, and M.W. Gardiner. 2011. "The Impact of Multiple Representations of Content Using Multimedia on Learning Outcomes Across Learning Styles and Modal Preferences." *International Journal of Education & Development Using Information & Communication Technology* 7(3):18-35.

Schein, E. 1983. *The Reflective Practitioner: How Professionals Think in Action*. New York: Basic Books.

Snowden, R., P. Thompson, and T. Troscianko. 2012. *Basic Vision: An Introduction to Visual Perception*. 2nd ed. Oxford, UK: Oxford University Press.

Stolovitch, H., and E. Keeps. 2011. *Telling Ain't Training*. 2nd ed. Alexandria, VA: ASTD Press.

Zacharis, N.Z. 2011. "The Effect of Learning Style on Preference for Web-Based Courses and Learning Outcomes." *British Journal of Educational Technology* 42(5):790-800.

What About the 90% of Learning That Occurs Beyond the Classroom?

Imagine you're at work and you've forgotten a step in a process that you haven't completed in the past few months. What do you do?

- Ask a co-worker for assistance?
- Check your organization's intranet?
- Review a previous task?
- Look in your employee handbook?
- Ask your boss?
- Google it?

Of course you do one of those listed or something similar. And you usually learn something new in the process. Ninety percent of what you learn is learned informally on the job. This 90 percent is two parts of the 70-20-10 guide for learning that I mentioned in chapter 2. Let's dig a little deeper into what 70-20-10 really means to you.

Experiential, informal, social, asynchronous, coaching, mentoring OJT, mobile learning: As today's talent development professional, you have multiple options for delivering learning to employees. The 70-20-10 model (70 percent hands-on experience; 20 percent developmental interactions; 10 percent formal learning) continues to serve as a valuable guideline for using a wide variety of developmental options. Trainers are experts in the 10 percent domain—delivering training or programs—but what's our role beyond instructor-led training? How do you deliver personalized developmental experiences? Can you support social learning? How can you ensure employees are immersed in experiential learning? What is your role in influencing interaction between employees and supervisors? Can you stimulate informal learning?

The world of work is changing. Trainers must provide shorter, more accessible, relevant, immediate, global learning experiences. They need to engage learners, ensuring that they have increased competence, confidence, and commitment. Today's organizations want the ability to drive greater individual and organizational performance. They need agility and speed, and they view a learning strategy that incorporates the 70-20-10 framework as a solution.

The Science and the Story Behind 70-20-10

The 70-20-10 model for learning and development is based on research that was conducted at the Center for Creative Leadership (CCL) in North Carolina beginning in the 1980s. The team leading the research included Morgan McCall Jr., Michael Lombardo, and Ann Morrison. Their research was reported in 1988. Michael Lombardo and Robert Eichinger then adapted the results of that research, leading to the current 70-20-10 framework. Today 70-20-10 is used as a talent development strategy aimed at improving workplace performance.

Other Science to Support 70-20-10

Beyond the work at CCL, what other evidence exists to support the 70-20-10 framework? Empirical studies and surveys on the topic first started in the late 1960s and demonstrated that employees acquire most of their knowledge and skills in the workplace and through others. Not all present an exact 70-20-10 split, but they consistently show a similar breakdown. Here are a few examples:

- In researching adult learning and personal change in the 1970s, Professor Allen Tough reported that "about 70 percent of all learning projects are planned by the learner himself." Although he didn't refer to a 70-20-10 split immediately, he later stated that is what he found.

- Mark Loewenstein and James Spletzer (1998) published a study conducted by the U.S. Bureau of Labor Statistics referencing research from 1993 and 1994. It stated that people learn about 70 percent of their jobs informally, although they found significant variation between both formal learning (13 to 46 percent) and informal learning (9 to 96 percent).

- In the 1990s, the Education Development Center of Newton, Massachusetts, summarized findings from a two-year study of corporate cultures, which was funded by the U.S. Department of Labor, state governments, and the Pew Charitable Trusts. An objective of the study was to "quantify formal training's contribution to overall job knowledge: 70% of what people know about their jobs, they learn informally from the people they work with." Study participants included Boeing Commercial Airplane Group, Siemens Power Transmission and Distribution, Reflexite North America, Data Instruments, Merry Mechanization, Ford Electronics, and Motorola (Dobbs 2000).

- Research by CapitalWorks, a human capital management service in Williamstown, Massachusetts, found that "not only do employee learning programs based on informal methods and self-study increase employee knowledge and productivity far more than more formalized methods, they also cost less." According to the study, employees learned about 75 percent of their skills on the job informally, through discussions with co-workers, asynchronous e-learning, and mentoring by managers. The other 25 percent were gained from formal training methods such as workshops, seminars, and synchronous classes (Lloyd 2000).

- Most recently DDI and The Corporate Board asked global leaders, "What percent of your time is spent in each of the three learning domains?" More than 13,120 responded (DDI 2014). The results? 52 percent learning on the job; 27 percent learning from others; and 21 percent from formal learning.

The Rest of the Story

As part of my preparation to write this book I contacted Michael Lombardo to confirm my content. I asked him about 70-20-10, his recollections, and to clarify some of my assumptions. For one thing I wanted to find out how the numbers should appear and what the categories should be called. Michael did not care. He stated that the most important part was that people understood the implications of the framework. How refreshing! Highlights of our discussion are embedded in the sidebar.

THE STORY BEHIND 70-20-10

Michael Lombardo shared with me that the original research was conducted with successful leaders. It was not originally meant to be called a model, formula, or a rule. Instead it was simply a rough guide to get everyone to think about how people develop. It is intended to provide a framework.

He said that the numbers project a solution that isn't as simplistic as it appears. For example, the pure 70-20-10 doesn't project the three essential ingredients to learning:

- Employees need challenging tasks. Development is a demand pull, "I want to grow because ___." Development occurs when the need and the solution meet.
- To learn, employees need to be assisted by others. Simply being exposed to new information is meaningless. Learning occurs when employees receive feedback and are helped by others—the social element of learning.
- Employees need fresh content and that is where courses come into the equation.

The 70-20-10 framework is a holistic approach and is powerful when everything is working together. It is more relevant today than ever before.

Follow-up studies have been conducted that replicate these or very similar results. The right balance will be different for each situation and each organization—even for different parts of the same organization.

People sometimes get distracted. Practitioners who argue that the percentages should be different—60-30-10, for example—are missing the point. It is meant to be a guideline, not a recipe.

It is disappointing to see the guide used for the wrong reasons, too; for example, to attack formal courses. I sometimes hear people attempt to justify spending a smaller budget on courses because it is the smallest percentage. Although only 10 percent or so, formal learning is critical for gaining new information and skills.

The best learning strategy is one that draws upon elements of all three categories.

Formatting 70-20-10

You have probably seen the 70-20-10 framework written as 70/20/10, 70:20:10, or even 70% 20% 10%. You've also seen the categories called different names, such as those in Table 4-1.

Table 4-1: 70-20-10 Categories

70%	20%	10%
Experience	Exposure	Education
Workflow	Social	Formal
Informal	Self-directed	Instruction
Practice	People	Programs
On-the-job assignments	Learning from others	New formal content

You can see that designers can be creative with the 3Es or the 3Ps. Whatever your organization decides to call it is fine, as long as it works for you and that you understand that these are guidelines. As you work with the framework you will see that there is some crossover between categories too.

But the real beauty is that no matter how the numbers are presented or what the categories are called, most people in the talent development profession recognize it as representing how we develop. The simplicity helps professionals and senior leaders quickly grasp the approach and benefits.

70-20-10 Learning Activities

So what activities might you expect to find within each of the three categories? Remember that I mentioned you will find some crossover between categories. For example, a research project could be a job assignment or learning from others.

Formal Content Activities—10 Percent

The low percentage may surprise you if you are reading about this framework for the first time. Supporters contend, however, that it is a critical element in development to ensure new concepts and innovative ideas are presented. The first activities that might come to mind are probably instructor-led courses, either in person or online virtually. The category also includes:

- courses, seminars, and workshops
- e-learning and virtual modules
- blended learning of classroom and e-learning
- certification or certificates
- professional accreditation
- college or university classes
- MOOCs, CMOOCs, and SPOCs
- reading books, articles, and whitepapers.

Learning From Others (Social)—20 Percent

The social element echoes the importance of receiving encouragement and feedback. The true value is that conversations stimulate learning. Others can be mentors, coaches, role models, capable supervisors, or even incompetent bosses. Receiving feedback is an important aspect of this development category. Without feedback we tend to settle into a complacent attitude that prevents us from becoming better and even sinking back to bad habit. No matter from whom we are learning, good examples or bad, we are learning from others every day. This category includes:

- accepting mentoring and coaching relationships

- encouraging peer feedback
- engaging as a mentor or reverse-mentor
- joining online professional communities
- seeking advice, opinions, and work debriefs
- curating and sharing work developments
- building internal and external networks
- initiating 360-degree feedback processes
- leading research projects
- training and teaching others.

On-the-Job Assignments—70 Percent

The experiential aspect may make this one of the most beneficial categories for employees because it enables them to discover, make decisions, and address challenges to ultimately refine their job-related skills. Matching the most appropriate challenging experience to the developmental need of the employee is powerful. When you think back to your career, certain events, tasks, or assignments most likely stand out as key developmental turning points. These developmental opportunities helped you decide what aspect of the work you liked and didn't and gain competencies in the process. This list encompasses just a few opportunities that are not only developmental, but also afford an employee to gain knowledge and skills, ultimately improving performance:

- solving problems (lead a project, action team member)
- handling a crisis
- participating in cross-functional activities
- accepting rotational assignments
- leading community or volunteer activities
- expanding the scope (new responsibility, acting role)
- accepting stretch assignments
- managing change
- championing a new product or service
- applying newly learned concepts

- increasing senior management interaction
- increasing the span of control.

Finally, remember that the true value of this model is using all three as a holistic approach to developing employees.

A Different Framework of Learning

In his book *Flat Army*, Dan Pontefract (2013) provides another view of learning ratios: 3-33, which stands for 33 percent of the learning is formal, 33 percent is informal, and 33 percent is social. What is most interesting is that the research behind his model revealed that when the learners were asked to give the percentages for how they thought they learned, the numbers were very different than when the researchers actually discovered how the learners actually learned. Pontefract calls his 3-33 approximation a Pervasive Learning model—learning is a collaborative, continuous, connected, and community-based growth mindset (Figure 4-1).

Although the Pervasive Learning model doesn't have the history or the traction the 70-20-10 has, it is worth reviewing. Remember the title of this book is *The Art and Science of Training*! You can read an overview of the model in Dan's chapter in the *ASTD Handbook*.

Figure 4-1: Pervasive Learning Model

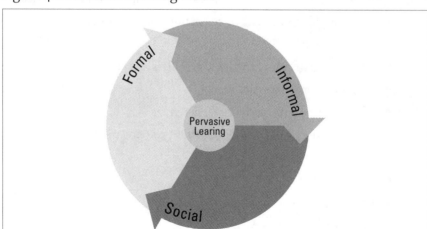

Put Learning Where the Work Is

No matter what numbers the model uses, you can envision that your job is to put the learning where the work is. Figure 4-2 adds another dimension to the 70-20-10, serving as a reminder that none of these elements stand alone. The framework needs to contribute to employees' development by weaving in and out of work and learning. Imagine that work and learning circle around the model ensuring that the right developmental activities are available at the right time.

Figure 4-2: 70-20-10

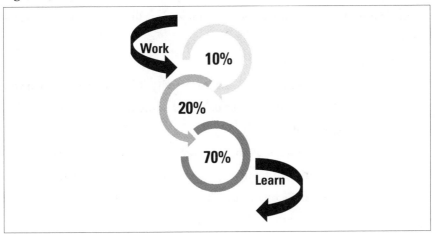

A Blended Perspective

I like to think of 70-20-10 as the first blended learning design. The 10 percent, or formal learning, includes classroom skill-building courses, simulations, instructor-led virtual classes, and reading. The 20 percent, or social learning, focuses on learning from others and includes how you can use communities of practice, coaching and mentoring, peer networking, and supervisory support. The 70 percent, or on-the-job assignments, includes new initiatives, increased responsibilities, and learning from mistakes. However, there are many crossover learning opportunities. For example, blogging or Twitter could be considered social learning but can also be paired with formal learning events.

On-demand learning such as webinars, videos, or job aids are other examples of how the three categories can work together. A webinar, for example, might be considered formal learning until your supervisor discusses it with you (social) and suggests that you implement what you learned on your new project (on-the-job assignment). This is blended learning that can (and should) occur naturally.

In addition, all of these need to be experiential in nature. The 70 percent category should not be renamed "experiential." *All* learning should be experiential. Imagine a transparent coating over the figure that represents experiential. How do you ensure your learners get these opportunities? What can you do to ensure learning is experiential? Here are a few ideas linked to each of the categories (Biech 2016):

- Formal—10 Percent
    - Use an experiential learning activity (ELA) model in which you follow activities with a debrief that includes What? So what? Now what?
    - Ensure you allow time for practice, reflection, observation, and conversation to "experience" what they are learning.
    - Build future relationships by encouraging learners to trade business cards and email addresses.
    - Design realistic role plays.
    - Demonstrate feedback.
- Learning From Others—20 Percent
    - Organize accountability relationships that extend beyond the classroom or virtual learning experience.
    - Encourage and establish mentors and coaches for learners.
    - Utilize apps and mobile learning; for example, could you text a challenge to a group of learners?
    - Connect learners through social media using discussion boards, incorporating Twitter feeds and allowing learners to share content on Facebook.

- o Enable watercooler learning by emailing a question of the day to an employee group.
- On-the-Job Assignments—70 Percent
  - o Work with managers to find challenging opportunities for employees.
  - o Encourage learners to seek out rotations, acting, and stretch assignments.
  - o Seek community and volunteer options.
  - o Communicate team prospects for those needing this experience.
  - o Help managers learn to ask the right questions such as:
    - What's on your mind?
    - What are your thoughts about *xx*?
    - What would you do differently next time?
    - What can you implement based on this experience?
    - What do you still need to learn/do/know?

"Personally, I'm always ready to learn, although I don't always like being taught."
—Winston Churchill

Organizational implementation of the 70-20-10 framework requires learning and development to team up with managers. There are two concerns here that only you and your organization can answer.

First, do your managers appreciate the importance of their role in developing their people? This framework requires that managers are coaches and recognize that they are primarily responsible for their employees' performance. It means that they foster an environment in which people can talk to them and to each other, share knowledge, and grow. The Brandon Hall Group found that "exposure to managers" was the second-most used development activity. Unfortunately its effectiveness was rated at 50 percent. You can't just toss the development task over the transom and expect supervisors and managers to know what to do. It is your role as a trainer to help them understand how to develop people.

Second, does your learning and development department understand what it needs to do to support supervisors and managers? Perhaps your learning and development department has a developmental opportunity. Jon Wolper (2016) reported in the May 2016 issue of *TD* that "DDI research shows that [two of] the most critical skills for leaders include coaching and developing others and identifying and developing future talent." This illustrates the important role managers have in developing employees. Put on your creative hat and paint a picture of how you could help.

Redefine Your Accountability and Relevancy

What is your role in the 70-20-10 framework? Would it surprise you to know that your talent development role is expanding? How can you target and shape learning beyond your classroom? How can you influence your learners' developmental experiences outside your classroom? And how can you integrate the framework to redefine your accountability to your organization and be more relevant?

Sound like too much work? You have at least four big opportunities to connect your session to the other 90 percent every time you lead a session (Biech 2016). You won't be able to implement all of these ideas for all of your learning events, but try a few—soon.

Prepare Before Your Session

Your preparation prior to the session is critical for you and your learners. Preparation takes on a new expanded and valuable part in the process when you begin to think about what you can do to connect to your participants and how they can continue to learn beyond the formal learning session. Contact or meetings with supervisors, learners, and others is key. You should:

- Meet managers and mentors to discuss what they expect from your training session, asking about the goals, measures, and changed behaviors.
- Collect messages from managers or leaders and share them during the session. The messages could be words of encouragement, offers of further development after the session, or anything else you deem useful to development.
- Ask participants to work with their supervisors to identify challenges related to the topic and arrive prepared to discuss the challenges.
- Pre-action plan with participants and their supervisors. What skills do they need to develop? What performance needs to be improved?

Engage During Your Session

Of course you are aware of the importance of engagement during your session. Be a good example during your session, because your learners watch what you do. This list addresses several specific ways that you can connect your instructor-led session with both on-the-job assignments and learning from others:

- Give feedback after all practice sessions. This accomplishes two things. Participants learn from your feedback and they learn the appropriate way to give feedback.
- Remember to use the debriefing questions. It is only a start to learning when participants hear the "what" of your message. The most important part comes with the debriefing questions or the "so what" (so what does that mean or relate to?) and the "now what" (now what are you going to do or change or implement as a result?).
- Allow reflection through journaling or designed activities. You may need to seed the reflection with possible questions.
- Assign accountability partners who work together during the session to encourage the social aspect of learning.
- Build in plenty of time for practice and rehearsal.

Focus Your Closing

Guard the time you have scheduled to close your session. Too often trainers get behind during an earlier part of the session and then rush through the closing. Many things come together and you'll want to ensure that participants have a sense of closure to the experience. Think about how you can create continued learning for all participants, how you can help learners stay connected, or what you can do to ensure that the skills are transferred to the workplace. These ideas will help you lead the all-important transition opportunity that occurs during the closing:

- Brainstorm barriers that may occur as they return to the workplace. Form small groups to identify ideas to overcome the barriers.
- Create learning communities. Support them with a wiki or a LinkedIn page to continue the experience by asking questions, sharing tips, giving advice, or celebrating successes. Seed the site with questions, links to videos, or short articles.
- Allow enough time so that learners can create action plans and discuss with someone else.
- Help your learners design a plan to meet one-on-one with their managers to ensure both understand what was taught and how it can be implemented.

The Aberdeen Group reports that almost half of all organizations struggle to ensure that what is taught in formal events is understood and used on the job. Only 26 percent of organizations say that employees are expected to have one-on-one meetings with their managers. However, they also found that 71 percent of best-in-class companies are more likely to have employees and managers meet following a formal event than all other companies (Moon 2015).

Apply After Your Session

It may be difficult to schedule time for follow up, but it is one of the most critical steps you can take to ensure that learners transfer what they learned to the workplace. Schedule your follow up prior to the session and ensure that you protect it. Remember that you helped participants start their journey; it's important that you follow up to assist them to reach their final destination. You can implement dozens of follow-up activities such as:

- Implement peer practice groups made up of the participants, or for a different dynamic add others in the department.
- Contact learners with tips, reminders, quizzes, articles, or other support materials through email, texts, discussion boards, Twitter, or personal visits.
- Meet with managers to discuss content and application. Remind managers about the skills taught so they can reinforce behaviors they observe. Revisit any discussions you may have held prior to the learning event. Answer any questions and provide tools that support managers to continue the learners' development.

This short list only scratches the surface of all of the things you can do to encourage development beyond the classroom. However, it will help get you started in your artist role so that you can develop yourself as you develop others.

As talent development professionals, we develop the capability for our organizations' future. Technology has opened exciting doors and we are inundated with new tools, technologies, and approaches. Organizations want us to provide learning that is faster, shorter, and more relevant. There is no shortage of ideas for *what* to do; the question is *how* to do it. Research conducted by ATD and i4cp in 2015, as reported in *Instructional Design Now: The Age of Learning and Beyond*, found that fewer than half in the learning profession think they are "highly effective at addressing learning needs."

Talent development professionals are experts at delivering formal learning as instructor-led training (ILT) in virtual and traditional classrooms. But the professional's role has broadened and expanded beyond the classroom. Based on the 70-20-10 model, this means that we need to learn innovative delivery methods in the 70 and 20 domains to step beyond our ILT roles. We need to put learning where the work is. According to Jane Hart (2014), talent development professionals are already increasingly incorporating informal and social learning into their repertoire of delivering learning.

In addition, talent development professionals need to learn how to help their supervisors and managers. They need to coach them to be better coaches, and stay on top of the changes. Superior results will occur when you implement all that 70-20-10 has to offer.

Expand Learning Opportunities

The challenge is to move your focus from the classroom to the workplace. This means you need to reframe what you do to more closely match how your employees learn and perform. Almost everyone is comfortable with technology and how it can be used to improve options and save time. A faster pace and strong competition have increased a need to be more nimble and customer focused than ever before. Increasing levels of work for everyone has created more pressure to improve performance.

What if your organization isn't ready to move to a 70-20-10 framework and you work primarily in an instructor-led role in a classroom or you are facilitating virtual learning? You can still implement some ideas. The grid in Table 4-2 (found on page 92) can help you create truly blended learning options that extend beyond your instructor-led classrooms (Biech 2016). It's an excellent way for you to get some experience stepping outside your instructor-led training role. You can use the activities as a transition for you and your learners' supervisors. Some of the activities share responsibility for the learning with the supervisors. You might call it a step in the right direction to putting the learning where the work is.

What We Know for Sure

Science tells us that we can rely on several proven facts.

- The 70-20-10 framework was not meant to be called a model. It was meant as a rough guide to influence those in the learning and development fields to think about how people develop.

- Employees need challenging tasks. Development occurs when the need and the solution meet.
- To learn, employees need to be assisted by others.
- Learning occurs when employees receive feedback and are helped by others—the social element of learning.
- The 70-20-10 framework is a holistic approach and is powerful when everything is working together. It is more relevant today than ever before.
- The best learning strategy is one that draws upon elements of all three categories.

The Art Part

Your success will depend upon how well you adapt to the situation and your learners' needs. Tap into some of these ideas to help your learners grow, to develop yourself, and to add your personal creative touch.

DIY design. Design your own 10 x 10 grid and fill in at least half of the cells with ideas. The next time you design or deliver a training session you will have 50 ideas from which to select.

Develop yourself. We all look for new opportunities. Complete this exercise and then use your experience to help other leaders in your organization. Think about how you could start something new or make a strategic change in your job. Create three columns on a page and title them: "Reshape My Job," "Temporary Assignments," and "Outside the Workplace." Under each of the headings, list four to five opportunities. For example, under "Reshape My Job" you could list "Take responsibility for a new project or process" or "Develop five-year business scenarios for my department." Under "Temporary Assignments" you could include "Volunteer my work group as a test site for a new organizational system" or "Seek seed money for an exploratory project." Under "Outside the Workplace" you could include "Establish a strategic plan for a community or professional organization" or "Volunteer for a task I've never done before in a community organization."

⚛ Art and Science Questions You Might Ask

These questions provide potential challenges for your personal growth and development:

- How can a 70-20-10 approach to development respond to your organizational challenges and priorities?
- What are the benefits of a workplace culture of continuous learning?
- How can you optimize on-the-job training in your organization?
- What can you do to help your organization transform into a learning organization?
- How can you create meaningful and impactful informal learning?
- What's your role beyond instructor-led training?
- What's your role to deliver personalized developmental experiences?
- How can you support social learning?
- How can you ensure employees are immersed in experiential learning?
- What is your role in influencing interaction between employees and supervisors?
- How can you stimulate and support informal learning?
- What kind of toolkit could you develop to support managers in their roles to develop employees (for example, tips, checklists, tools, discussion starters)?
- How can you help encourage collaboration and cooperative learning to actively transfer knowledge and skills?
- How do you coordinate formal learning with on-the-job assignments and learning from others?
- How could you socialize the framework across your organization?
- How can you support managers in their role as talent developers?
- How can you best encourage managers and supervisors to develop talent?

What About the 90 Percent of Learning That Occurs Beyond the Classroom?

The 70-20-10 framework can be used to assess how employees learn and develop in your organization. It is not prescriptive, but a guide for what seems to work in most organizations under most circumstances. It is not meant to be one more thing for you to do. It is not meant to be a distractor or antitraining. And finally it is not a perfect ratio. It can help you redefine your accountability and relevancy.

The other 90 percent? The 70-20-10 framework *is* the reality that we all need to promote and encourage as our key responsibility. We need to become more adept at supporting and enhancing the other 90 percent.

Table 4.2. 100 Design Combinations to Expand Learning Beyond the Classroom

Method Objective	Twitter	Text or Email	Peer or Supervisor	Pinterest/ Instagram	Social Media and Internet
Opening				Send photos ahead as introductions	YouTube introductions
Meet Others	140-character intro		What my boss knows (pre-class)	Collaborative group project	
Content-Related Icebreaker		Text a question for icebreaker			
Needs Assessment	Twitter NA p. 137				
Gather Data				Assign research boards	
Evaluate Skills					
Practice			Peer action learning team		Google your organization p. 277
Review	140-character summary			Visual journal	
Job Aid					Make and share on a discussion board
Follow-up Engagement	Ask what is needed after class	Learning buddies	Peer coaching circles		

© 2016 Elaine Biech. Page numbers refer to activities in *101 Ways to Make Learning Active Beyond the Classroom*.

External Experience	Personal Improvement	Video	On-the-job	Personal Introspection
		Pre-welcome by trainer on YouTube		
		Participants video selves and share		
				Preassign one concept I must learn
Assign department NA				
				Preassign interviews with leaders
	Establish life goals p. 229		Academy p. 275	
Volunteer in community organization			Rotational request	
		Video/share company examples		
				Create personal post-use job aid
	Virtual or local book club			

Resources

Biech, E. 2014. *ASTD Handbook: The Definitive Reference for Training and Development*. 2nd ed. Alexandria, VA: ASTD Press.

———. 2015. *New Supervisor Training*. Alexandria, VA: ATD Press.

———. 2016. "101 Ways to Expand Learning Beyond Your Classroom." Presented at the ATD 2016 International Conference & Exposition, May 2016, Denver.

Bozarth, J. 2010. *Social Media for Trainers: Techniques for Enhancing and Extending Learning*. Hoboken, NJ: John Wiley & Sons.

Dobbs, K. 2000. "Simple Moments of Learning." *Training* 35(1):52-58.

Hart J. 2014. *Social Learning Handbook*. London: Centre for Learning and Performance Technologies.

Lloyd, R. 2000. "Informal Learning Most Effective." *Knowledge Management*. http://www.kmmagazine.com.

Loewenstein, M.A., and J.R. Spletzer. 1998. *Formal and Informal Training: Evidence From the NLSY*. Washington, D.C.: U.S. Bureau of Labor Statistics of the U.S. Department of Labor. www.bls.gov/ore/abstract/ec/ec940090.htm.

Lombardo, M., and R. Eichinger. 2011. *The Leadership Machine: Architecture to Develop Leaders for Any Future*. Minneapolis: Lominger International: A Korn/Ferry Company.

McCall, M.W. Jr., M. Lombardo, and A.M. Morrison. 1988. *The Lessons of Experience: How Successful Executives Develop on the Job*. Lexington, MA: Lexington Books.

McCauley, C. 2006. *Developmental Assignments: Creating Learning Experiences Without Changing Jobs*. Greensboro, NC: Center for Creative Leadership.

McCauley, C., D. DeRue, P. Yost, and S. Taylor. 2015. *Experience-Driven Leader Development: Models, Tools, Best Practices, and Advice for On-the-Job Development*. Hoboken, NJ: John Wiley & Sons and Center for Creative Leadership.

Miller, L. et al. 2015. *Instructional Design Now: The Age of Learning & Beyond*. Alexandria, VA: ATD.

Moon, M. 2015. *The New 70:20:10: The Changing Face of Learning*. Aberdeen Group, September 30. www.aberdeen.com/research/11040/11040-RR-newalearning-framework.aspx/content.aspx.

Pontefract, D. 2013. *Flat Army: Creating a Connected and Engaged Organization*. San Francisco: Jossey-Bass.

Raybould, R. 1995. "Performance Support Engineering: An Emerging Development Methodology for Enabling Organizational Learning." *Performance Improvement Quarterly* 8(1):7-22. www.imamu.edu.sa/Scientific_selections/Documents/IT/Raybould.pdf.

Ruderman, M., and P. Ohlott. 2000. *Learning From Life: Turning Life's Lessons Into Leadership Experience*. Greensboro, NC: Center for Creative Leadership.

Sinar, E., R.S. Wellins, R. Ray, A.L. Abel, and S. Neal. 2014. *Ready-Now Leaders: 25 Findings to Meet Tomorrow's Business Challenges*. DDI. www.ddiworld.com/DDI/media/trend-research/global-leadership-forecast-2014-2015_tr_ddi.pdf?ext=.pdf

Tough, A. 1971. *The Adult's Learning Projects: A Fresh Approach to Theory and Practice in Adult Learning*. La Jolla, CA: Pfeiffer and Company.

Wolper, J. 2016. "Developing Effective Leaders." *TD*, May.

What Can You Expect of Technology?

Smartphones, smart cars, smart homes, virtual reality. Growing corporate networks, exciting technology, and the Internet have created expectations for "smart" learning everywhere. And the ability to integrate tools is nothing short of amazing. As we move to a world without computers, only smart networked objects, everything will be connected.

Organizations are pushing the boundaries of artificial intelligence. They are planning to use the wealth of data that will soon be available to them to do everything from innovate their services and products for a competitive advantage to reverse engineering customer dissatisfaction.

And in talent development? We will see more wearables that support learners, a stronger emphasis on gaining employee experience, and mainstreamed virtual reality. The downside is that experts predict a skilled labor shortage in the near future like we've never seen (Desmarais 2016).

But what about today. What do we know now?

Using Technology as a Learning Strategy

The 2016 ATD *State of the Industry* reported that technology-based learning expanded from 41 percent in 2014 to 42 percent in 2015. Technology-based learning as defined by ATD includes online instructor-led learning, self-paced online, mobile, and non-computer technology such as DVDs.

Currently the majority of technology is focused on e-learning. We use e-learning in both synchronous and asynchronous situations. We are still getting comfortable with the technology and how to best use it, while at the same time recognizing that the world of technology isn't waiting for us to adapt; it's moving forward.

If you design or conduct virtual training sessions, take a look at *The Serious eLearning Manifesto* developed by Michael Allen, Julie Dirksen, Clark Quinn, and Will Thalheimer (several of a group I call the e-Learning Elite). The group observed designers taking shortcuts and ignoring evidence-based design techniques like those I have presented in this book. They wanted to remind training designers to focus on quality and proven scientific techniques to create the most valuable learning experiences. The authors have created a statement of what they believe are the best principles for e-learning design and development. You can see the short version in the sidebar.

THE SERIOUS E-LEARNING MANIFESTO

The Serious eLearning Manifesto—developed by Michael Allen, Julie Dirksen, Clark Quinn, and Will Thalheimer—focuses on some of the core principles of instruction. This shortened list of best practices and principles for e-learning establishes a guide to follow when you design virtual learning sessions:

- performance focused
- meaningful to learners
- engagement-driven
- authentic contexts
- realistic decisions
- individualized challenges
- spaced practice
- real-world consequences.

Additional supporting principles, which provide more detail about how each of these ideas should be realized, are included in the manifesto. *The Serious eLearning Manifesto* is a free online resource with an open creative commons license so you can use it any way that's helpful (http://elearningmanifesto.org).

Is Online Training Effective?

Have you enrolled in a webinar lately? Did you check your email, eat lunch, answer co-workers' questions, or finish writing that overdue report while the facilitator talked through her well-designed, informative slides? Yes? Well, me too. So you might ask, how can online learning be effective?

A report from MIT researchers states that online classes are at least as effective as traditional classroom courses—and they found that this is true regardless of how much preparation and knowledge students start with (Pritchard 2014). In fact, those students who were the least prepared as demonstrated by their pretest scores learned as well as everyone else. In another study in 2012 of more than 6.7 million students, 77 percent of academic leaders rated the learning outcomes for online education the same or superior to face-to-face learning experiences (Babson 2012).

Ruth Clark (2015) weighs in on the subject of effectiveness of online learning as well. She suggests that research shows that learning outcomes improve in asynchronous e-learning if you ensure that the important topics and examples are the default rather than an option to be selected. The "continue" selection should lead to the most important content. Another beneficial design feature is to provide advisement during the lesson based on responses. Clark reminds us that control over pacing should be available to all learners, allowing them to manage their rate of progress.

Finally Cindy Huggett (2013) reminds us that to be truly effective we need to continue using all the excellent learning tools and techniques we use in a physical classroom in our virtual classrooms, too.

There Are Benefits

Online training is available in most organizations and has been proven to be effective. So, what are the benefits to the organization and learners? Five of the most favorable are:

- **Saves time.** It is delivered in shorter chunks, with little or no travel time.
- **Is convenient.** It is easy to take a course at your desk. It can be delivered 24/7. You can study anywhere at any time.
- **Is tailorable.** It is possible to tailor asynchronous content to move beyond "one-size-fits all." Support is readily available.
- **Saves money.** It decreases travel costs.
- **Expands reach.** It ensures that more learners can benefit from the training. It's also easy to include a variety of facilitators.

Where We're Heading

Today, more emphasis is placed on informal and social learning than ever before. You've probably felt this shift already, as your organization begins to move from today's expectations into the demands of tomorrow. One example is The Persistent Classroom. Developed by David Powell, founding member of the Innovation Lab at the Center for Creative Leadership, The Persistent Classroom provides learners with anywhere, anytime learning. Table 5-1 provides additional examples.

Table 5-1: Moving Learning From Today to Tomorrow

From Today's Expectations	To Tomorrow's Demands
Learning departments push courses	Employees pull what they need to learn
Focus is on knowledge, skills, and attitudes	Increased use of experiential learning
Focused on e-learning, classes, individual development plans, and learning from experts	More dependence on informal, on-the-job, and social interaction
Emphasis is on closing performance gaps and gaining competencies as defined by supervisors	Emphasis is on learning to learn and finding ways to answer immediate requirements
Learning is contained and approved internally by the organization	Learning is done internally and far beyond into the community, perhaps outside the country

Apply Adult Learning Theory to Technology

What technology you use will not affect the fundamentals of good learning design. Do you conduct virtual training? Virtual requires the same tactics as the traditional classroom. In fact, the two delivery methods are more alike than different, according to Cindy Huggett. Let's consider how we apply Malcolm Knowles's learning principles in an e-learning event:

- **Share the purpose.** Learners will want to know why the content is important. Encourage questions during the first session. Keep it informal.

- **Maintain self-concept.** Find ways to build on learners' existing knowledge or invite them to share during an open mic period. Invite submissions of short self-videos or written introductions to share with everyone. Encourage small group exercises between online sessions, and have an e-learning support system in place for questions. You can also post learners' pictures on a slide at the beginning of the session (but be sure you have their permission).

- **Acknowledge experience.** Tap into expertise. Anticipate that your group will have a broad array of skills and skill levels. Use polls and quizzes to draw out their memories. If you send out a precourse survey, you can learn about their technical knowledge limitations to prevent discomfort in the first session.

- **Make it relevant.** Learners are looking for support for immediate concerns. Share how the content can be used immediately, and use chat so that others can chime in. Allowing time for reflection is also useful. Establish your own credibility and how you can help.

- **Deliver solutions.** Use an example of an instance you overcame a hardship or situation that required these skills. Make it easy for them to relate your solutions to their problems.

- **Respect self-motivation.** Adults are self-motivated and are more likely to participate and learn if they feel camaraderie. Consider using Google Hangouts or asking everyone to turn on their cameras during an early session.

Performance Support

The MASIE Center defines performance support as "any learning modality, resource, or asset that is accessible and applicable at the moment of need. It is embedded in the work process such that the learning is accessed in the context of the work flow and helps solve a very specific problem."

When you think about performance support, computer-aided support and performance support tools probably come to mind first. But is that all that is available? No. In the sidebar, Patti Shank (2014) provides examples of performance support.

WHAT IS PERFORMANCE SUPPORT?

Performance support can be anything from looking up information about a patient's healthcare coverage at a doctor's visit, to getting help diagnosing a car's problems, to looking up prices at other stores, to downloading maps and directions. It may be in the form of text, graphics, audio, or video, and include:

- **Information:** contract numbers, error codes, prices, warehouse locations, names, or addresses
- **Assistance:** a decision tree, an expert system that asks questions and suggests the best course of action
- **Instructional support:** a link to a video showing how to do a task, a simple list of steps to take, or a practice simulation
- **Tools:** spreadsheets, databases, online calculators, company programs used for a specific purpose.

Performance support tools give employees what they need at the right time to make their jobs easier. You might use an interactive PDF, video, whiteboard animation, or something else. At what point might you use a performance support tool? Consider introducing one when your learners:

- are learning a skill or process step for the first time
- want to learn more about what's happening or why
- want to apply or remember a step they've forgotten
- need to solve a problem or address an issue

- face changes in a process, the system, or in the organization.

Performance support is relevant, convenient, and user-friendly.

Getting Excited About Technology All Over Again

Social media is expanding your options for talent development. Are you taking advantage of all that's available? You may want to revisit the design combinations table at the end of chapter 4. It may jog the creative side of your brain to think of how you could use Twitter, YouTube, Facebook, wikis, blogs, Instagram, and other formats in your training. Essentially you can create every part of a learning event using social media tools and technology.

"Unless you try to do something beyond what you have already mastered, you will never grow."

—Ralph Waldo Emerson

Tweet Your Training

Social media and smart mobile devices such as phones, tablets, and watches have firmly established their place in our society. Consider how you can use these technology resources to make training more effective and fun. Right now, Twitter appears to be the most mainstream, and it is more likely to be approved by your IT team now than in the past.

Thanks to the addition of image attachments and its intrinsic value of limited size messages, Twitter is perfect for concise, relevant training nuggets delivered right to your learners' devices. Here are 10 things you could Tweet that would enhance a face-to-face or virtual training program (Biech 2015; Bozarth 2010):

- short, snappy descriptions of the training programs for potential learners
- reminders of dates and times of the program
- a QR code of the webpage with more details on the program

- a message from your CEO about the importance of the training
- pictures of books you are reading that will enhance the content
- images evoking a training class that future participants won't want to miss
- follow-up job aids using a shortened URL or QR code
- reminders of new behaviors or knowledge you want to make stick
- tips for supervisors to ensure new training behavior is observed
- a link to the program evaluation immediately after completion.

Should You Use QR Codes?

QR code is short for quick response codes. These handy little tools can be used in multiple ways. Initially an alternative to bar codes in the automotive industry, this matrix of dots or lines can now be used to reference a specific website. QR codes can be created and read by anyone with Internet access and a reader (a smartphone camera).

So, how can you use QR codes? They provide a simple solution to ensure training content is always available for your learners. Suppose you needed to make a forklift safety training video accessible to your team 24/7. You could simply create the QR code with the URL of the training video, print the code, and attach it to the forklift. Then your learners can scan and watch the video anytime they need it. If you wish to track who uses the QR codes and when, you can implement a data analysis system, such as Google Analytics.

Here's another example. You could deliver training content to your sales staff's smartphones while they are on the road. This allows you to provide up-to-the-minute resources and new data at any time of the day or night.

There are many options and many books that define some very creative activities. For now, I will leave you with 15 activity stems to consider the next time you are asked to facilitate a learning program. They are not completely defined (thus the name "stem"), but that's half the fun. Check out the sidebar on the next page and use the artist in you to focus on how you can incorporate the concept.

ACTIVITY STEMS TO USE ONLINE

- Engage with a poll immediately.
- Post a rolling quote slide show.
- Use chat rooms for paired intros.
- Submit photos and intros to Instagram, LinkedIn, a Facebook group, or other social media site.
- Use analogies on a whiteboard.
- Follow a case with several discussion questions in chat pods.
- Ask volunteers to role play.
- Find corporate facts on the company's website.
- Use SurveyGizmo to create questions for other groups to answer.
- Email a short video clip before the session and use breakout groups to discuss.
- Conduct a Point-Counterpoint on a discussion board.
- Create a Poll Everywhere question.
- Post "How I will apply what I learned" on the whiteboard.
- Have participants create a DIY job aid.
- Create a key concepts Pinterest board.

What We Know for Sure

Science tells us that we can rely on several proven facts:

- Social media, e-learning, and technology that we haven't even heard of yet can make learning more fun, less expensive, and more immediate than in the past.
- Conducting a virtual instructor-led training program has the same requirements as conducting an instructor-led class.
- The adults you are training are guided by the same principles as those that Malcolm Knowles studied.
- You are moving into a learning environment in which learners will be expected to know what they need to learn.
- Your job is changing!

The Art Part

Your success will depend upon how well you adapt to the situation and your learners' needs. Tap into some of these ideas to help your learners grow, to develop yourself, and to add your personal creative touch.

Field trip. Take a field trip around the offices you support. What quick references have people created that might be hanging next to their computers? Is there something you can do to make these homemade job aids more useful to the designer? Can you distribute them to others?

Create a tool. Yes, computerized performance support would be nice, but that isn't always possible. When it isn't, create job aids or tools to help your learners remember key concepts, formulas, intranet sites, or other helpful lists, examples, or processes. You could create an e-version and email it to them so they can store it conveniently. And you can give a laminated copy to those learners who like to tape tools to their computer.

Knowles meets virtual learning. It's one thing to say that a virtual learning event should demonstrate the same things as a traditional classroom setting. It's harder to actually make it happen. You can start with these questions to build Malcolm Knowles's adult learning principles into your next virtual learning event:

- How can I engage learners during the session?
- When can I encourage learner-to-learner collaboration?
- How can I make short bursts of information interesting in a three- to five-minute segment?
- How can I tap into the knowledge and expertise of the learners?
- How can I ensure 100 percent participation?

 # Art and Science Questions You Might Ask

These questions provide potential challenges for your personal growth and development:

- How can you help your organization use technology as a learning strategy?

- Regarding technology, where is your organization now and where does it want to be?
- What's the best way to start your technology journey?
- What do you need to learn about technology and learning in the future?
- What support will learners of the future need to find their way through the content maze?
- What are the opportunities for mobile application in your organization?
- How well is social learning being adapted as a learning strategy?
- What is your ongoing e-learning strategy?

So What Can You Expect of Technology?

You can expect everything and nothing of technology. Everything because new tools, processes, and strategies are expanding daily. There are spectacular examples of how social networking is changing the way we conduct business and develop people. M-learning has just started to shine, and virtual reality is on the cusp of exploding. A limitless source of new tools and technologies is on the way.

You can expect nothing from technology unless you avail yourself of the options, learn about the tools, experiment with new activities, and engage in social networks yourself. As stated, there will be a limitless number of available tools and technologies, but you have to reach out and grab them.

Resources

ATD. 2015. *State of the Industry*. Alexandria, VA: ATD Press.

Blair, B.S. 2013. "Babson Research Study: More Than 6.7 Million Students Learning Online." "Babson College, January 8. www.babson.edu/news-events/babson-news/Pages/130107-2012-survey-of-online-learning-results.aspx.

Biech, E. 2007. 90 *World-Class Activities by 90 World-Class Trainers*. Hoboken, NJ: John Wiley & Sons.

——. 2011. *The Book of Road-Tested Activities.* Hoboken, NJ: John Wiley & Sons.

——. 2014. *ASTD Handbook: The Definitive Reference for Training and Development.* 2nd ed. Alexandria, VA: ASTD Press.

——. 2015. *Training and Development for Dummies.* Hoboken, NJ: John Wiley & Sons.

Bozarth, J. 2010. *Social Media for Trainers: Techniques for Enhancing and Extending Learning.* Hoboken, NJ: John Wiley & Sons.

Clark, R. 2015. *Evidence-Based Training Methods: A Guide for Training Professionals.* 2nd ed. Alexandria, VA: ATD Press.

Colvin, K.F., et al. 2014. "Learning in an Introductory Physics MOOC: All Cohorts Learn Equally, Including an On-Campus Class." *The International Review of Research.* www.irrodl.org/index.php/irrodl/article/view/1902/3009.

Deloitte. 2016. *Global Human Capital Trends 2016, The New Organization: Different by Design.* Westlake, TX: Deloitte University Press.

Desmarais, C. 2016. "10 Tech Trends to Expect in 2016." *Inc.,* January 4. www.inc.com/christina-desmarais/10-tech-trends-to-expect-in-2016.html.

Dirksen, J. 2012. *Design for How People Learn.* Berkeley, CA: New Riders Publishing.

Huggett, C. 2010. *Virtual Training Basics.* Alexandria, VA: ASTD Press.

——. 2013. *The Virtual Training Guidebook: How to Design, Deliver, and Implement Live Online Learning.* Alexandria, VA: ASTD Press.

Powell, D. 2014. "The Persistent Classroom." In *ASTD Handbook: The Definitive Reference for Training and Development,* edited by E. Biech, 873-887. Alexandria, VA: ASTD Press.

Quinn, C. 2011. *Designing mLearning.* San Francisco: Pfeiffer.

——. 2005. *Engaging Learning: Designing eLearning Simulations and Games.* San Francisco: Pfeiffer.

Shank, P. 2014. "Supporting Worker Performance in the Workplace." In *ASTD Handbook: The Definitive Reference for Training and Development,* edited by E. Biech, 447-459. Alexandria, VA: ASTD Press.

How Do You Prepare for Your Delivery Role?

W e are all trainers. We are all learners.

Sure you are a trainer; a facilitator of content. But when you are *preparing* to deliver your learning—whether face-to-face, online, one-on-one, in a video, or through some other method—you are a learner. The more you learn, the more you know about your client, the participants, the content, the expectations, the location, and even yourself, the better you will be when you switch to the role of trainer.

I've always felt that the creators of ADDIE forgot one of the most important steps—preparation. I think it should be ADDPIE.

"Audience interest is directly proportionate to the presenter's preparation."
—Nancy Duarte

Not ADDIE, but ADDPIE: Preparation

Few trainers put enough emphasis on the preparation required for a successful training program. When I first started as a trainer, I followed a 10:1 practice rule. That meant that for every hour in the classroom, it was necessary to practice the material for 10 hours. I refer to practicing the presentation only. This does not take into account room preparation, client preparation, participant preparation, or audiovisual preparation. Yep, that's pretty old school. Today, trainers are lucky to have a ratio of 1:1—and it shows. They may not appear as comfortable with the content, may not have a clear perspective of what the organization requires, and may not be familiar with the participants' competencies.

The Bob Pike Group believes that 80 percent of being a good trainer and getting participant involvement depends upon adequate preparation. In fact, the Pike 6 Ps remind us of the importance of preparation. The expression is, "Proper preparation and practice prevent poor performance" (Pluth 2016).

The best thing you can do for your participants is prepare for their success. If you do not need to worry about your delivery, you can focus on your participants, which is most important.

Training is like an iceberg. Most participants see the top 10 percent, what surfaces as a result of preparation: the error-free PowerPoint slides, the well-designed participant materials, a welcoming room set up, your professional facilitation skills, and your organized presentation. It all looks so easy! Consider that a compliment to your preparation. This chapter addresses the other 90 percent that's below the surface, including:

- how to prepare the physical environment
- how to prepare a positive learning environment
- how to prepare your participants
- how to prepare your client
- how to prepare yourself.

Prepare the Physical Environment

Your participants walk into your training room 30 minutes before you start. What do they see? Extra chairs stacked up against one wall? Empty boxes in a corner? Blinds askew? IT staff scurrying around trying to get the projector to sync with your computer so you can display your PowerPoint slides? You searching through your briefcase looking for your remote? Materials stacked haphazardly on the tables? Put yourself in your participants' shoes. How would that make you feel? Yes, there will always be those times when something goes wrong, but proper preparation helps you eliminate most of the problems.

There are two reasons to spend time preparing the environment:

- Participants will learn more, better, faster if the environment is conducive to learning. That means more than orderly; we'll address that further.
- You will feel more confident in your ability if you are organized. You will be better able to meet your participants' needs if you aren't worrying about the room details.

Room Arrangements

Let's begin with room set up. What's the foundation to any training design? The learning objectives. What's the foundation to how you set up your room? The learning objectives. The objectives will tell you:

- how much participation is required
- whether participants will have the best experience working in one team or working with many different people or a mixture of both
- whether a secondary goal of the session is to get the entire group to work more as a team (that is, as a department or functional group)
- if individual reflection is necessary.

Ideally you want to consider those four bullets, but the reality is that you may not have a choice when it comes to rooms, so you will have to make do with what you have.

Size

The room should be the appropriate size for the number of participants. Too small and everyone will be crammed in, which will make it difficult to conduct activities. And it is going to get really hot! Too large and it will be difficult to build a comfortable, welcoming environment—and do you hear that echo, echo,

echo? Watch out for windows placed on a west wall without shades, which will wash out your projected images when the afternoon sun comes streaming in. If the learning objectives require small group work, make sure there's enough room to form small groups that do not disturb others as they are working. If not, request a breakout room or two.

Location

The room should be in a place that is easy to find and easy to reach. This means both within the building and also by vehicle. Parking two blocks away and walking in the rain is not a good start to a day of training. Ensure that the room is easily accessible to everyone, including those with limited mobility.

Structure and Furniture

Sometimes the temporary walls in conference centers or hotels are paper thin. If there is a sales conference booked next to you, your participants may have a difficult time hearing. Check out what furniture is available. Do you want round tables, but can only get rectangular ones? You'll probably need to make do. If you are in a hotel, there will probably be cloths on the tables. Do they "skirt" the tables? This is the extra fabric that is placed around the edge of the table that goes to the floor. Skirts are useful because they cover scratched-up table legs; however, if they get tangled up in your participants' legs they become a distraction.

If your tables do not have table cloths, check them for cleanliness. I've scrubbed some pretty nasty looking tables in my career. How about the chairs? You'll want to provide the most comfortable chairs possible. And by the way, that's not the typical classroom stacking chair. The room arrangement should satisfy the needs of your agenda.

Electronics

Ensure that lighting is adequate. Is the light bright enough that your partici-pants will not fall asleep in a dimly lit, romantic atmosphere? Are you using a PowerPoint presentation? Too many trainers dim the lights when they do not need to. The lumens of light in the projectors used today do not require the dimming of room lights. Keep your participants energized and enthused (and awake). Keep the lights on bright. Having said that, be sure that you know where the light switches are located. Check out the location of outlets and placement of the screen. Will you need to jump cords throughout the presentation? Even worse, if your participants are expected to present to the group—as they will in a Train the Trainer class—untaped cords can become a hazard.

Climate Control

A third of your participants will always be too hot, a third too cold, and a third just right. You won't be able to please everyone, but if you have the ability to adjust the temperature yourself, you can try. When you are setting up the room the day before your session, experiment with the controls. Do they respond quickly? Does one degree make a big difference? Do you need to contact someone to help you? Remember, it is usually best to change thermostats one degree at a time. A room that was too cool can become too hot if you are not careful.

Walls

Do you have adequate wall space to hang flipchart pages? Sometimes walls are filled with windows and pictures, which leaves no space for hanging anything. I have removed artwork from the walls on more than one occasion. The most you will need to deal with is a nail that sticks through a flipchart.

Even if you have adequate wall space, they may not be usable. If they are covered with a felt-like fabric, it may be impossible to hang your flipcharts with masking tape. If they don't fall down immediately, they will slowly drift down during a time when you are trying to make a critical learning point. Sometimes you can use pins on these walls. Some conference centers will not allow you to use tape on the walls, so for times like those I carry blue painter's tape. It isn't pretty, but it is guaranteed to leave the paint intact. Finally, make sure you are using markers that will absolutely not bleed through.

Equipment and Visuals

If anything is going to go wrong, it will probably be something related to your equipment or visuals. The projector isn't compatible with your computer, the flipchart does not have paper, the DVD player is missing its electrical cord, the extension cord does not reach, your memory stick was damaged in transit. Whatever it maybe, it can prevent you from conducting the session that you had envisioned.

Although these suggestions do not ensure nothing will go wrong, following them will certainly increase the chances of success.

Conduct a Dry Run One Week Before

Set up the equipment, go through every PowerPoint slide, prepare your flipchart pages, and check out the visibility of the screen for everyone in the room. If you have anything tricky, such as an embedded video clip, sound bites, or animation, run through your presentation a few times. If you have never used a flipchart, practice flipping, ripping, and hanging techniques. (Have you ever spent a day staring at a flipchart page that has been hung crookedly?) If you have a new remote, try it out, especially the laser pointer. This is a good time to learn just how far you can stray from your computer while using it.

Set Up the Day Before

Probably your best hedge against something going wrong is to set up the day before. If something is missing or not compatible or was damaged in transit, you still have time to adjust. Focus all equipment and set the volume appropriately. Check the volume throughout the room—especially if you are relying on a laptop for sound, because they typically do not have the best sound system. Turn on everything to ensure it all works at the same time. Make sure the projector has the correct lens and it is clean. Check that the screen is large enough and mark the location of the projector with masking tape so that it is easy to reset if it is moved (for example, if it needs to be locked up or because someone cleaned the floors). Sit in the seats to ensure that everyone can see the screen, for example, to make sure your flipchart stand isn't blocking anyone's view of the screen. If you are using a computer, make sure you have the login ID and password to access it.

Have the Right Materials Available

I mentioned using markers that do not bleed through paper onto walls; water-based ones work best. Also, do not use dry erase markers on paper; they were meant to be used on whiteboards only. Dry erase markers dry out fast and do not allow you to write clearly.

Be Prepared for an Emergency

It's important to have extra batteries for your remote, an extra bulb for the projector, and an extra extension cord for anything electrical. Also, learn a few troubleshooting tricks for the equipment you use most often. The next time a technician fixes something, ask what was done and why. Pack a roll of duct tape to fasten unruly electrical cords. Be sure that you have the name and contact number (cell phone is best) of the person who will assist you if you are not using your own equipment. And finally, have an alternative plan in case all else fails. All trainers can conduct a successful session without their PowerPoint presentations. You just need to be prepared and think through what you might do ahead of time.

So that takes care of the tangible things you can do to prepare a traditional classroom environment. How about the virtual classroom?

It's Virtual: I Don't Have a Room

A virtual training session requires just as much set up, so you should leave an equal amount of time for preparation. Of course you don't have a room, but almost all of the advice for physical classroom trainers also pertains to virtual classroom trainers: Find out who's in your session, practice, create your personal checklist, and stay organized during the session. There are a few things that are unique to your set up. You should:

- Meet with your producer.
- Test your audio.
- Write and post marketing content through your selected method.
- Ensure that the registration and enrollment are tracked.
- Distribute materials through email or a central repository.

- Communicate with participants to ensure that they know how to set
  up and test their computers, disable pop-ups, close their email, post
  an out-of-office message, and other steps that will allow them to focus
  on their professional development.

If your organization has a LMS, most of the preparation before the session
will be automated, which saves you time. The drawback, however, is what
training is built on—personalization and connecting with your learners. There
may be times when you want to reach out to your learners, especially if some
are new to the technology, if this is the first of several consecutive events, or if
your audience is global.

Prepare a Positive Learning Environment

You must focus on your participants and ensure that the environment is positive. Create a learning environment of trust and respect. (Remember Malcolm
Knowles's adult learning principles?) Although the following items are an
important part of your session, you should address them ahead of time for a
couple of reasons:

- You need to be prepared to make the environment safe and
  comfortable without thinking about it.
- You need to be prepared so that you aren't thinking about setting up
  the next activity or where you left the special handouts.

The better you prepare a positive learning environment (safe, comfortable, and reliable), the more participants will want to talk with you during the
breaks. And the more they talk with you during breaks, the less time you have
to prepare for the activities after the break. Therefore you need to be prepared.

Make the Environment Safe

Every participant will arrive with a different mindset. Your job is to make the
environment safe for everyone. I try to set up the room the day before a training session, and arrive two hours prior to start time on the first day and at least
one hour prior to start time for the rest of the program. This is by far the most

important advice; part of your preparation is to plan how you can make the environment safe. You should:

- Be prepared early enough to greet participants at the door.
- Display a sign or a PowerPoint slide that tells participants they are in the right location and it is "safe" to enter the room.
- Learn participants' names and ask them to tell you something about themselves.
- Share the objectives of the training early, so they know what to expect.
- Let participants know what's in it for them.
- Use names and sincere reinforcement to build rapport.
- Learn techniques to get learners to open up.
- Create experiential learning activities in which the learners discover their own "ahas!"

Make the Environment Comfortable

Plan to arrive two hours early to welcome the learners. Arriving early is one way you demonstrate professionalism. Remember, the learner should be your focus. It is difficult to focus on your learners if you are not fully prepared physically and mentally for them.

In a traditional classroom you should:

- Turn the lights on bright. There is nothing more depressing than walking into a ballroom where the lights have been left on "romantic-dim" from the party the night before. I like to request a room with natural light. Even on a sunless day, natural light is more pleasant.
- Ensure that the environment looks comfortable. Hide empty boxes, make sure chairs are straight, and place materials neatly and uniformly at each seat. This order tells the learners that you care and went to the trouble of getting ready for them.
- Ensure that everyone has adequate personal space.
- Supply extra pens, paper, and other materials.

- Provide coffee, tea, and water in the morning and throughout the day.

In a virtual classroom, you should:

- Use a preclass communication to connect with your participants to assure them that you are there to help facilitate their learning.
- Confirm that participants received any handouts or other materials they need before the class.
- Help participants manage the environment in which they will attend the virtual session by suggesting that they close their doors, shut down their email, and remove other distractions. This can be included in your preclass communication.
- Do whatever it takes to put all learners at ease about participating in your virtual classroom.

USE PARTICIPANTS' NAMES

In a traditional classroom, I like to use table tents on which participants write their names. Some facilitators prefer to use name badges. Whatever your choice, be sure that you can read them. For example, ask participants to use a marker and write their first names large enough on the front and back so that everyone can read them from across the room. If you use preprinted table tents, make sure that the type size is bold and can be read from 40 feet.

In a virtual classroom, keep a list of all participant names next to you. Even if you have a host or administrative person who "opens" the classroom by checking audio connections and other tasks, you should welcome participants. This builds rapport. I suggest you encourage participants to join 10 minutes early. You should be there to greet each person by name, and add a short comment such as "Welcome back" or "What is your location?" or "How's the weather in Madison today?" Call on people by name during your virtual session, too.

Make the Environment Reliable and Trustworthy

Initiating ways to build trust with your participants makes the difference between simply attending training and absorbing knowledge. You should:

- Plan for small breakout groups to overcome early reluctance to share ideas or concerns.

- Think of how you will use body language to encourage participation—positive nods, smiles, and eye contact all show that you are interested in others' ideas.

- Remember when I mentioned in chapter 3 that participants learn more when materials and learning are presented in a conversational first- or second-person tense (Moreno and Mayer 2000)? I think it also helps to build rapport with your participants.

- Plan to share something of yourself to begin a trusted exchange of ideas.

- Stimulate discussion among the learners.

- Show that you value their opinions and ideas.

- Pair individuals as sounding boards for each other.

Prepare Your Participants

Touch base with your participants before the session. This makes it easier to develop rapport, build trust, clarify the purpose of the training, and initiate the learning. Other than sending them a reading assignment—which a third will skim, a third will forget to do, and a third will claim they never received—what can you do? The following ideas will prepare participants for the topic and help them accept you as a credible resource:

- Email the objectives of the session. Provide a phone number or email address and encourage them to contact you with any questions. Better yet, send a letter or a welcome card that includes the same information.

- Ask participants to complete an action, for example, interview a few leaders with questions you've sent, survey colleagues, or ask co-workers for feedback. For a train-the-trainer session, you could provide three questions to ask current trainers in their work area. Or you could ask them to bring a design project they are currently working on.

- Send a self-assessment ahead of time and ask participants to complete it before attending the session.
- Mail an agenda and attach a handwritten note telling participants how they can reach you. State that you welcome any questions they may have.
- Send a cartoon, puzzle, brain teaser, or thought-provoking question that is pertinent to the session and arouses their curiosity.
- Meet their "safety needs" by sending the logistics of the session, such as the location of the site, room number, telephone number for emergencies, plans for lunch, email access, available parking, available public transportation, a roster of fellow participants, and other pertinent material that will help them feel comfortable and prepared about attending the session.
- Speak with the participants' managers or supervisors to determine what they want the participants to be able to do when they return to the workplace. Encourage them to speak with their employees prior to the session. You may also wish to include discussion notes for the supervisor to address with the participant.
- Invite participants to send you any pertinent questions or topics they would like you to cover during the session.
- Get participants involved early in adjusting the agenda by sending them a brief questionnaire that focuses on their unique needs.
- Conduct a mini needs assessment on SurveyMonkey.com or Zoomerang.com. Share the results with participants before the session or early in the session.
- Call participants, introduce yourself, and inform them of the objectives and purpose of the course. Ask if they have anything specific they would like you to address during the session.
- Consider assigning reading ahead of time, even though some participants may choose not to read the assignment.

Prepare Your Client

Your focus is on the participants, and they will benefit most if there is clear communication among you, the participants, and the client (customer or manager). These ideas set the stage to ensure a transfer of learning occurs:

- Contact your client prior to finalizing the training plans and ask for issues or concerns that your client hopes to resolve with the training. What performance improvement does the client expect? You may be able to use these ideas to personalize the training or to address special issues. Often the information is just what you need to develop a new role-play situation or critical incident.

- Meet with your client to review the materials. Sometimes the participants' managers may not agree with a new concept or may not understand it. It's better to discuss this before you conduct the training.

- Discuss with your client his role in supporting and reinforcing the training.

- Ensure that supervisors are verbally supportive. One negative comment by a team leader can damage what's been learned during the training session (Smith-Jentsch, Salas, and Brannick 2001).

- Offer to coach your client after the training session is over.

- Before the training session, provide a template of a pretraining agreement on which the client and the participant can spell out exactly what the participant is to learn during the session and implement upon returning.

- Invite your client to kick off the session, thereby sharing ideas for her vision for the session.

Prepare Yourself

The better prepared you are, the more smoothly your session will go and you should encounter fewer problems. Even if something does go wrong, your preparation will pay off because you will be better able to address it. You need to know more than your participants regarding the subject because you won't know what questions they will ask. You also need to be flexible because your participants will lead their own learning—not you. Here's a general process I follow when I prepare to conduct a training session.

My preparation begins the day I find out I am conducting a training session. At that time I add it to my calendar, open a file, and pull the materials (if I have presented a similar session in the past) or begin collecting books or articles I might use as a resource (if it is a new session). I find out if I can observe the class being conducted and make the necessary arrangements if that's possible. I also ask if there is a subject matter expert I need to talk to or any background reading that would be helpful.

You will likely have three elements of materials to review: the participant handouts, the facilitator's guide, and the PowerPoint slides or other media. If the participant handouts have been created and finalized, I read all of them and think about what I read. Then I take a break from it and in a week or so scan the participants' handouts again. This is the spacing that I mentioned in chapters 2 and 3.

Next, I place the handouts beside the facilitator guide and the PowerPoint slides as I read it. If the PowerPoint slides are professionally done, they should not be filled with information, so they will not be very detailed. However, they will help you organize your thoughts; you can organize your presentation later.

Thus far I've been concerned with the details, but now it is time to look at the course from the big picture perspective. I look at the agenda if it has been provided and then print a copy and fill in the actual times that my session will take place. Next, I print a final copy of the schedule on brightly colored paper (I prefer bright yellow) so that I can always find it on my training table. This task gives me a better idea of the general topics I will complete in chunks, which was also covered in chapters 2 and 3.

Finally, I make a copy of my handouts, add my notes, and begin practicing with the PowerPoint slides.

General Preparation to Ensure a Smooth Session

Here's a quick checklist of what I do to prepare for the logistics prior to every training session:

- ☑ Review the training session thoroughly and list all the logistical details that need to be addressed. Create a checklist of these details and begin to address the items at least a week before the session.
- ☑ Create a packing list of all the things you need to take to the training session, such as markers, index cards, prizes, and tape.
- ☑ Complete all participant material and visuals early enough so that they can be proofed by someone else and corrections can be made. I suggest that you three-hole punch all materials and put them in a binder. You may also need to print evaluations and certificates, and you may need to locate resources (articles or books).
- ☑ Learn who will be attending your session to help you customize and plan the focus of your training. You might be able to learn their position, their understanding of the subject, the reasons they are attending, their opinions, any baggage they may bring with them, or negative concerns they may have about the content.
- ☑ Check on your room about a week before your session. Rooms have a way of rescheduling themselves or double booking with other groups if you do not give them enough attention.
- ☑ Provide a detailed drawing of how you want the room to be set up. Don't assume, however, that it will be correct. I change my room setup more often than not. It seems that if you ask for a room to be set up for 20, facilities people tend to err on the side of caution and set it up for 25. You do not want extra spaces set up, even though this is the practice at most convention centers and training rooms. Empty chairs make it appear that there were participants who did not show up.
- ☑ Begin to make contact with those in charge of the logistics at least a week before to confirm that they have your requests on record.

Contact them again the day before reminding them that you intend to arrive either two hours before the session begins, or the night before to go over final logistics. Remind them that you will want your AV equipment set up so that you can try it out. Get the name and phone number of the contact person who will be available to let you in the room, as well as a contact for the AV equipment.

☑ Set the room up the day (or evening) before the session; this is part of my preparation. Oftentimes people offer to help, but I prefer to do it myself. This process helps me feel prepared: I know where things are, and I know if I have forgotten something. It is a great way for me to give the room my personal touch and to take ownership of the space and be ready to welcome my guests the next day.

☑ Arrive one to two hours before the session begins to set up materials, finish last-minute details, tidy the room, rearrange furniture, set up and test equipment, and anything else that may arise. After you do this, you will be free to greet your participants as they arrive.

☑ Due to the possibility of last-minute crises or participants who arrive early, be sure you are fully prepared and rehearsed and your materials are in ready-to-go order.

No amount of preparation will avert all the problems, but the better prepared you are, the better you will be able to address them.

Tips for Practicing Your Delivery

Practice makes perfect—or so my grandmother would say. As a trainer you have lots of things to practice. You can start with these:

- Practice setting up and debriefing the activities with colleagues.
- Practice the mechanics, especially if you need to use two kinds of audiovisuals at the same time.
- Practice the theatrics if you tell a story with a punch line that needs certain pauses or inflection. Tell your story to colleagues or your significant other to get feedback.

- Practice aloud to ensure you have no enunciation problems.
- Practice in the room where you will conduct the training so that you feel comfortable—so comfortable that it becomes your room.
- Anticipate questions participants may ask, as well as your responses to them.
- Practice the questions you will ask participants.
- Practice in several different ways:
  - in front of a mirror
  - with your colleagues
  - with your family, friends—even your dog (who will make great eye contact!)
  - in front of a video camera or your smartphone.

Practice and preparation can make your training session all that you had hoped it would be. It will help you focus on your participants. It will ensure that you look professional.

"Learning is not compulsory, but neither is survival."

—W. Edwards Deming

It's About Time

A few organizations provide guidelines for their employees about the amount of time trainers should spend to prepare for a workshop. For example, the IRS has regulations stating that instructors must spend two to four hours of preparation per hour of training. The University of California, Berkeley, and Harvard Business School Press both recommend two to four hours. I spoke with two vendors who stated that their standard when learning a new course was at least five days of preparation for every day of instruction.

In 1985 Dugan Laird, a pioneer in the learning and development field and member of the HRD Hall of Fame, listed these instructor preparation times based on U.S. Civil Service estimates:

- Course is five days or less: three hours of preparation for each hour of training.
- Course is between five and 10 days: 2.5 hours of preparation for each hour of training.
- Course is more than 10 days: two hours of preparation for each hour of training.

I can tell you exactly how much time it takes me to develop, design, prepare, and practice for every one-hour webinar I've completed during the past year. I knew it took me a long time. In fact it was surprising, but each one required an investment of time from 70 to 100 hours. It certainly makes me rethink the profitability of webinars!

What We Know for Sure

Science tells us that we can rely on several proven facts:

- Preparation is important for success.
- Preparation is not just about the content, but also about preparing the environment, the participant, the client, and yourself.
- Preparation takes longer than you would think.
- Negative comments from supervisors can damage what's been learned during the training session.
- Preparation is valuable for both in-person and virtual training, although there are different tasks for each.

The Art Part

Your success will depend upon how well you adapt to the situation and your learners' needs. Tap into some of these ideas to help your learners grow, to develop yourself, and to add your personal creative touch.

Find the time. Chances are you will not have as much time to prepare as you would like. Find ways to squeeze it in whenever you can. For example, you might be able to record some of the information you need to learn and listen to it on the way to work. You could maintain a list throughout the day of the questions you think participants might ask you.

Create a checklist. You will never have enough time for preparation. That's the reality. One thing that will save you physical time as well as worry time is a preparation checklist. Create your own and include everything you know that you need to remember. It could have categories such as "what to pack," "AV check," or "room arrangement." Then under each heading add what you know you'll need. The "what to pack" list could include such things as DVDs, markers, tape, a remote control, and extra batteries. I have developed my list over the years—often because I'd forgotten something!

Pick a preparation practice. Select one of the ways from the list to prepare your participants. Do it before your next training session.

Be mindful. Practice mindfulness techniques when you begin to feel frustrated.

Art and Science Questions You Might Ask

These questions provide potential challenges for your personal growth and development:

- What can you do to build a strong, trusting, and positive dynamic with the participants?
- Which practice techniques will work best for you?
- What's your plan to build collaborative and supportive relationships among participants?
- Have you designed good questions that will encourage meaningful discussion among participants?
- What's unique about your organization that you should consider when you prepare participants?
- What's unique about your organization that you should consider when you prepare clients?
- What's the best way to discuss preparation and practice time with your manager?

- What creative ways can you find to practice?
- How can you and your colleagues practice collaboratively?
- What did you learn about being a learner while preparing?
- How are you going to find time to prepare and practice?

How Do You Prepare for Your Delivery Role?

Do you get nervous before conducting a training session? Preparing for your delivery role will lessen the irrational thoughts and make those butterflies in your stomach fly in formation. Practicing and being prepared help to ensure that you are ready for anything.

Remember, preparation isn't for you; it's for your learners. This chapter has given you ideas to prepare your learners, your client, your environment, and yourself. We are all busy—too busy. Implementing what you can will be valuable. You are a learner as you practice. You are a trainer once delivery starts. Preparation leads the way to excellence.

Resources

Biech, E. 2014. *ASTD Handbook: The Definitive Reference for Training and Development.* 2nd ed. Alexandria, VA: ASTD Press.

———. 2015. *Training and Development for Dummies.* Hoboken, NJ: John Wiley & Sons.

Campos, J. 2014. "The Learner-Centered Classroom." *TD at Work.* Alexandria, VA: ATD Press.

Chapman, B. 2006. *PowerPoint to E-Learning Development Tools: Comparative Analysis of 20 Leading Systems.* Sunnyvale, CA: Brandon Hall Research.

———. 2010. *How Long Does It Take to Create Learning?* Chapman Alliance, September. www.chapmanalliance.com/howlong/.

Clark, R. 2015. *Evidence-Based Training Methods: A Guide for Training Professionals.* 2nd ed. Alexandria, VA: ATD Press.

Duarte, N. 2010. *Resonate: Present Visual Stories That Transform Audiences.* Hoboken, NJ: John Wiley & Sons.

eLearning Guild. 2002. "The e-Learning Development Time Ratio Survey." The eLearning Development www.elearningguild.com/pdf/1/time%20to%20 develop%20Survey.pdf.

Huggett, C. 2010. *Virtual Training Basics*. Alexandria, VA: ASTD Press.

——. 2013. *The Virtual Training Guidebook: How to Design, Deliver, and Implement Live Online Learning*. Alexandria, VA: ASTD Press.

Laird, D. 1985. *Approaches to Training and Development*. 2nd ed. Reading, MA: Addison-Wesley.

Moreno, R., and R.E. Mayer. 2000. "Engaging Students in Active Learning: The Case for Personalized Multimedia Messages." *Journal of Educational Psychology* 93:724-733.

Pluth, B. 2016. *Creative Training: A Train-the-Trainer Field Guide*. Eden Prairie, MN: Creative Training Productions.

Salas, E., S. Tannenbaum, K. Kraiger, and K. Smith-Jentsch. 2012. "The Science of Training and Development in Organizations: What Matters in Practice." *Psychological Science in the Public Interest* 13(2): 74-101.

Smith-Jentsch, K.A., E. Salas, and M.T. Brannick. 2001. "To Transfer or Not to Transfer? Investigating the Combined Effects of Trainee Characteristics, Team Leader Support, and Team Climate." *Journal of Applied Psychology* 86:279-292.

How Do You Align Delivery to Your Learners' Needs?

Remember my refrain in chapter 1, "It's all about the learner?" Well when you deliver training you are face-to-face with the learner. Aristotle (yes, him again—and he's not even my favorite philosopher) stated that, "Art completes what nature cannot bring to finish. The artist gives us knowledge of nature's unrealized ends."

If we think of our learners as "unrealized ends," trainers are the artists who help people see that they have more potential than they think they do. The most effective trainers facilitate processes that encourage learning and create an environment that is conducive to learning. They ensure the absorption of knowledge and skills, and provide a setting that instills confidence and courage.

You've probably heard the statement that humans use only 10 percent of their brains. Turns out it is a myth. Barry Gordon, a neurologist at Johns Hopkins School of Medicine, says that couldn't be further from the truth (Boyd 2008). What may be true is that scientists only understand about 10 percent of *how* the brain functions. Throughout the day we use virtually all of our brain for different tasks.

Think about how much you are capable of doing. You can walk, talk, listen, smell, laugh, swim, work, touch, write, read, sing, dance, build, drive, calculate, compose, design, learn, and create. You have the potential to do many things. It is the artist in you who sets the stage for learning, helping learners see all the possibilities.

"We need our arts to teach us how to breathe"

—Ray Bradbury, *Zen in the Art of Writing*

Help your learners by establishing the processes and setting an environment in which they can learn all they are capable of learning. Then use the artist within to teach your learners "how to breathe." Let's examine your two key tasks and end by putting it all together:

1. Create an environment that is conducive to learning.
2. Use cognitive learning tactics customized for individual learners.

Yes, there are hundreds of other tasks as well. But let's only focus on these two critical areas. And there will be a bit of crossover between them.

DID YOU NOTICE?

You may not have noticed, but I have tried to embed learning concepts throughout this book. In this case, my focus is on cognitive overload—providing you, the learner, only what you need. Our brains can only process a specific amount of information at a time. Cognitive load theory provides guidelines that help to define the amount and in what manner content should be presented to ensure maximum learning (Sweller, Van Merrienboer, and Paas 1998).

Create an Environment Conducive To Learning

You have the ability to raise your learners' self-esteem and confidence. You can help them become the best version of themselves. I referenced Malcolm Knowles in several chapters. Remember his adult learning principles? This is key to the environment you create, so let's start there.

Apply Adult Learning Theory

It's important to circle back to Knowles's work and become grounded in his assumptions by answering the six key questions that your learners will be asking themselves before they attend your learning event. With any typical science, his principles make sense, but how do you artfully apply them? It is not enough to just know adult learning principles. When you are conducting training for a group, you must be able to implement them. They should become a part of your trainer persona. Think about how to incorporate each of Knowles's principles in your future designs and in your delivery. How will you respond to the questions that participants bring to your sessions?

1. "Why do I need to know this?" Adults have a need to know why they should learn something before investing time in a learning event.

   Share the purpose. You could incorporate these into your delivery:

   - Write the purpose on a flipchart page and post it on the wall.
   - Give participants time to vent if necessary.
   - Be prepared to respond to comments such as, "my boss should be here."
   - Link the content to the participants' jobs and particular issues they may be facing.
   - Encourage questions from learners.

2. "Will I be able to make decisions or are you going to re-create my grade school memories?" Adults enter any learning situation with a self-concept of themselves as self-directing, responsible grown-ups.

   Maintain self-concept. You could incorporate these into your delivery:

   - Welcome participants with a warm greeting and a cup of coffee.
   - Announce that participants can get up, move around, get a cup of coffee, or whatever it takes to be comfortable.

- Make the point that questions are encouraged—all questions.
- Allow participants to establish their own ground rules.
- Lead learners toward inquiry before supplying too many facts.

3. "Why am I here? How do I fit? What do they think they can teach me?" Adults come to a learning opportunity with a wealth of experience and a great deal to contribute.

   Acknowledge experience. You could incorporate these into your delivery:

   - Allow participants to add to the learning objectives.
   - Use teach-backs as a learning method.
   - Allow for differences of opinion.
   - Customize and personalize. If everyone in the session understands the content, speed up. If most do not understand, repeat the portion. If some know it and some don't, find ways to tap into the expertise in the room to be beneficial to everyone.

4. "How is this going to simplify my life? How will this make my job easier?" Adults have a desire to learn those things that will help them cope with daily life effectively.

   Make it relevant. You could incorporate these into your delivery:

   - Allow time for participants to ask questions about implementation back on the job (Salas, Tannenbaum, Kraiger, and Smith-Jentsch 2012).
   - Make yourself available at breaks, at lunch, and after the session to discuss unique situations with individuals.
   - Allow time for reflection on how the concepts can simplify their lives or make their work easier.
   - Establish your own credibility without bragging, and couple this with an I-want-to-help-you attitude.

5. "Do I want to learn this? Do I need to learn this?" Adults are willing to devote energy to learning those things that they believe will help them perform a task or solve a problem.

    Deliver solutions. You could incorporate these into your delivery:

    - Use yourself as an example to share why you wanted to or needed to learn the information.
    - Organize a problem-solving clinic.
    - Establish a "parking lot" to encourage participants to post their questions and add ideas.

6. "Why would I want to learn this? Does this motivate me? Am I open to this information and if not, why not?" Adults are more responsive to internal motivators such as increased self-esteem, than to external motivators such as higher salaries.

    Respect self-motivation. You could incorporate these into your delivery:

    - Create a safe learning climate that allows participants to be themselves.
    - Get to know all participants in some one-on-one time.
    - Build time in for reflection.
    - Acknowledge the wealth of experiences in the room.
    - Regard learners as colleagues who are equal in life experience.

Creating rapport and establishing a climate conducive to learning cannot be overemphasized. This is particularly true when you facilitate a virtual session. When done right from the start, it means that participants will be enthusiastic about the learning activities that follow, because they know what to expect. You can set the tone for the rest of the training session by what you accomplish at the beginning.

If you want to create a participative climate, the opening should put people at ease—including you. Participants may be reluctant to get involved unless the trainer provides structure that includes a purpose. They may be shy or may not want to appear vulnerable in front of their peers or strangers.

In a physical session the trainer should greet people as they arrive and chat with them. This can also occur in a virtual session—greet each person individually with a comment such as, "Welcome, Karl; it's cold in Bismarck this morning. How's it in Flagstaff?" or "Good morning, Amy, did you fix the problem with your computer interface?" Don't delay your delivery; be ready to start the agenda on time. Determine the climate that will be the most conducive to learning. Then begin to establish it from the first moment the session begins.

"The degree to which I can create relationships that facilitate the growth of others as separate persons is a measure of the growth I have achieved in myself."

—Carl Rogers

Create a Safe Haven for Learning

Some learners may arrive excited about the training. Others may arrive thinking that training is punishment. Yet others may arrive bringing burdens. To create a safe haven, you should:

- Be prepared early enough to greet participants at the door, welcome them, learn their names, and allow time for them to tell you something about themselves.
- Share the objectives of the training early, prior to the session if possible.
- Let participants know how they will benefit from the information.
- Demonstrate your respect for each individual.
- Incorporate whimsy to pique curiosity and add a smile; for example, use crayons, clay, or brightly colored paper.
- Use names and sincere reinforcement to build rapport.

Create a Comfortable Atmosphere

Arrive in a training room early enough to make it yours so that you can welcome the learners in as your guests. To create a comfortable environment, you should:

- Have lights on bright; it's depressing to walk into a room when the lights are dim.
- Learn how to adjust the thermostat for the most comfortable level.
- Make sure the room is clean and organized, which will eliminate distractions. An orderly room says that you went to the trouble of preparing for your participants.
- Ensure that you and your visuals can be seen and heard by all learners. Try it out the night before.
- Have coffee, tea, and water available throughout the day, and plan for ample breaks.
- Pair individuals to work together.

WHAT'S AN ENGAGING FACILITATOR?

"She's an engaging facilitator!" What exactly does that mean? Are you born that way? Well, you may have natural proclivity, but being more engaging is a learnable skill. Try out some of these actionable tips to be even more engaging. (Or just check them off to affirm that you already are!) These ideas from trainer extraordinaire Halelly Azulay of TalentGrow will inspire you.

- **Be enthusiastic.** Enthusiasm is the secret sauce that separates the most successful people in any profession from the rest. It's not the only thing you need, but it is required.
- **Be authentic.** People can smell fake from a mile away. You will not be able to gain participants' trust unless you show up as real and authentic.
- **Show confident benevolence.** Let's break it down: Benevolence means having others' best interests in mind, approaching others with an assumption that they mean well, and expecting the best of others. Confident benevolence means showing your confidence without it trumping your humility and other focus. So confident benevolence means respecting your own worth while respecting others'.

WHAT'S AN ENGAGING FACILITATOR? (CONT.)

- **Be approachable.** Sometimes when you are concerned about being seen as credible you can come across as aloof, cold, self-important, or detached. So humility and an intent focused on others' welfare will help you come across as approachable. Smile, make eye contact, and relax!

- **Show interest to be interesting.** In your quest to be seen as an expert or to gain respect you can put excessive emphasis on what you came to share. Instead, shift your focus to the learners and activate your curiosity. Ask questions. Be genuinely interested in their ideas, questions, objections, concerns, or perspectives. People are instantly drawn to those who show interest in them.

- **Use self-deprecating humor.** If you show that you don't take yourself too seriously, you will allow learners to relax and take themselves a little less seriously, too. This will help them be more open to learning and experimentation and less concerned about keeping up appearances.

- **Be congruent in body and voice.** When we perceive that the verbal and non-verbal messages don't match, we tend to trust the non-verbal part of the message to be more credible and trustworthy. Don't present learners with different messages and make them guess what you really feel or mean. Be congruent and make sure your words and actions align.

- **Be upbeat and high energy.** Your energy level needs to be a couple levels above that of the participants. If you sit or you feel lethargic, you can be sure that it will affect how learners perceive you. If you exude energy it will help learners feel energized. Remain standing, keep moving, and be energetic.

- **Be trustworthy.** To truly grow and learn, your participants need to show vulnerability and even share personal or uncomfortable stories or examples. The more you convey that you can be trusted to keep confidences and honor their trust in you, the less learners will feel at risk, and the better able they will be to take chances and move outside their comfort zone, which is where real learning takes place.

- **Be open to feedback.** Actively solicit feedback from learners and not just on Level 1 evaluation at the end of the session. Ask at a midway point, such as after lunch, at the end of the first day, or on the morning of the second day: What should I keep doing? What else can I do to make this a successful and comfortable learning environment for you? Listen openly and attentively to the feedback, and demonstrate that you are taking it to heart by implementing course changes that make sense.

Use Cognitive Learning Tactics Customized for Individual Learners

Brain-based learning has certainly received a lot of attention. Journal articles and conference presenters make it sound as though the research is brand-new. But it is not: Malcolm Knowles, Howard Gardner, Robert Gagné, and other early adult learning theorists have touted what is best for learners for decades. The brain-based knowledge we have today has been acquired over the past 200 years and comes from the field of cognitive science. What is new is that brain imaging, a noninvasive way to view how the brain responds, has become so precise that we can more accurately identify the brain's responses to various stimuli.

The recent emphasis on brain-based learning is a good reminder to all of us that if we want our participants to learn, we cannot just push content at them; we must use strategies that enhance the brain's learning power! You've seen some of these strategies throughout this book. These examples should lead you to think about how you can help your learners learn faster and better and retain content longer.

Enhance Learning With Visual and Verbal Context

Stories, pictures, and metaphors increase retention. Use stories and metaphors to anchor the content in your delivery. Use pictures and images in your Power-Point slides, handouts, and job aids (Clark 2015; Medina 2008).

Participation Is Necessary

Involvement in activities or even talking and writing enhances learning. This participation encourages focus on the content. You should at least change your lectures into discussions (Ericsson, Krampe, and Tesch-Romer 1993; Salas et al. 2012).

Present Content in Bite-Sized Pieces

Chunk or offer content in small pieces because our brains cannot process too much in a short period of time. While it was once believed that our brains could process seven chunks of information, new research states that two to four chunks is more realistic because the hippocampus has a limited capacity and gets overloaded quickly. Think of this part of the brain as a holding tank for information. Allow participants to practice their new skills before learning more (Miller 1956).

Implement Learning Immediately

Long-term memory relies on the use of new information, which is known as the theory of plasticity. New learning must be transferred to the workplace for memory to remain. Without application, the new skills are lost because our brain "prunes" unused new cells. Even before you agree to conduct a training program make sure that the learners' supervisors will ensure the new skills are put to use immediately (Clark 2015).

An Exciting Curriculum

Enrich your learning environment with controversy, novelty (more about novelty in chapter 8), and creativity. Stimulate all five senses. Your delivery is not just about stating content—you must also make sure your learners are committed to implement what they learn. You must instill confidence in your learners to change their performance back on the job. Engage emotions through stories, interactions, visuals, and other stimuli (Jensen 2008; Rock 2009).

Give Feedback

In chapter 2 I suggested several opportunities for your learners to receive feedback. In chapter 3 I discussed Ruth Clark's findings about feedback. Here, I'll offer you an easy to remember process: SBI. SBI reminds you of the three things you should include when providing feedback to your participants: The situation, behavior, and impact that you observed (Fleenor and Taylor 2005; Salas, Tannenbaum, Kraiger, and Smith-Jentsch 2012).

No Music

Several studies show that music adversely affects learning, so I'd suggest that you not use it except for social enhancement, and even then be aware that some in your group will not see the value (Moreno and Mayer 2000; Jensen 2008).

Movement Gives a Cognitive Boost

This means that recess at school and breaks during training are important. Physical activity such as using relay races, or even simply moving participants from one group to another, enhances learning (Medina 2008).

Cognitive Load

Cognitive load refers to the maximum amount of mental effort used in the brain's working memory. The theory espouses that there are three types of cognitive load:

- intrinsic—difficulty and the effort associated with a specific topic
- extraneous—how the information is presented to the learner, including unnecessary or distracting materials
- germane—the effort required to create a permanent store of knowledge.

Evidence shows that we have individual differences in how we process capacity. Experts, for example, have more knowledge or experience, which reduces the load. What's true for everyone is that our brains have limits to how much they can process. When we overload the brain, people get frustrated, quit, make errors, or at the least do not learn as well. (Ericson, Krampe, and Tesch-Romer 1993; Medina 2008).

Some solutions to cognitive overload include spacing, chunking, and knowing what each person can handle. For example, address intrinsic cognitive load sequence content in a simple-to-complex order, or introduce a concept separately before introducing the complete task. You can also reduce intrinsic load by removing ambiguity and clarifying the relationship of the content elements (van Merriënboer 2006). You can address extraneous load by eliminating unnecessary learning material—although it may not be evident which characteristics of the material are extraneous. You can increase capacity by addressing both visual and auditory working memory (Low and Sweller 2005). Address germane cognitive load using techniques that stimulate learning, such as game-based learning, collaborative learning, or experiential learning. Cognitive load theory presents three design principles that have been around since the 1980s: align material to learners' prior knowledge; avoid unnecessary and confusing information; and find ways to stimulate rich knowledge (de Jong 2009).

Space Practice and Review

Allow processing time. Don't just whip through an activity because it is fun; learners need to know how it relates to them. Learning takes place when an activity is processed immediately and also when discussion and practice time are spaced between activities. Ebbinghaus was the first to report that when practice is distributed over time, learning is better (Rohrer and Taylor 2006).

Allow Choice

Giving participants choices can improve performance. In one study the choice was as simple as the color of markers and the topics. The result was that those who were given a choice completed twice as many tasks and continued the task on their own into the break. The researchers concluded that when participants were given autonomy they were more meaningfully engaged and they improved their performance (Ivengar 1999). Think about the choices you can give participants, such as developing their own ground rules, whether to take a break or finish a project, or manage their time for a longer activity. However, although the research recommends providing choices, be careful what you ask for. Offering to start an hour earlier so that participants can leave early may deteriorate into a no-win situation (Salas et al. 2012).

Summary

What can you take away from this section? Focus on fewer topics with short explanations. Segment content into smaller chunks and allow time to process and practice—spaced apart. Make it visual, participative, and interesting. Allow participants to make choices and conduct the training as close to implementation as possible.

The Art of Delivery: Putting It All Together

How do you create an environment that is conducive to learning, while at the same time using cognitive learning tactics customized for your learners into your training delivery? This section will take you from start to finish and show you how.

Your First Words: Start With Excitement

First contacts create lasting impressions. Most people have discovered that the first 10 minutes of any initial meeting between two people lays the groundwork for almost all assumptions and decisions about the ensuing relationship. If first impressions are critical, how does a good trainer hold participants' attention from the beginning? Here are five features that will get your training session off to the right start:

- Grab learners' interest and enthusiasm for the training-session content. Perhaps you can build an element of surprise into the opening using props or introducing a creative activity.
- Clarify participants' needs—both content and personal—by learning something about participants' experience and expertise.
- Identify the ground rules and administrative needs so that guidelines can be established to ensure the training session runs smoothly. In a virtual session, discuss how to use the chat feature; in a traditional session, determine when breaks will occur and where restrooms are located.
- Clarify expectations by introducing the agenda and the objectives for the session. The opening also identifies other expectations participants have that may or may not be addressed.

- Help everyone get to know one another through the use of icebreakers, discussions, or other activities. When people participate immediately, it sets the stage for full participation throughout the session.

How can you accomplish all of these in a short amount of time? Try some of the following suggestions for traditional and virtual settings.

Indicate What's in Store

What happens in the opening should indicate whether participants will be moving around or sitting most of the time. It should set the tempo and tone of the session. Fast paced? Slow? Jovial? Serious? Interactive? Passive? Creative? Cerebral? Exciting? Calm? All of these describe a potential training climate. Decide what yours will be, and then begin to establish that climate during your opening. Even if participants can't see you in a virtual setting, smile when you open. Your participants will hear the smile in your inflection.

Clarify Participants' Expectations

Participants expect you to ask about their expectations for the session and there are numerous ways to accomplish this. The most straightforward way is to simply ask, "What are your expectations for the session?" List them on a flip-chart page and post them on the wall. In a virtual session you can ask participants to post on the whiteboard. There are also other ways to get the same information. Try twisting the question a bit to get learners to look at their questions or concerns from a different perspective. You could ask:

- "What are your hopes and fears?"
- "What are your dreams and desires?"
- "Why are you here?"
- "What questions did you bring with you today?"
- "What do you need to happen today for this training to be worth your investment of time?"
- "How well do your needs match the learning objectives?"
- "What else do you need?"

What if the participants' expectations go beyond the scope of the training design? It's better to let them know early on how you intend to handle this. You may respond in three ways:

- You can add time to the agenda to address the additional expectations. However, this most likely means eliminating or shortening something else.
- If the additional expectation is something that concerns only one or two individuals, you could meet with them after the session or during a break.
- You may need to tell them that you're not prepared or that time doesn't allow for the added content, but that you will follow up with them after the session. You could email them additional resources, put them in touch with someone who has expertise, or do something else that will address their concerns. In a virtual setting that runs over several weeks, you have the potential to build some of the expectations into future sessions.

Possibly the most important thing you can do for participants no matter your format is to help them understand how the session relates to them. Participants who understand why they are involved in a training session, how it will help them do their jobs better and faster, and how the content relates to them will get more out of it.

Introduce the Content

Related to clarifying the participants' expectations is introducing the content. You provide an overview for participants by reviewing the agenda and the purpose of the training session. It's important to know what your learners know so that you can tailor the content to their needs. Telling them what to expect provides a foundation for the content and establishes a common starting point for everyone in the room.

Ensure that participants know other aspects of the training program as well: Will they be required to take a test? Will they receive a grade for the course? Will the grade affect their jobs? They may want to know what kind of participation will be expected and whether there will be assignments. For example, in a virtual setting you can tell them that you will call on them by name periodically, but start calling on them by name while you review the agenda, "Pierre, is that what you expected to see on the agenda?" Some learners may be new to virtual training and not realize that you do expect them to participate.

I generally present the content and then ask participants whether they were anticipating different or additional content. You can do either first. I find my process saves time because I do not have to repeat the content later as I present the agenda. On the other hand, sometimes it is more important for the participants to establish their own agenda than to save time. For example, during a team-building effort I facilitate a discussion of the team's expectations and needs first. It takes a bit longer, but there is more buy-in, which leads to better end results. By the way, your icebreaker should relate to the content.

Surprise!

Add an element of surprise right from the start. Do something unconventional to send a message to participants that this session may be different than what they have experienced in the past. You may introduce props in your opening or state something unusual or shocking about the topic (just make sure you can prove it later). You can also start with an activity, rather than addressing the logistics of the session. Here are a few examples:

- During introductions most trainers start at the front and go clockwise around the room. You could plan to start someplace else, such as the middle back and go counterclockwise. Even better, ask for a volunteer to start, then ask for a second volunteer, and continue to select or call on learners randomly. This takes a bit of practice on your part to remember who was introduced. When all else fails, you can always end by saying, "Who has not been introduced yet?" to pick up anyone who was missed by this scatter approach.

- Save administrative comments until just before break. No one needs to know most of the information until then anyway. Because most sessions start off with a discussion about lunch, parking, and sign-up sheets, you will surprise your participants if you do not begin the same way.

- Ask participants to use crayons instead of pens or pencils to generate lists, draw something, write their names on their table tents, or anything else they would typically complete with a pen.

Doing something unique or in a different sequence introduces an element of surprise that energizes participants, adds interest and excitement to the session, and communicates that your session will not be boring. As you already know, this is important to maintain your participants' attention. This technique is backed up by research, which states that providing learners with variation helps to boost learning, sometimes by double digits (Barcroft and Sommers 2005; Quilici and Mayer 1996; Rost and McMurray 2009). Learners stay more engaged and memory retrieval is improved when we vary the learning materials, so use this tactic throughout your training delivery.

Introduce Participants

An opening is not complete unless the participants learn who else is attending the session. Whether you use an icebreaker or a quick round of introductions will depend upon the amount of time you have and how you want the participants to interact during the rest of the training session.

Allow participants to become acquainted with one another. Establish a way they can begin to understand who else is in the training session and what their attitudes, values, experience, and concerns are.

Use this time wisely. Before deciding how participants will meet each other, determine what you want them to be able to do as a result. You may just want them to be able to match names and faces, but you may want to consider whether other results will help to further the training session. What else do you want your participants to know about one another? Make a list of what you want to accomplish. These may help get you started:

- Have a continuous contact for other content.
- Practice solving problems.
- Understand attitudes, beliefs, likes, and dislikes.
- Practice a creative experience.
- Begin to build a learning team.

There are many legitimate aspects for what you hope participants will learn about one another and how they actually interact based on this introduction experience. At the least, I suggest that everyone in the group accomplish two things:

- All participants hear all other participants' names.
- All participants speak at least once.

In virtual sessions use a participant list as you call on individuals. In a physical session I highly recommend using table tents—the cards folded like a tent—that have people's names written on both sides, which allows you and other participants to see their names from any angle. They will help you remember participants' names and help participants remember and use one another's names.

Learn About the Group

Be sure to build time into the opening so that you can observe the group and learn something about its dynamics and individual personalities. Conducting an icebreaker provides this opportunity.

It may be tempting to have your head in your notes during the icebreaker to prepare for the next section. However, if you do, you will be doing your participants and yourself a disservice. Take the time to determine how you perceive the group as a whole. Circulate among the participants and observe how they work together. Listen to their conversations. Who seems to be taking the lead? Who is reluctant to join in? What strong personalities exist in the group? Who seems to be dominating the discussion?

This time gives you a chance to think ahead to the rest of the program design and alerts you to potential difficulties in which you may consider changing the process. For example, if you have planned a risky activity and the group appears to be risk-adverse, you may want to make a mental note about that. It is certainly too early to make the change now, but it may give you a heads up that a change may be required.

Obviously you cannot "see" your participants in a virtual setting, but you can see what they do. For example, if you ask them to write on a whiteboard or engage in a chat session, you can tell who participates and who does not. Use this time to discover as much as you can about the group and individuals.

Establish Ground Rules

Establishing ground rules as a part of your opening shapes the parameters of behavior that the participants expect of one another and from the trainer for the session. This is one way in which you can demonstrate giving them a choice. I generally present the group with a few givens to get started, such as start and end time. Sometimes I'll make a commitment, such as "If we start on time each day (or after each break), I guarantee we will end on time." Then encourage them to identify other ground rules (Salas et al. 2012). Capture the same words participants used. You need buy-in to the ground rules from everyone, so you may need to modify the list to get agreement.

In a physical session, post the ground rules in a location where everyone can see them, usually near the front of the training room. This facilitates your ability to reference them if you need to manage disruptions or to use as a reference point to facilitate group dynamics.

In a virtual setting you also have ground rules, but because your session most likely won't last more than 90 minutes, the time allotted to discuss them will be shorter too. You can email them prior to the start of the class, along with other information I like to call "What to Expect." You may also wish to post them on the screen prior to the start of the session.

Address Any Issues

If you know issues exist around the training session, confront them during the opening and plan time to address them. In fact, your icebreaker may incorporate the concerns. If something is happening in the organization that led to this training session, address it head on. If it is troublesome to participants, allow enough time to discuss. You will find that if you do not address the issues immediately, participants will not be able to focus on the content you're presenting. And besides, you will most likely have to use time to address it later anyway.

Encourage Participation

Convincing learners to actively participate is the most important thing you can do to enhance learning. Here are a few thoughts to get you started:

- Use small break-out groups to overcome early reluctance to share ideas or concerns.
- Use body language to encourage participation—positive nods, smiles, and eye contact all show that you are interested in the learners.
- Share something of yourself to begin a trusted exchange of ideas.
- Make it fun.
- Plan celebrations, such as distributing certificates, team applauses, or "moments in the sun."

Take a Break!

Yes, remember the breaks; don't skip or shorten them because social learning occurs during these times. Breaks maintain the energy level, provide participants an opportunity to follow up with other participants, and give people a chance to take care of personal needs. They also allow for some of the spacing required for learning.

A Dynamic Delivery

Trainers walk a fine line between being proactive and responsive, between being flexible and sticking to the agenda, and between presenting content and facilitating discussion. They must be adaptive to the many learning styles in the room and supportive of the various requirements of all the participants. How do they do all this, act as a role model for the participants, and ensure that the participants have learned all they need to learn?

Throughout this book I emphasize that training is all about the learner. You must provide opportunities to actively engage participants. Of course the goal is not just activity and participation; it is to ensure that the participants gain the knowledge or learn skills to effectively improve performance. Active learning may be incorporated in hundreds of methods such as role plays, simulations, and games. Active learning is also required when you coach a manager to support an employee, when you create a peer-mentoring group, or when you follow up with one of your virtual learners to provide additional resources.

It is not enough for a trainer to cover the content and involve the learners. A trainer must ensure that learners practice the skills, that learning occurred, and that the learners are both competent and confident to perform the skill or use the knowledge when they return to the workplace (Salas et al. 2012).

The experiential learning process is often used by facilitators to ensure that learning occurs and that learners are ready to perform on the job. Participants learn inductively; that is, they discover for themselves by experiencing the activity. A more thorough explanation is included in the sidebar.

EXPERIENCE IS THE BEST TEACHER

Experiential learning occurs when a learner participates in an activity, reviews the activity, identifies useful knowledge or skills that were gained, and transfers the result to the workplace. This is the natural learning process, called life experience.

Experiential learning activities (ELAs) attempt to duplicate life experience. Participants "experience" what they are supposed to learn before they discuss it. Ideally, learners participate in actual on-the-job situations. When this is not possible or when learners need some guidance before the actual situation occurs, trainers can create ELAs, which are based on several characteristics, including:

- They are directed toward a specific learning goal.
- They are structured; that is, they have specific steps and a process that must be followed to ensure results.
- There is a high degree of participant involvement.
- They generate data and information for participant analysis.
- They require processing or debriefing for maximum learning. Debriefing is considered one of the most effective yet underused tools for stimulating and reinforcing learning (Brock, McManus, and Hale 2009).

The five steps in William Pfeiffer and John Jones's experiential learning cycle explain what must occur to ensure maximum learning results: experiencing, publishing, processing, generalizing, and applying (Pfeiffer and Jones 1975; Kolb 1984).

EXPERIENCE IS THE BEST TEACHER (CONT.)

1. **Experiencing: Do something.** This is the step that is associated with the "game" or fun of the experience. Participants are involved in completing a defined task. If the process ends here, all learning is left to chance and the trainer has not completed the task.

2. **Publishing: Share observations.** The second step gives the learners a chance to share what they saw, how they felt, and what they experienced. The trainer can facilitate this in several ways, including recording data in the large group, asking participants to share or interview in subgroups, or leading a variation of a round robin. The facilitator typically begins with a broad question and then focuses on more specific questions. The facilitator may also probe for turning points or decisions that affected the outcome. This stage is important because it allows the participants to state their thoughts and feelings or to vent or express strong emotions.

3. **Processing: Interpret dynamics or concepts.** This step gives the participants a chance to discuss the patterns and dynamics they observed during the activity. Observers may be used to discuss this step. The facilitator begins with broad questions and then homes in on more specific questions. During this stage, participants can test various hypotheses preparing them to apply what they learned—"Why do you think that happened?" This stage also gives the facilitator a way to observe how much the participants have learned from the experience.

4. **Generalizing: Connect to real life.** The key question in this step is "So what?" Participants are led to focus their awareness on situations that are similar to what they have experienced. It makes the activity practical and ensures that the participants grasp the lesson and learning that was intended—"How does this help you understand _____?"

5. **Applying: Plan effective change.** The last step presents the reason the activity was conducted: "Now what?" The facilitator helps participants apply generalizations to actual situations in which they are involved. The group may establish goals, contract for change, make promises, identify how something will change at the workplace, or any other actions that may result from the experience. They frequently follow this step with an action plan or at least spend some time noting their thoughts about how life might be different as a result of the ELA. Two of my favorite questions for this step are, "What will you do differently as a result of this experience?" and "How will you transfer this learning to the workplace?"

The ELA is a powerful debriefing tool, but it takes time and is therefore used sparingly. If you decide to facilitate an ELA, don't take any shortcuts. The value is truly in the process.

Asking and Answering Questions

There is an art to asking questions as well as an art to encouraging questions from learners. Questions often uncover things others in the group did not know. Encourage your participants to ask questions to ensure learning, prompt interest, and to create interaction.

Encourage Questions

Probably the best way to ensure that your delivery is meeting your participants' needs is to encourage questions and then demonstrate that you genuinely appreciate them. Try out these tips:

- Tell participants that you want to hear their questions.
- Stop at natural points in your presentation and ask for questions.
- Pause long enough for participants to formulate questions.
- Give signals such as, "Let's pause here so you can ask questions." Then wait for questions.
- Watch facial expressions; if a participant looks puzzled, stop and ask if there is a question.
- If two or more participants are talking among themselves, ask if there is something they would like clarified.
- Make sure there is time for participants to ask their questions privately. They may be too shy to ask in front of the group.

Ask Questions

Asking questions helps you determine whether your learners understand the critical content you are delivering. Here are some suggestions for asking questions:

- Plan some questions in advance.
- Increase participation by including them early in the session.
- Include questions to create discussion, introduce controversy, obtain a correct response, review information, or offer a hypothetical comment.
- Keep questions short.

- Know whether you want opinions or information.
- Consider whether it should be an open- or closed-ended question.
- If asking a direct question, say the participant's name first, then ask the question.
- Pause for answers; do not continue to repeat the question; and most important, do not answer your own questions.
- Use follow-on questions to further clarify or expand the initial response.
- Paraphrase responses, especially when the response was not focused.
- Use a round-robin discussion if you wish to hear from everyone.

Answer Questions

Of course answering questions is the corollary to encouraging participants to ask them. Be sure you include everyone in your response. If you are responding to one person's question, there is a good chance that someone else has the same one. Use some of these suggestions when you answer questions:

- Anticipate participants' questions.
- Paraphrase questions to ensure that everyone heard and understood the question.
- Ask for clarification if necessary.
- Be brief.
- "I don't know, but I will find out," is a perfectly good response.
- Redirect questions or encourage other responses from the entire group.
- If the question is not relevant, invite the participant to discuss it during a break.
- Include the entire audience in your response with body position and eye contact.

Create an expectation of asking and answering questions to encourage learning.

Facilitate More Than You Present

There will be times when you must present information or content, but as a rule of thumb, you will most likely want to facilitate more. Facilitation creates a two-way discussion that keeps your learners involved and ensures you stay connected with your learners and their needs. Here are a few tips for successful facilitation:

- Create discussion. Not just between you and the learners, but among the learners.
- Get opinions and ideas out in the open before you deliver your message. You may be surprised at how much "training" the learners can do for you.
- Provide opportunities for participants to evaluate their own learning throughout the session. Create experiential learning activities in which the learners discover their own "ahas!"
- Create individual check points in the program.
- Build in a group review of learning.

End With Excitement

Design your ending as specifically as any other part of the training. Plan a formal send-off message for the participants. You opened the training with excitement! End it with the same kind of fanfare. Try some of these closers:

- Help participants remember the experience.
- Give them encouragement for their next steps.
- Send them off with something to think about after the session, such as a call to action, a poem, a quote, a moral to a story, a visual, a reference to the introduction, a rhetorical question, a demonstration, a challenge, a magic trick, or something that makes the point.
- Make sure that they leave with competence, confidence, and commitment to perform back on the job.

Finally, stand at the door, shake participants' hands, wish them luck, and say good-bye.

What We Know for Sure

Science tells us that we can rely on several proven facts:

- We teach for competence, but unless we ensure that learners have confidence and commitment to do the task outside the training setting, the skill will not likely transfer.
- Malcolm Knowles's adult learning principles are a critical foundation to excellent delivery.
- Participants need to feel safe, comfortable, and appreciated to learn best.
- The 11 cognitive science tactics help to ensure we are using a process that makes learning easier; we need to implement things such as maximizing participation, delivering learning in bite-sized chunks, and providing feedback.
- Cognitive load research should guide how we align delivery to our learners.
- Every step in training delivery is tied to creating an appropriate environment and helping participants learn.

The Art Part

Your success will depend upon how well you adapt to the situation and your learners' needs. Tap into some of these ideas to help your learners grow, to develop yourself, and to add your personal creative touch.

Lectures they'll like. It's easy to say that your learners should be 100 percent engaged all the time. However, there are times when you just have to tell it like it is. You may need to deliver the information as a short lecture when a procedure has critical steps, for safety reasons, or to obey the law. Try some of these suggestions to encourage participation:

- Ask questions regarding predictions or recall of information.
- Create a conversation among participants.
- Include pop quizzes in the middle of a presentation.

- Ask participants what they need or want.
- Intersperse demonstrations.
- Pass out props, such as photos showing correct or incorrect ways to address the content or products your organization produces for new employee orientation.
- Stop for an impromptu role play with one of the learners.
- Develop a guided note taking page in the form of questions or fill in the blanks (Pluth 2016).
- Develop keyword outlines of the presentation, leaving room for additional ideas.
- Use visuals to go with all presentations; participants can follow your words visually.
- Plan points to stop midway to ask if everyone is with you.
- Introduce a partial story at the beginning and complete it at the end.
- Find ways to interject humor, such as creating a cartoon to match the content.
- Challenge them.

Art and Science Questions You Might Ask

These questions provide potential challenges for your personal growth and development:

- What's the best thing you can do to build relationships with learners?
- What will you do to help learners practice and deepen their understanding of new skills and knowledge?
- How can you ensure learners translate content into performance?
- What creative methods can you use to ensure learners have time to reflect on content and that they are reflecting on the most important elements?
- How can you grab and hold learners' attention?
- How can you minimize the load placed on working memory by limiting distractions and avoiding asking learners to process vast amounts of information at one time?

- How will you engage learners? How successful have you been in the past? What can you change in the future?
- What can you do to help learners build confidence about using the skills and knowledge?
- How can you ensure that participants will be committed to using what they learn?
- Would you want to be a learner in your training session?

How Do You Align Delivery to Your Learners' Needs?

The learner sits in front of you literally or figuratively when you deliver training either in person or virtually through your laptop. You align your delivery with all your learners when you invest the time to create an environment that is conducive to learning. You need to address both the content and the process you use—what you deliver and how you deliver it.

Cognitive science provides us with excellent data about how participants learn best. You need to utilize what has been proven to make a difference in learning. Yes, you have many things to juggle. Practicing makes a difference. You need to train yourself! Remember Aristotle's quote, "Art completes what nature cannot bring to finish." Your delivery role summons the best of your scientist and the best of your artist to help learners reach their greatest potential.

Resources

Barcroft, J., and M.S. Sommers. 2005. "Effects of Acoustic Variability on Second Language Vocabulary Learning." *Studies in Second Language Acquisition* 27(3):387-414.

Biech, E. 2014. *ASTD Handbook: The Definitive Reference for Training and Development*. 2nd ed. Alexandria, VA: ASTD Press.

———. 2015a. *101 More Ways to Make Training Active*. Hoboken, NJ: John Wiley & Sons.

———. 2015b. *Training and Development for Dummies*. Hoboken, NJ: John Wiley & Sons.

Boyd, R. 2008. "Do People Only Use 10 Percent of Their Brains?" *Scientific American*. February 7. www.scientificamerican.com/article/do-people-only-use-10-percent-of-their-brains.

Brock, G., D. McManus, and J. Hale. 2009. "Reflections Today Prevent Failures Tomorrow." *Communications of the ACM* 52:140-144.

Clark, R. 2015. *Evidence-Based Training Methods: A Guide for Training Professionals*. 2nd ed. Alexandria, VA: ATD Press.

De Jong, T. 2009. "Cognitive Load Theory, Educational Research, and Instructional Design: Some Food for Thought." *Instructional Science* 38(2): 105-134.

Ericson, K., R. Krampe, and C. Tesch-Romer. 1993. "The Role of Deliberate Practice in the Acquisition of Expert Performance." *Psychological Review* 100(3):363-406.

Fleenor, J., and S. Taylor. 2005. "Closing the Loop: Getting the Most From 360-Degree Feedback." Greensboro, NC: Center for Creative Leadership.

Ivengar, S., et al. 1999. "Rethinking the Value of Choice: A Cultural Perspective on Intrinsic Motivation." *Journal of Personality and Social Psychology* 76(3):349-365.

Jensen, E. 2008. *Brain-Based Learning: The New Paradigm of Teaching*. Thousand Oaks, CA: Corwin Press.

Kolb, D. 1984. *Experiential Learning as the Science of Learning and Development*. Englewood Cliffs, NJ: Prentice Hall.

Low, R., and J. Sweller. 2005. "The Modality Principle in Multimedia Learning." In *Cambridge Handbook of Multimedia Learning*, edited by R.E. Mayer, 147-158. Cambridge, UK: Cambridge University Press.

Medina, J. 2008. *Brain Rules: 12 Principles for Surviving and Thriving at Work, Home, and School*. Seattle: Pear Press.

Miller, G.A. 1956. "The Magical Number Seven, Plus or Minus Two: Some Limits on Our Capacity for Processing Information." *Psychological Review* 63(2): 81-97.

Moreno, R., and R.E. Mayer. 2000. "A Coherence Effect in Multimedia Learning: The Case for Minimizing Irrelevant Sounds." *Journal of Educational Psychology* 92:117-125.

Pfeiffer, W., and J.E. Jones. 1975. *A Handbook of Structured Experiences for Human Relations Training*. La Jolla, CA: University Associates.

Pluth, B. 2016. *Creative Training: A Train-the-Trainer Field Guide*. Eden Prairie, MN: Creative Training Productions.

Quilici, J.L., and R. Mayer. 1996. "Role of Examples in How Students Learn to Categorize Statistics Word Problems." *Journal of Educational Psychology* 88(1):144-161.

Rock, D. 2009. *Your Brain at Work: Strategies for Overcoming Distraction, Regaining Focus, and Working Smarter All Day Long*. New York: HarperCollins.

Rohrer, D., and K. Taylor. 2006. "The Effects of Overlearning and Distributed Practice on the Retention of Mathematics Knowledge." *Applied Cognitive Psychology* 20:1209-1224.

Rost, G.C., and B. McMurray. 2009. "Speaker Variability Augments Phonological Processing in Warly Word Learning." *Developmental Science* 12(2):339-349.

Salas, E., S. Tannenbaum, K. Kraiger, and K. Smith-Jentsch. 2012. "The Science of Training and Development in Organizations: What Matters in Practice." Psychological Science in the Public Interest 13(2): 74-101.

Sweller, J., J. Van Merrienboer, and F. Paas. 1998. "Cognitive Architecture and Instructional Design." *Educational Psychology Review* 10(3): 251-296.

Van Merriënboer, J.J.G., L. Kester, and F. Paas. 2006. "Teaching Complex Rather Than Simple Tasks: Balancing Intrinsic and Germane Load to Enhance Transfer of Learning." *Applied Cognitive Psychology* 20:343-352.

How Can You Address Training Challenges?

With all the cognitive research, the emphasis on neuroscience, and solutions in general, there shouldn't be any challenges to training. Science has fixed everything that might have been broken. Right? Not quite. This is the time as a facilitator when you may really need to be creative and artful!

Challenges still exist in the field of training. Besides that, many in the profession have not implemented what they've learned—not because they don't want to, but because they don't know the facts or they may not know how to change. Many may still be operating under old myths, such as "people have different learning styles" or "schools kill creativity."

The first step is to recognize that there is a challenge. The profession is changing; it's important to understand why it's changing and how to prepare for the changes. Certainly understanding the science of training is a start, but with that comes challenges, both old and new, and knowing how to address them.

The Multitasking Muddle

Many people refuse to believe it, but the brain cannot attend to two attention-rich stimuli simultaneously. Multitasking doesn't work. A 2000 study led by Moshe Naveh-Benjamin, a psychology researcher at the University of Missouri, helps us understand what this means for trainers. The researchers learned that there were important differences between the encoding and retrieval activities involved in processing information created when multitasking. Encoding requires more attention than retrieval, which means that lack of focus or undivided attention during the encoding (intake) phase of learning significantly inhibits memory.

Encoding is the first of three memory stages, followed by storage and retrieval. The research implies that the quantity and quality of our memory is influenced by multitasking. In another study, a team led by Karin Foerde—a research scientist from New York University who specializes in cognitive neuroscience, learning, memory, and decision making—discovered that memories acquired when multitasking use the striatum (Foerde, Knowlton, and Poldrack 2006). Unfortunately this region of the brain is poorly suited to long-term memory and understanding, which means that learning that happens during multitasking can't be generalized and probably can't be recalled when needed. Even if it can be recalled, there is doubt that the content could be understood.

The bottom line is that learning that happens while multitasking cannot be generalized and does not result in understanding or the ability to recall when needed.

MULTITASKING, MEMORY, AND DISTRACTIONS

In the Foerde study, young adults were tasked to sort shapes into different piles based on trial and error. The same people completed the exercise two times under two different conditions:
- without distractions
- while listening to high and low beeps and counting the high ones.

Participants were tested about what they learned in each situation. fMRI results showed that learning occurred in both scenarios, but how the brain processed the information and the parts of the brain that were involved were different.

When they performed the sorting task without multitasking, the hippocampus was active. This region of the brain is involved in sorting, processing, and recalling information. It is considered critical for memory about facts and events. While multitasking, however, the participants' knowledge was less flexible. They couldn't extrapolate their knowledge to different situations. This is because the distracting beeps shifted activity away from the hippocampus to the striatum, which is necessary for procedural memory (things we do naturally or by habit, such as eating, walking, or biking).

Memory that resides in the hippocampus makes it easier to recall in various situations; whereas, memories stored in the striatum require the specific situation in which they were learned to remember. This suggests that learning with the striatum leads to knowledge that cannot be generalized as well in new situations (Foerde, Knowlton, and Poldrack 2006).

Continuous Partial Attention

Linda Stone (2008), former Microsoft vice president who became an educator and speaker, coined the term *continuous partial attention* to describe how many people use attention today. The term goes beyond multitasking, referring to a person's desire to connect and be connected at all times. This is the reason people scan their current situation for the best place to be connected at any given moment.

People pay continuous partial attention because they do not want to miss anything. This creates an artificial sense of continuous crisis, which puts us in a constant place of high alert. This artificial sense of constant crisis is more typical of continuous partial attention than it is of multitasking.

"We live in an age of information overload, where attention has become the most valuable business currency."

—Thomas Davenport and John C. Beck

While this behavior can be useful on occasion, Stone warns that it eventually increases stress and prevents people from being able to effectively reflect, make decisions, and think creatively. Technology contributes to the stress and even a sense of being unfulfilled in the always-on world we live in. We focus on managing our time, but the real opportunity is to focus on how we manage our attention.

Whether you call it multitasking or continuous partial attention, the message for trainers is that more and more multitasking and attention studies demonstrate the importance and value of grabbing and holding your learners' attention. Let's consider how to do this.

Can I Grab Your Attention?

A multipart experiment studied the effects of novelty on the brain (Bunzeck and Duzel 2006). In the first part, participants were shown images of different scenes and familiar and unfamiliar faces. Some of the images were unusual, appearing rarely. Others contained negative emotional content, such as an angry face or a car accident. The subjects showed increased production of dopamine when they saw new images, but not the unusual or emotional ones. You've probably heard of dopamine—it's the chemical that controls our reward and pleasure centers.

Then the experiment was repeated, with some of the images being more or less familiar. In this segment of the study, only brand-new information caused robust activity in the brain, stimulating the production of dopamine.

The third segment of the experiment focused on testing the participants' memory on the new, familiar, and very familiar images. This segment was conducted two more times—20 minutes after viewing and a day later. Subjects performed best when new information was combined with familiar information. Surprisingly, even the familiar information was easier to remember when it was learned in conjunction with new facts. While novelty and tapping into prior knowledge may seem contradictory, they are both parts of learning. Novelty helps the brain initially attend to a stimulus; once the novelty is acknowledged, the brain makes connections so the content can take root.

This tells us that the brain needs to make connections, but it also likes things that are new and unique. Our brain is actually quite fickle; it quickly begins to recognize that the stimulus is not new and, through a process called habituation, the idea becomes less exciting. When we see something new, we think it could reward us in some way. This expectation motivates us to explore our environment for rewards. Once the stimulus becomes familiar, it has no reward associated with it and so it loses its prestige. As a result, only new objects increase our levels of dopamine (Duzel 2006).

So tapping into prior knowledge and introducing "novelty" are two powerful strategies to gain attention. This suggests that:

- You should learn as much as you can about your participants' experiences and expertise. Certainly surveys work, but have you thought of speaking with their supervisors? Have you ever tweeted a simple assessment question? Have you visited your participants' workplace? Or have you asked them an unusual question before the session, such as "What can you contribute to our discussion?" or "What's your greatest fear about this class?" or "What do you think your boss wants you to bring back to the workplace?"

- How about novelty? In her book *Creative Training*, Becky Pike Pluth (2016) tells a story of placing an industrial sized roll of bathroom tissue on the front table and asking each participant to take "as much as they need," with no further instruction. She later uses it as a recall mechanism to review the content.

How Can I Hold Your Attention?

So how can you hold someone's attention and manage it? While we generally think that focus is good—in fact, scanning is often better (Jonassen and Grabowski 1993). It may seem counterintuitive, but the human brain is more proficient at noticing detail by scanning rather than by focusing intently. The brain evolved this way to enhance our probability of survival.

We exhaust our neurons if there is a constant demand on the same ones for a long period of time. So what can you do to help your learners attend to new concepts? Two things:

- Instead of requiring learners to "pay attention," you can offer ways to look at something from various perspectives. How about from their boss's perspective? Or the customer's perspective? Or how about finding the most creative, the most ideal, or the most realistic?
- Instead of expecting learners to sit in one place, ask them to move around so that they can see details (Zull 2002). Have participants form a pair with someone at a different table, or plan a gallery walk after small groups brainstorm ideas on flipcharts.

Be aware of what is involved when learners shift their attention from one topic to another. Shifting attention requires three discreet brain processes:

- Disengaging or concluding the current topic and content.
- Moving from the present content and preparing to switch to new information.
- Re-engaging or initiating a new topic.

Each process activates different parts of the brain and engages working memory. Richard Wright and Lawrence Ward's (2008) award-winning book *Orienting of Attention* shows us that this process takes time and is energy depleting.

When you use these shifts in your classroom or asynchronous learning event, you must allow learners enough time to make the switch effectively and efficiently (Wright and Ward 2008). This is equally true if you have a group of "task-switching" learners who are eating up neuron energy by shifting from the discussion to their smartphone to the PowerPoint slide and back to a text.

"I have come to believe that a great teacher is a great artist and that there are as few as there are any other great artists. Teaching might even be the greatest of the arts since the medium is the human mind and spirit."

—John Steinbeck

So, back to your participants who truly believe they can multitask—research supports that our brains cannot multitask. When you think you are multitasking, you are really only task-switching, which is energy draining. To prevent task-switching, find ways to grab and hold your learners' attention.

Changing Mindsets and Attitudes

What is a mindset, why is it important, and what can we do for our learners? According to Peter Senge (2006), mental models are conceptual frameworks consisting of generalizations and assumptions from which we understand the world and take action in it. We all have mental models that explain our thought process about how something works in the real world. They represent our surrounding world and our perception about our own behaviors, beliefs, and the consequences. Within that mental model we develop mindsets and attitudes about its value and effectiveness. This mindset influences our choice of behavioral strategies, and our attitudes toward the mental model support the strategies we create for how to react in specific situations. This is a very brief overview of a complex topic, but you get the idea: What we believe today is based on our past experiences. It may or may not be accurate. Often we have not examined our mindsets in any depth, but a strong and wrong mindset can interfere with learning (Dweck 2008).

Researchers haven't figured it all out and there are plenty of debates, but you will know when you are working with learners whose mindsets, beliefs, and attitudes collide with the data. No matter how much data you present, your learners will insist that their way is better. Can you change their minds? Can you persuade them?

Visuals

Numerous studies demonstrate the persuasive power of visuals. Are they as powerful as Ruth Clark tells us? The brain has an extraordinary capacity to remember images. Memory experiments with pictures have shown that people can recall seeing hundreds, even thousands, of pictures (Standing, Conezio, and Haber 1970). Some believe that pictures may operate as "chunks." Because the brain can hold only a few chunks in working memory at one time, visuals incorporate more details and help the brain grasp and expand the scope of those chunks. Our visual processes have evolved over millions of years, making the brain highly efficient (Medina 2008). So yes, they are effective and persuasive.

One study at Dartmouth University showed the persuasive power of visuals by using highly emotional topics (the war in Iraq and unemployment, for example) to convince individuals to change their minds. The researchers:

1. made the case using words
2. added flattering comments, such as, "You're a reasonable person"
3. presented information in the form of charts and graphs.

Option three was most effective. The researchers reasoned it was because the brain is more likely to see visuals as "true," but words as "debatable" (Nyhan et al. 2011). Visuals work best because that's how the brain prefers to receive information. More of our brain is devoted to visual processing than to verbal processing.

Visuals aren't only good for persuading, they are also good for locking in learning. If your learners need to change their mindset and remember why, use graphs, images, and tangible examples. In another experiment, researchers tested subjects' visual and auditory memory three times after an initial learning event (same-day, next-day, and a week later). In all three tests, learners remembered significantly more of what they saw than what they heard (Bigelow and Poremba 2014).

What About the Other Senses?

"Multimodal" or "multisensory" learning is also effective for changing mindsets, according to several studies. In one study, participants were trained for five days on a task that had either congruent audiovisual stimuli, incongruent audiovisual stimuli, or only visual stimuli. The results showed that training with congruent audiovisual stimuli resulted in significantly better results than training with incongruent audiovisual stimuli or with only visual stimuli (Kim, Seitz, and Shams 2008). I'm not sure about you, but this gives me rationale to add pictures to my PowerPoint slides!

How Can You Help Your Learners?

Attitudes are formed or changed during a training session. Sometimes the differences are obvious, sometimes not. But how does this change take place? Is it the change caused by the content or the activities or the other participants? The answer is, of course, all three. A mindset may be difficult to measure, define, and explain, even so, it's important for transfer of skills and knowledge. Facilitators must consider what they can do to support their learners.

In previous books I've written that we can't train or change attitudes and mindsets, but we can influence them. During these times it's important to remember that our job also consists of coaching and mentoring our learners. It starts with building a foundation of trust and truly recognizing that we require permission from learners to help in this area. We also need to recognize that we can't predict the outcome. Carol Dweck's (2008) research describes various mindsets and reactions to them. Consider these ideas if you need to influence your learners' mindsets, refocus their attitudes, or help edit their "story":

- Lay a foundation of trust.
- Be authentic and consistent.
- Maintain a positive classroom setting.
- Listen, listen, listen—ask questions and listen some more.
- Demonstrate the benefits of changing.
- Use visuals and graphics to make the point.
- Design experiential learning activities, allowing enough time to process what happened, determine what it means, and identify what learners will do differently as a result.
- Use role plays, especially reversed roles to explore positions from a different perspective.
- Conduct self-assessments to help participants understand their priorities or values.
- Encourage journaling and schedule reflection time.
- Allow for spacing, as discussed in chapters 2 and 3.

- Create various small groups to provide a variety of attitudes and thoughts.
- Encourage discussion and ways that learners can acknowledge what a change could mean.
- Plan for follow up, such as making an appointment for a discussion, helping establish reminders, or assigning accountability partners.

Do you face a mindset challenge? Use a variety of visuals, engage participants in discussion, and use experiential learning that allows learners enough time to process what they learned, why it's important, and what they will do as a result. Mindsets are often invisible, below the awareness level. They extend beyond the body in the classroom and the hours in learning. Encourage participants to surface, explore, discuss, and reconsider their mindsets. It's your job.

Dealing With Disruptive Participants

Related to changing mindsets is addressing difficult participants, who may act like dominators, comedians, attackers, or deserters. Begin by ignoring the behavior. If the behavior is disruptive to others, stop it, but keep your cool; don't take it personally.

Many people have written books about how to manage difficult participants. The following strategies will help you manage them:

- Stop talking until the behavior ends.
- Use nonverbal cues such as talking between two people who are having a side conversation or holding up your hand.
- Refer to the ground rules if appropriate.
- Directly ask for the behavior to stop or change.
- Take a break.
- Discuss the behavior with the individual at a break.
- Continue to respect the individual; consider that perhaps he does not know he is being disruptive.
- Keep the individual involved since you don't want her to disengage.
- Maintain the involvement of the rest of the group. They want you to succeed and will judge how you handle the situation.

Relying on Subject Matter Experts

People think that because they are experts on a topic they can train others to acquire the same knowledge. Excellent trainers invest a huge amount of time and energy in preparing—even when they know the content well. Subject matter experts (SMEs) who are excellent at what they do may be rewarded with the opportunity to show others how to do what they do so well. But just because they are experts in a topic, it does not necessarily mean that they are experts in training others about the concepts. Just like any profession, training has its own expert techniques and processes that ensure that learners assimilate the content.

SMEs can actually be harmful to learners because they know too much. They are training because they have deep content knowledge and experience, which has earned them credibility. The risk is that people at this level may have forgotten what it was like to be a beginner. They will be tempted to deliver too much content and too many details. They will want to lecture at the learners. How do you ensure that your SMEs will be successful?

Chuck Hodell (2013) recommends that SME selection should be based on content and noncontent criteria.

- In the content portion, consider the relevance, depth, timeliness, location, and training or teaching experience.
- In the noncontent portion, consider communication ability, writing ability, and sociability.

Before the training session help them out by providing guidance; experts and leaders can be trained to be better teachers and coaches (Zsambok et al. 1997). You can begin by providing tools, training, and support. It could take the form of a short handout or booklet of tips and tools for the nontrainer. You could also develop a short checklist to:

- Help them remember what it was like when they first learned the subject they have now mastered.
- Clarify the exact content, objectives, and expected results.
- Review the material to ensure they are not trying to squeeze too much content in too short of time.

- Think about how to be effective, such as:
  - arriving early
  - establishing a rapport with learners
  - using activities instead of lecture
  - involving your learners
  - scheduling a practice session.

Hodell suggests several best practices, including showing appreciation, providing clear guidelines for roles and responsibilities, making SMEs part of the design team, attending to the SMEs' needs, and celebrating project milestones.

Few strategic relationships are more important than the one you create with your SMEs. Anecdotal data suggest training conducted by SMEs can be more effective than that facilitated by professional trainers. I predict this is the direction our organizations need to move; supervisors and managers will soon need to spend more of their time in a teaching and coaching role. If that is the case, we must start getting ready now.

What We Know for Sure

Science tells us that we can rely on several proven facts:

- Information and stimulation overload are here to stay.
- It is important to:
  - Manage attention shifts, allowing learners sufficient time and space to make the shift.
  - Utilize novelty and surprise while allowing learners to make connections with existing knowledge.
  - Help learners apply attention management strategies back on the job.
  - Call attention to productivity-sapping practices, such as multitasking and continuous partial attention.
- Learning as much as possible about the participants before you train them gives you the flexibility to customize a learning event that taps into the patterns in learners' brains.

- The brain cannot multitask.
- Task-switching requires a great deal of energy and does not allow input to go to the most efficient part of the brain for later recall.
- Patterns in the brain are useful to accelerate learning by providing a "filing system" for new content. However, the prior experiences and beliefs of a learner that form these patterns can also create mindsets that interfere with learning.
- SMEs are a valuable resource to learners.

The Art Part

Your success depends upon how well you adapt to the situation and your learners' needs. Tap into some of these ideas to help your learners grow, to develop yourself, and to add your personal creative touch.

Manage attention. If you provide learners with awareness and skills training in attention management, it could make a huge difference in how people learn to learn. Think of how you could make that happen.

Free your creativity. Go through a novelty catalog, such as *Oriental Trading*. Set your creativity free and think of ways that you can add interest to your learning event—think about new ways to keep learners focused. For example, if you are teaching change management skills, the theme could be "staying afloat," symbolized by little yellow ducks. You could purchase yellow duck pads of paper, erasers, pencil toppers, candy, keychains, or baseball caps.

Virtual needs novelty, too. If you are conducting a virtual session, surprise your learners by mailing them something to open during your virtual training. It could be a booklet, gizmo, or gadget you found at a dollar store or in a novelty catalog.

Smartphone smarts. They'll have them out anyway, so use your participants' smartphones, tablets, and computers to search for data or concepts during your training events. How? Try these:

- Use Poll Everywhere to take minute surveys, brainstorm, or vote.
- Ask them to research content.

- Have them look for answers.
- Suggest they tweet comments that are pertinent to their learning.

SME toolbox. Build a useful toolkit for your SMEs, including things such as a list of acronym meanings, a simple ADDIE flowchart, a list of active learning methods and when to use them, training dos and don'ts, index cards with activities that can be used in various situations, a room set-up diagram, and a list of additional resources.

Art and Science Questions You Might Ask

These questions provide potential challenges for your personal growth and development:

- How can you actively incorporate attention management strategies during learning design?
- How can you ensure that learners' self-esteem remains intact while eliminating multitasking?
- Can you minimize the load placed on working memory by limiting distractions?
- How can you help learners apply attention management strategies?
- How can you explain how multitasking and continuous partial attention hurt our ability to learn?
- How can you honor the need for flexibility so participants can focus on tasks without interruption?
- Are your visuals relevant and stimulating?
- How skilled are you in addressing mindsets and attitudes?
- What tools are in your toolbox to address participant disruptions?
- How can you best support your SMEs?

How Can You Address Training Challenges?

Science tells us emphatically that the human brain cannot multitask. Yet one of the biggest challenges we face is participants who check their devices an average of 74 times per day. A *Time* magazine article (2015) states that Americans collectively check their smartphones eight billion times per day. While we can establish ground rules that would prevent this behavior, it probably wouldn't work anyway. So, what can you do? Keep learners busy. We know that movement and discussion enhance learning, so use that to your advantage. Constantly seek out creative and interesting ways to grab and maintain learners' attention, and incorporate those when you train.

No matter what is happening with technology, we still have strong mindsets and disruptive participants to address. SMEs can be extremely beneficial if we invest the time upfront to ensure that they are successful.

Science hasn't solved all our challenges and never will. Cognitive science has, however, provided proven research that can make our jobs easier. We can address many training challenges by implementing the resulting best practices.

Resources

Biech, E. 2009. *ASTD's Ultimate Train-the-Trainer: A Complete Guide to Training Success*. Alexandria, VA: ASTD Press.

———. 2014. *ASTD Handbook: The Definitive Reference for Training and Development*. 2nd ed. Alexandria, VA: ASTD Press.

———. 2015. *Training and Development for Dummies*. Hoboken, NJ: John Wiley & Sons.

Bigelow, J., and A. Poremba. 2014. "Achilles Ear? Inferior Human Short-Term and Recognition Memory in the Auditory Modality." *PLoS ONE* 9(2):e89914. doi:10.1371/journal.

Bunzeck, N., and E. Duzel. 2006. "Absolute Coding of Stimulus Novelty in the Human Substantia Nigra/VTA." *Neuron* 51(3):369-379.

Clark, R. 2015. *Evidence-Based Training Methods: A Guide for Training Professionals*. 2nd ed. Alexandria, VA: ATD Press.

Davenport, T., and J. Beck. 2002. *The Attention Economy: Understanding the New Currency of Business*. Boston: Harvard Business School.

DeBruyckere, P., and P. Kirschner. 2015. *Urban Myths About Learning and Education*. London: Academic Press.

Dweck, C. 2008. *Mindset: The New Psychology of Success.* New York: Ballantine Books.

Eadicicco, L. 2015. "Americans Check Their Phones 8 Billion Times a Day." *Time*, December 15.

Elliot, B. 2009. "E-Pedagodgy." *Scribd*, January. www.scribd.com/doc/932164/E-Pedagogy .

Foerde, K., B.J. Knowlton, and R.A. Poldrack. 2006. "Modulation of Competing Memory Systems by Distraction." *PNAS* 10:11778-11783.

Hemp, P. 2009. "Death by Information Overload." *Harvard Business Review*, September.

Hodell, C. 2013. *SMEs From the Ground Up.* Alexandria, VA: ASTD Press.

Jonassen, D.H., and B.L. Grabowski. 1993. *Handbook of Individual Differences, Learning, and Instruction.* Mahwah, NJ: Lawrence Erlbaum Associates.

Kim, R.S., A.R. Seitz, and L. Shams. 2008. "Benefits of Stimulus Congruency for Multisensory Facilitation of Visual Learning." *PLoS ONE* 3(1): e1532. doi:10.1371/journal. pone.0001532.

Kolb, D.A. 1981. *Experiential Learning: Experience as the Source of Learning and Development.* Upper Saddle River, NJ: Prentice-Hall.

Medina, J. 2008. *Brain Rules: 12 Principles for Surviving and Thriving at Work, Home, and School.* Seattle: Pear Press.

Miller, G.A. 1956. "The Magical Number Seven, Plus or Minus Two: Some Limits on Our Capacity for Processing Information." *Psychological Review* 63:81-97.

Naveh-Benjamin, M., F.I.M. Craik, J.G. Perretta, and S.T. Tonev. 2000. "The Effects of Divided Attention on Encoding and Retrieval Processes: The Resiliency of Retrieval Processes." *The Quarterly Journal of Experimental Psychology* 53A (3):609-625.

Nyhan, B., et al. 2011. "Opening the Political Mind? The Effects of Self-Affirmation and Graphical Information on Factual Misperceptions." Unpublished manuscript, Dartmouth University, Hanover, NH.

Pluth, B. 2016. *Creative Training: A Train-the-Trainer Field Guide*. Eden Prairie, MN: Creative Training Productions.

Rock, D. 2008. "SCARF: A Brain-Based Model for Collaborating With and Influencing Others." *NeuroLeadership Journal* 1:1-9.

Senge, P. 2006. *The Fifth Discipline*. 2nd ed. New York: Currency Doubleday Books.

Society for Neuroscience. 2007. "Mirror, Mirror in the Brain: Decoding Patterns Reflecting Understanding of Self, Others May Further Autism Therapies." Society for Neuroscience, November 4. www.sfn.org/Press-Room/News-Release-Archives/2007/MIRROR-MIRROR-IN-THE-BRAIN?returnId={0C16364F-DB22-424A-849A-B7CF6FDCFE35}

Standing, L., J. Conezio, R.N. Haber 1970. "Perception and Memory for Pictures: Single Trial Learning of 2500 Visual Stimuli." *Psychonomic Science* 19: 73-74.

Stone, L. 2009. "Continuous Partial Attention." Linda Stone, November 29. https://lindastone.net/qa/continuous-partial-attention.

Understanding What Makes People Tick: Applying Discoveries in Neuroscience to Optimize the Potential of People. 2009. Fenton, MO: The Maritz Institute.

University College of London. 2006. "Novelty Aids Learning." *Medical Express*, August 3. www.physorg.com/ news73834337.html.

Wright, R., and L. Ward. 2008. *Orienting of Attention*. Oxford, UK: Oxford University Press.

Zsambok, C.E., G.L. Kaempf, B. Crandall, M. Kyne, and Klein Associates Inc. 1997. "A Comprehensive Program to Deliver on-the-Job Training (OJT)." (ARI Contractor Report 97-18). Alexandria, VA: U.S. Army Research Institute (DTIC: ADA327576).

Zull, J. 2002. *The Art of Changing the Brain*. Sterling, VA: Stylus Publishing.

How Can You Guarantee Transfer of Learning to the Workplace?

Transfer of learning has long been a concern for professionals in the field of talent development. After all, we do not exist to merely "train"; we exist to improve performance in the workplace. How well learning is applied on the job is the ultimate goal.

In *Telling Ain't Training*, Harold Stolovitch and Erica Keeps write:

> A great deal of controversy exists about the exact amount of training that gets transferred to the workplace. This is a futile argument as a number of factors affect transfer: utility of the training, the workplace environment, inhibitors and facilitators that occur post-training, and even the attitudes of supervisors and colleagues. What appears to be the consensus of researchers is that the training event is one thing. The application is quite another. Some influencing factors relate to the quality and relevance of the training; most reside outside of the trainee (2011, 277).

I agree. However, not knowing the exact percentage isn't a reason for you to throw in the towel. In research that I referenced in chapters 6 and 7, authors Salas et al. (2012) used meta-analysis to determine how to design and deliver training as effectively as possible. Their research is filled with valuable information for you. They state that, "The research on training clearly shows two things: (a) training works, and (b) the way training is designed, delivered, and implemented matters."

This is good news! I'm sure you've heard the few detractors who would like us to believe that training doesn't work. So it is good to read solid research stating unequivocally that it does work. It's up to you to make sure you are doing everything necessary in your design and delivery to stand behind that claim. You need to ensure performance and the transfer of learning to the workplace.

Ensuring Performance and Transfer of Learning

A training program alone will not lead to long-lasting learning and change. What happens prior and follows after the training program ends are equally critical to success. What separates effective from ineffective training is the attention given to on-the-job application. Unfortunately the application is often the most neglected part of a training design. What do you do before, during, and after training are all equally important to ensure the learning is applied on the job. I have addressed each of these in other chapters about design and delivery. This summary incorporates what Salas and his colleagues (2012) address in their report.

Involve the Team Before the Training Occurs

Eduardo Salas and his colleagues (2012) summarize three steps to take before training: conduct a training needs analysis; prepare the learning climate; and prepare supervisors and leaders. Since I've already discussed the first two, I'll focus on the third. Besides, "preparing supervisors and leaders" is probably the area most of us need to shore up.

Involve each participant's team before the training session. Start by pretraining participants' supervisors—this is especially important when the organization is going through a major change. When they receive such training, supervisors are able to serve not merely as managers but also as mentors, coaches, role models, and encouragers.

Of course, this step may initially be expensive, time-consuming, and hard to implement. This is an instance in which virtual training programs can be beneficial. If you cannot pretrain supervisors, you may want to brief them about the training their employees are receiving. In such briefings, it is important for you to discuss the following:

- the objectives of the training program
- the course outline
- the kinds of training activities utilized in the program
- course materials
- suggestions for facilitating further practice and application of skills.

But this pretraining meeting is not just for you to provide information, it is also about getting information. Meet with the participants' managers to discuss what the manager expects from the workshop. Dana Robinson (2008) offers her suggestions on the type of questions you can ask when exploring a manager's request for a training program:

- What are the goals for your employees?
- What are the measures you use to determine an employees' success?
- What must employees do more, better, or differently if your department or function is to be effective?
- What have you observed employees do that needs to change?

This approach is valuable to build your training program with organizational objectives in mind. It helps managers and supervisors trust that learners will find a connection between their new skills and the organization's goals and priorities.

Another way to make supervisors your allies is to enlist their cooperation with regard to any precourse preparation you may ask of their employees. Giving participants time from their regular responsibilities to read advance materials or complete precourse assignments is a real contribution. It is even better when supervisors sit down with their employees and help them define a personal case situation or two to bring to the training program. This can become the basis for real-life problem solving during the training session.

There are other things you can do prior to the training program to build supervisor support. Here are some ideas to get you thinking in that direction:

- Partner with supervisors to help them determine how they can help their employees upon returning from the workshop. Ask questions to determine the link between the workshop and the performance results. At the very least, leave them with a list of skills that you intend to discuss in the workshop. Managers can use this list to help reinforce these new skills when they see implementing them on the job, or as stated in the *One Minute Manager*, "catch them doing something right."

- Inform participants' managers about any action plan activities.

- Collect messages of support from participants' managers describing how they will support transfer of the skills after the workshop. Weave these messages into your workshop.

- Ask participants to bring challenges they have that they hope will be resolved by what they learn.

- Ask participants and their supervisors to select a project to undertake as a result of what the participants learn. If you do this for a virtual training session, be very clear in your written directions and offer assistance and clarification by phone or email. When participants come to the training program with a project that has already been discussed with their management or team, on-the-job application is built into the program design.

Of course, the best way to obtain management support is to invite supervisors to conduct training programs for their own team. While once uncommon, this is occurring more frequently. Fei Liu has worked for COFCO in China for 12 years and states that the company is very successful using this technique. Participants report that manager-led training is successful as long as managers are well prepared to conduct training on their own (Biech 2015). In many instances, you may be asked to help managers prepare.

Support During the Training Program

Salas's research demonstrates that during training you should enable the right mindset and follow appropriate instructional principles, such as building in engagement opportunities and using computer-based training correctly. I've discussed most of this in chapters 6, 7, and 8, so here's a summary of ideas you can facilitate to ensure application:

- Allow enough practice time for skill mastery. Some trainers have a tendency to move quickly from skill to skill without enough rehearsal. For example, you can give participants the opportunity to role-play a skill and have peers provide feedback on their performance. Some degree of overlearning is required for participants to feel confident about exercising a new skill. Confidence grows even more when participants master exercises of increasing levels of difficulty. Eventually, they believe that they truly own the skill.

- Use realistic practice. The more similar the training situation is to the situation on the job, the more likely it is to last. Even re-creating the physical environment of the job can be helpful. For example, call center training is greatly enhanced if recordings of actual customer calls are used and the training takes place in an actual call center.

- Share successes. Tell participants how past training sessions have had a positive impact in the workplace.

- Read messages of support from key people from the organization. If you are an internal facilitator or working with just one organization, you might include statements from participants' line managers describing how they will support transfer after the workshop.

- Remember to use the debriefing questions. It is only a start to learning when participants hear the "what" of your message. The most important part comes with the debriefing questions or the "so what" (so what does that mean or relate?) and the "now what" (now what are you going to do or change or implement as a result?).

This reduces the gap between talking and action, and forces the learning to be focused on implementation.

- Build in a final module that addresses what they will do. It may be in the form of an action plan or how to develop yourself. Once learners leave the training session they need to continue to learn.

- Provide participants with a range of strategies for how to continue to learn.

- During the workshop learn when participants will have an opportunity to implement what they are learning. Tell them that they should watch for follow-up reminders when the event occurs. Prepare your follow up so it is ready to send just in time. For example, just prior to performance reviews, email your participants reminders about how to conduct successful reviews.

- Encourage participants to express their opinions about the skills being taught and how they performed. They are less likely to resist changes if they have the chance to express their reservations and trepidations. Some trainers hard-sell the value of the skills, ideas, and procedures they are advocating. But, it's far better to encourage participants to draw their own conclusions. For example, invite participants to examine their thoughts about the skills they are learning and the environment they will practice them in. Ask the rest of the class to take turns listening, observing, and communicating their own perceptions.

- If you are able to arrange for time back on the job between training sessions, give participants assignments to complete in their own work settings. When you resume the training, you can ask them to share how well the real-life practice went, and pose any questions they may still have about their new skills.

At the Close of the Training

Many things come together at the end of your training. Allow enough time to discuss next steps. This is not the time to rush participants through an evaluation form and push them out the door. Instead use the closing of your training program to help ensure transfer of learning. The following list contains options that will work for both traditional and virtual training sessions.

At the end of the training session you could:

- Ask participants to assess themselves and identify a "buddy" in the session who could help coach them or encourage them to practice specific skills.

- Provide job aids.

- Ask participants to voluntarily opt into a continuing learning group. Create a wiki or a LinkedIn page where they can ask questions, share tips, give advice, or celebrate successes. You can seed the site with questions, links to videos, or short articles.

- Ask participants to commit to trying one new skill within the week. If it was a supervisory skills training, perhaps they could meet with one of their employees to conduct a developmental discussion. Ask them to publicly commit to their plans and have them text the entire group once they complete their actions.

- Plan at least an hour for participants to brainstorm a list of barriers they anticipate that may prevent them from implementing some of the skills that were discussed in the workshop. Form small groups to tackle each of the barriers and report out ideas to overcome them. Do the group a favor and compile the lists and email them to the group shortly after the session.

- Suggest that participants discuss their action plans with their managers upon returning, and ask for support in achieving their goals.

- Organize peer practice groups to support one another as they perfect their skills and competencies. They may be self-organizing or you may wish to attend the first meeting to get them started and provide resources and a suggested meeting format to ensure the peer groups are productive.

- Near the end of the workshop ask each participant to partner with an individual with whom he has worked closely (and ideally is in the same physical location). Call these pairs *support buddies, accountability partners, peer coaches,* or *peer mentors,* depending on your audience. Ask them to select one topic from the training session that they want to focus on in the coming month. Then have each partner interview the other about strategies he will use to implement that topic daily at work (and at home if applicable) for the next 30 days. Have the partners schedule four weekly meetings over the coming month.

- At the close of the workshop, provide participants with a postcard and ask them to address it to themselves. Have participants write two MVTs (most valuable tips) and two things they intend to implement from the workshop. Tell the participants to select a learning accountability partner to contact and debrief upon receipt of the postcard. Mail the postcards out to arrive two to four weeks after the workshop.

Follow Up After the Training Session

After training, Eduardo Salas and his research team (2012) recommend that trainers remove obstacles to transfer; provide tools and advice to supervisors; encourage use of real-world debriefs; and provide reinforcement and support mechanisms. According to Cal Wick (2010), a few enlightened organizations have begun to recognize that making time for ongoing support results in more learning implemented back on the job. While many trainers deliver back-to-back learning sessions without time for follow up, the responsibility for follow up can be shared between the trainers and managers. Here are a few suggestions:

- Follow up the session by emailing a resource to participants. It could be something that came up during the session, an article you think will be pertinent, or a link to a YouTube presentation.

- Follow up the session with a quiz. Share responses with everyone and offer prizes for the best ones.

- About a week after the session, tweet a simple question that participants can respond to. For example you could ask what new skill they have tried and to give themselves a score of how successful they were. You could use a 100 percent scale or an A, B, C, D, F scale. Follow up to find out what you can do to help.

- Several months after the workshop, invite the participants to return for a review and celebration session during which they share their successes and review situations they needed additional knowledge or skills to complete.

- Facilitate a book club that meets over lunch once or twice each month to continue learning about your topic. You could also create a discussion forum or arrange a webinar or conference call for the discussion.

- Create short videos or a podcast about some of the topics presented in the workshop, and then send the link to participants. Interviews are a great and easy way to do this.

- Reinforce the content using workplace communication processes. Use the workplace employee newsletter, intranet, or posters to reinforce key training concepts. Provide tips, funny self-assessments, and other means for your employees to apply and refine what they've learned.

Transfer of learning to the workplace often requires that you follow up with participants as either a mentor or a coach. Mentoring and coaching are effective ways to ensure the development needs are transferred. Training sessions that are followed up with on-the-job support result in a higher return on every dollar invested.

"It is a great nuisance that knowledge can be acquired only by hard work."
—Somerset Maugham

On-the-Job Support Ensures Transfer

Most organizations expect their managers to develop people. However, few clearly specify people development as a key item on their performance review forms. Organizations that are clear about this responsibility also generally link the performance management system with talent development, as well as the compensation and benefits package. Most organizations and managers believe that talent development should be linked to managers' promotion and performance evaluation. They just have not taken the time to do so. I anticipate this changing rapidly in the near future.

One of the new roles for trainers is to have solid coaching and mentoring skills so that they can support managers and supervisors in their new "coaching" roles. In these instances they will act in two roles. They will be a coach to the managers and they will help managers learn to be good coaches to their direct reports.

Engaging Leaders in Development and Performance

The next training event is a perfect time to begin practicing your new role. Your responsibility to your organization is to ensure transfer of learning back to the workplace. But it doesn't end there.

You can't be on the job with your learners all the time, so for on-the-job support to occur, the supervisor needs to be involved. Here are a few things you can do in your new role as a coach to the supervisors:

- Suggest that the supervisors find other ways for the learner to practice the skills. Serving on an internal cross-functional team or in a volunteer activity are helpful because they allow the learners to experiment with their new skills. Make sure managers meet regularly with their learners to provide coaching along the way.

- Familiarize supervisors with the skills taught in the session so they can correct or reinforce any behaviors they observe.
- Recommend that supervisors ask participants to review key concepts learned in training with others in their position once they return to the workplace.
- Suggest that supervisors discuss any problems in transferring skills and knowledge from the workshop to the job. Tell them to ask what barriers need to be removed to allow the learner to practice new skills.

Competency Is Nothing Without Commitment and Confidence

As a trainer you may think that your key role is to provide competence and expertise. You are expected to facilitate a process so that learners acquire new knowledge and behaviors as a result of practice and the content you provide. In fact, isn't that the purpose of writing objectives and incorporating KSAs (knowledge, skills, attitude)? Actually, it's only a portion.

Your learners can leave your training event with perfect scores in the content you have delivered. Common sense, however, tells us that for your learners to implement the acquired skills and knowledge on the job, they have to be committed to the change and confident in themselves to take the first steps to try out the skills.

Your job is to ensure your learners have not only the competence, but also the confidence and commitment to make the change and apply what they learned in the workplace. How does that happen? You already know how to facilitate competence, and I have presented ways to encourage confidence and commitment. Your learners gain confidence when they receive feedback from you, practice the skills, role play, or work in small groups to experiment with the skills. They gain commitment when they complete an action plan, resolve a case study, commit to a change to the rest of the group, or have a chance to ask questions about or discuss their concerns.

Performing Under Pressure

Some jobs require you to perform under duress. Trainers have long believed that it was not possible to train individuals to react under pressure. Is it possible to ensure that learners do not freeze when confronted with a stressful situation and remember to apply what they've learned? Can you train them to perform under pressure? Recent research confirms it is possible.

People freeze in high-stress situations because their working memory becomes overwhelmed by the emotional reaction. Your brain is built for immediate responses when threatened and as a result your body automatically releases adrenaline and cortisol. These emotions overwhelm what you've learned for how to deal with these situations. For a long time trainers believed there wasn't much they could change. However, a recent study demonstrates that learners can be trained to control their emotions under stress, which means they'll be able to utilize what they learned to perform under pressure (Schweizer et al. 2013).

Researchers in the study conducted a series of experiments with two subject groups. The first was trained using emotionally neutral material to match geometric shapes. The second group was given emotionally loaded tasks, including matching words such as *evil* and *dissent* to pictures of facial expressions.

After training, the subjects viewed highly emotional videos; for example, news coverage of natural disasters. They were asked to regulate their emotions, stay calm, and emotionally detach while watching. Using brain scans and self-reporting, the team found that those who had trained with the emotional content were better able to regulate their emotions (Schweizer et al. 2013).

What does this tell us as trainers? If you want to help people perform better under stress, train them under stress. Make training challenging. Emotional working memory improves when it's operating at capacity. Don't make training too easy or learners won't experience the stress that occurs in real-life situations. Add emotional content to role plays. Ask learners to identify their emotions as they progress through a role-play exercise or hypothetical situation.

Is Learning Transfer About Recall and Retention?

Let's think about this. No single area of your brain is completely responsible for memory. Memories are spread out and generated from throughout the brain (Jensen 2008). Our brain is complex, and retention starts with the messages that grab our attention based on memories, level of interest, and awareness (Medina 2008).

Retention depends on how well our brain processes, stores, and retrieves the information. Hundreds of things affect how we gain and retain information, and there are a few things to focus on regarding retention (Jensen 2008; Medina 2008):

- **Patterns.** Our brain looks for patterns based on prior experiences to fill in the blanks. If the pattern is clearly defined, content can be readily retrieved. How much background information we have affects how readily our brain takes in new information and places it in the pattern.

- **Forgetting.** German psychologist Hermann Ebbinghaus showed that a great deal of memory loss occurs in the first hour or two of initial exposure. He most likely created "forgetting curves" so that we wouldn't forget (Loftus 1985; Schacter 2011).

- **Repetition.** Ebbinghaus also demonstrated the power of repetition to move content from short-term to long-term memory (Loftus 1985).

- **Novelty.** Repetition is critical, but the brain really craves novelty, which causes the dopamine system to send the chemical throughout the brain (Barcroft and Sommers 2005; Quilici and Mayer 1996; Rost and McMurray 2009).

- **Basics.** Sleep, exercise, rest, and food all affect how well our brain works and play a role in retention (Jensen 2008; Medina 2008).

- **Spacing.** Learning that is spaced over time with intervals between allow us to internalize and process new information to ensure that it moves into our long-term memory. Darryl Bruce and Harry Bahrick

(1992) reviewed more than 300 studies, demonstrating the potency of spacing.

- **Emotions and stress.** Creating emotional arousal and a limited amount of stress all aid in retaining memories (Jensen 2008).
- **Tools.** Mnemonic devices are like job aids for our brains. They help us remember because they take a large amount of information and put it into a single chunk (Stolovitch and Keeps 2011). For example, you remember the colors of the spectrum using the acronym ROY G. BIV: Red, Orange, Yellow, Green, Blue, Indigo, Violet.
- **Cognitive load.** Your brain can only process a specific amount of information at a time. Don't overload it (Ericson, Krampe, and Tesch-Romer 1993; Medina 2008).
- **Use it or lose it.** Your brain generates more cells than it needs, and only those that receive chemical stimuli survive. Information that isn't used is lost as the neural pathways weaken over time (Diamond 1996).

What about the social aspects of recall? Isn't readiness to learn a critical element? While there are other aspects of learning that affect retention, you can see that these encompass many important aspects of the transfer of learning. They're all useful. What I want you to take away from this section is that even if you facilitate the best training ever and attend to all the necessary cognitive steps, transfer of learning is dependent upon what happens before training, what happens after training, and the involvement of the learner's immediate team.

I opened this chapter with the lament from Stolovitch and Keeps that we can't really measure how much gets transferred. But there are other opinions too. Some theorists argue that transfer doesn't occur at all. They believe that transfer is a passive notion and that participants actively transform what they have learned into a new context, constructing knowledge so that they understand it themselves (Larsen-Freeman 2013). They believe that learners change the information they have learned so that it makes sense to them. In addition, if the learner does not find the information necessary, it isn't likely that the knowledge will ever transfer. Well, that makes sense to those of us who are trainers too!

Can Learning Transfer Be Predicted?

Precise measures of learning transfer are nearly impossible to find. Whether you call it transfer or not, it is a key step in improving performance in the workplace. Therefore, it would be nice to be able to predict the chances of success. Ensuring learning transfer is one of the most critical challenges facing our profession today. Twenty-five years of research by Rob Brinkerhoff (2006), an internationally recognized expert on training effectiveness and evaluation, demonstrates that the best predictor of learning transfer is "expectation." If learners expect to be held accountable for using what they learned, they are more likely to transfer their skills and knowledge to the workplace. Most often this expectation of accountability is based on interactions with the learners' managers.

Can leaders be trained to be better coaches? Research says they can be taught and also demonstrates the importance of why effective developmental discussions between supervisors and their employees are so critical (Zsambok et al. 1997; Eddy et al. 2006). When supervisors have developmental discussions, coach employees, and support employees as they implement new skills, it clearly enhances the predictability of learning transfer and retention. I see this nuance as a part of talent development's changing role. We must help our organizations identify the tools, training, and support to help supervisors coach employees and use on-the-job assignments to reinforce training and to enable employees to continue their development.

Brinkerhoff's conclusion is a valuable scientific nugget we must keep in mind. We have to make sure that time is available for the learners, their managers, and ourselves to create the expectation of accountability. After all, it's what happens before and after the training that is the most important to ensure learning transfer. We must be more involved in the solution. We must make the time.

What We Know for Sure

Science tells us that we can rely on several proven facts:

- Transfer of learning and improved performance demonstrates training success.
- What you do before and after a training event is equally important for transfer of learning as what you do while training.
- Transfer of learning is enhanced when you conduct a training needs analysis, prepare the learning climate, and prepare supervisors and leaders prior to the training event.
- Few organizations recognize the value of making time for ongoing support before and after a training session.
- Transfer of learning is rarely about retention and recall.
- You can train people to respond well and recall learning in emotionally charged or stressful situations.

 # The Art Part

Your success will depend upon how well you adapt to the situation and your learners' needs. Tap into some of these ideas to help your learners grow, to develop yourself, and to add your personal creative touch.

Where's the money? Perhaps it's time for you to consider reviewing how your organization invests training and development dollars and whether every delivery option will lead to transfer of learning.

Skill or will? Trainers sometimes discuss whether it is the learner's skill or will that prevents top-notch performance following a training session. This refers to the fact that an employee may have learned the skill but is unwilling to use it. Therefore, the real reason an employee may not be using what was learned may not be skill-based at all. Identify ways you can inspire employees to stay motivated to use what they've learned.

Read it yourself. Download "The Science of Training and Development in Organizations: What Matters in Practice" by Salas and his colleagues, which is listed in the resource section for this chapter. You will appreciate the confirmation of best practices.

Pick an idea. This chapter shared dozens of ideas for how to encourage transfer of learning. They may not all work in your situation, but many will. Select one from each category—before, during, at the close, and after the training—to implement in your next workshop.

Add emotion. Don't be afraid to add an emotional twist to learning to make it as much like real life as possible. Try adding deadlines to create a scenario similar to the workplace; for example, you could:

- Use a ticking clock during timed quizzes or exercises.
- Ask learners to brainstorm as many ideas as possible in two minutes.
- Ask salespeople to discuss how they feel when they're trying to close a high-stakes deal.

Art and Science Questions You Might Ask

These questions provide potential challenges for your personal growth and development:

- What are you doing to ensure learning transfers to the workplace?
- How are you getting supervisors and managers involved to ensure you are providing accurate and required content for learners?
- What are you doing before and after training to ensure that learners can and will use what they learned in the workplace?
- How clear are you about required competencies and performance on the job?
- What evidence do you see that training is making an impact in the workplace?
- What role do you play in ensuring that you have created a learning environment?
- How can you make your organization more conducive to learning?

How Can You Guarantee Transfer of Learning to the Workplace?

Can you guarantee transfer of learning? Well, *guarantee* is a very specific word and you probably can't guarantee it—but you can come pretty darn close. It all depends on what you do before, during, and after the training session. Training produces value when it is applied to your organization's work. A critical part of your job is to ensure that participants transfer what they have learned from classroom to the job.

Yes, this means going the extra mile to help supervisors and managers better understand their role in developing employees. It's our responsibility to see that this happens. Our focus needs to change to ensure our organizations are building a culture of learning. The ATD research report *Building a Culture of Learning: The Foundation of a Successful Organization* states that, "Robust cultures of learning are distinct hallmarks of organizations that consistently produce the best business results" (ATD 2016). Isn't that what we all want for our organizations?

Transfer of learning is not an event. Like change, it is a process. And it is a critical part of having a culture of learning.

Resources

ATD. 2016. *Building a Culture of Learning: The Foundation of a Successful Organization*. Alexandria, VA: ATD Press.

Barcroft, J., and M.S. Sommers. 2005. "Effects of Acoustic Variability on Second Language Vocabulary Learning." *Studies in Second Language Acquisition* 27(3):387-414.

Biech, E. 2014. *ASTD Handbook: The Definitive Reference for Training and Development*. 2nd ed. Alexandria, VA: ASTD Press.

——. 2015a. *Training and Development for Dummies*. Hoboken, NJ: John Wiley & Sons.

——. 2015b. *Training Is the Answer: Making Learning and Development Work in China*. Fairfax, VA: Trainers Publishing House.

Brinkerhoff, R. 2006. *Telling Training's Story*. San Francisco: Berrett-Koehler.

Bruce, D., and H.P. Bahrick. 1992. "Perceptions of Past Research." *American Psychologist* 47(5):674.

Clark, R. 2015. *Evidence-Based Training Methods: A Guide for Training Professionals*. 2nd ed. Alexandria, VA: ATD Press.

Diamond, M. 1996. "The Brain . . . Use It or Lose It." Johns Hopkins School of Education. http://education.jhu.edu/PD/newhorizons/Neurosciences/articles/The%20Brain...Use%20it%20or%20Lose%20It.

Eddy, E.R., C.P. D'Abate, S.I. Tannenbaum, S. Givens-Skeaton, and G. Robinson. 2006. "Key Characteristics of Effective and Ineffective Developmental Interactions." *Human Resource Development Quarterly* 17:59-84.

Ericson, K., R. Krampe, and C. Tesch-Romer. 1993. "The Role of Deliberate Practice in the Acquisition of Expert Performance." *Psychological Review* 100(3):363-406.

Jensen, E. 2008. *Brain-Based Learning*. Thousand Oaks, CA: Corwin Press.

Knowles, M.S. III, E. Holton, and R. Swanson. 2015. *The Adult Learner: The Definitive Classic in Adult Education and Human Resource Development*. 8th ed. Burlington, MA: Elsevier/Butterworth-Heinemann.

Larsen-Freeman, D. 2013. "Transfer of Learning Transformed." *Language Learning: A Journal of Research in Language Studies*, 63:S1. http://online-library.wiley.com/doi/10.1111/j.1467-9922.2012.00740.x/abstract.

Levin, H. 1996. *Innovations in Learning: New Environments for Education*. Mahwah, NJ: Lawrence Erlbaum Associates.

Loftus, G.R. 1985. "Evaluating Forgetting Curves." *Journal of Experimental Psychology: Learning, Memory, and Cognition* 11(2):397-406. doi:10.1037/0278-7393.11.2.397.

Lombardo, M., and R. Eichinger. 2011. *The Leadership Machine: Architecture to Develop Leaders for Any Future*. Minneapolis: Lominger International: A Korn/Ferry Company.

Medina, J. 2008. *Brain Rules: 12 Principles for Surviving and Thriving at Work, Home, and School*. Seattle: Pear Press.

Pluth, B. 2016. *Creative Training: A Train-the-Trainer Field Guide*. Eden Prairie, MN: Creative Training Productions.

Quilici, J.L., and R. Mayer. 1996. "Role of Examples in How Students Learn to Categorize Statistics Word Problems." *Journal of Educational Psychology* 88(1):144-161.

Robinson, D., and J. Robinson. 2008. *Performance Consulting: A Practical Guide for HR and Learning Professionals*. 2nd ed. San Francisco: Berrett-Koehler.

Robinson, D., J. Robinson, J. Phillips, P. Phillips, and D. Handshaw. 2015. *Performance Consulting: A Strategic Process to Improve, Measure, and Sustain Organizational Results*. 3rd ed. San Francisco: Berrett-Koehler.

Rost, G.C., and B. McMurray. 2009. "Speaker Variability Augments Phonological Processing in Warly Word Learning." *Developmental Science* 12(2):339-349.

Salas, E., S. Tannenbaum, K. Kraiger, and K. Smith-Jentsch. 2012. "The Science of Training and Development in Organizations: What Matters in Practice." *Psychological Science in the Public Interest* 13(2): 74-101.

Schacter, D.L., D. Gilbert, and D. Wegner. 2011. *Psychology*. 2nd ed. New York: Worth Publishers.

Schweizer, S., et al. 2013. "Training the Emotional Brain: Improving Affective Control Through Emotional Working Memory Training." *The Journal of Neuroscience* 33(12):5301-5311.

Silberman, M., and E. Biech. 2015. *Active Training: A Handbook of Techniques, Designs, Case Examples, and Tips*. Hoboken, NJ: John Wiley & Sons.

Stolovitch, H., and E. Keeps. 2011. *Telling Ain't Training*. 2nd ed. Alexandria, VA: ASTD Press.

Wick, C., R. Pollock, and A. Jefferson. 2010. *The Six Disciplines of Breakthrough Learning: How to Turn Training and Development Into Business Results*. 2nd ed. San Francisco: Pfeiffer.

Zsambok, C.E., G.L. Kaempf, B. Crandall, M. Kyne, and Klein Associates Inc. 1997. "A Comprehensive Program to Deliver On-the-Job Training (OJT)." (ARI Contractor Report 97–18). Alexandria, VA: U.S. Army Research Institute (DTIC: ADA327576).

How Do You Align Learning With Organizational Requirements?

M ost organizations view learning as a strategic enabler, making it imperative that talent development aligns with organizational requirements and strategic objectives. Unfortunately, *Managing the Learning Landscape*, a whitepaper by ATD and PMI (2014), suggests that only 45 percent of organizations have "significant" or "good" alignment of talent development to organizational strategy.

What difference does it make? Untrained employees may lack knowledge about company resources or procedures that affect customer retention, ultimately leading to waste or decreased profits. *The Value of Training*, a research report funded by IBM (2014), demonstrates these data:

- 84 percent of employees in best performing organizations are receiving the training they need, compared with 16 percent in the worst performing companies.
- 71 percent of CEOs (4,183 leaders in 70 countries) identified human capital as a key source of sustained economic value.

- 62 percent of new hires intend to stay at companies that offer training for their current jobs; however, 21 percent do not intend to stay if training is not provided.

Organizations need to take measures to drive performance. Skilled employees are a strategic part of an organization's performance.

Linking Learning to Performance

Aligning learning with your business needs starts by building a business case and cost justification for the investment. Organizations whose learning strategy is aligned to organizational requirements are more agile and competive. Learning and development exists to drive business value rather than to only provide training.

To align with your organizations' business objectives, you might consider these questions:

- Do you speak the language of business?
- Do you understand and communicate with all your stakeholders—business leaders, line managers, and employees—especially about their learning needs?
- Can you help to quantify the potential impact of the solution? What are the key metrics of business success? What difference would these key performance indicators make to your organization's bottom line?
- Review your capacity. What are the capabilities required to achieve your business goals based on defined metrics? Does your current infrastructure support talent development goals?
- Can you show evidence that you have the ability to measure the impact of learning activities against the business goals?
- Have you involved key stakeholders in generating and championing the agenda?
- How will you create a plan to ensure that learning and development activities reflect the demands of the business goals?
- How can you ensure the learning evaluation metrics align with the valued business measures?

- How can you use data to help justify your budget, using relevant indicators important to your organization and stakeholders?
- How can you be proactive in both tactical and strategic organizational goals and analyze the business problem before recommending a solution?
- Who will work with senior managers to identify specific business metrics that need to be improved?
- On what timeline might you demonstrate value back to the business by revisiting objectives with senior managers and reporting on the results?

Throughout the process, stay focused. Business moves rapidly and strategies change quickly. This means that you need to deliver knowledge and skills for any new direction. Of course this isn't easy, but it is critical. One final thought: You need to determine what you will not do to make time for what you will do for your organization. A good resource for more details is the third edition of *Performance Consulting* by Dana Robinson and her colleagues (2008). Linking learning to your organizational needs will coincide with beginning to create a culture of learning.

Building a Culture of Learning

The ATD research report *Building a Culture of Learning* reveals that only 31 percent of organizations have well-developed learning cultures (ATD 2016). Essential traits include closely aligned business and learning strategies; values that affirm the importance of learning; and an "ingrained learning atmosphere." Change is embraced and employees have developmental and growth mindsets.

The report determined that a culture of learning pays off in many ways:

- Top companies are almost five times more likely than lower performers to have extensive learning cultures.
- High performers are nearly two times more apt to say their learning functions help meet organizational business goals.

- Employees at high-performing organizations share knowledge with their colleagues at a rate four times greater than that of workers in lower-performing firms.
- Communication is supported by rewarding workers for learning, providing tools and resources for creating and sharing learning content, and making knowledge sharing a performance expectation at all levels.
- Discussing an employer's commitments to ongoing talent development during prehire interviews is a distinguishing trait.
- Three practices related to supporting a learning culture are performance standouts:
  - regularly updated personalized development plans for every employee
  - worker accountability for the learning specified in those plans
  - nonfinancial rewards and recognition for employee learning.

The study also found that top performers are three times more likely to use the learning culture for recruitment and three times more likely to hold leaders accountable for demonstrating learning's importance.

What's involved in building a culture of learning? First and foremost, make time for learning and create accountability from the top down. These two steps will result in personalized development plans.

The time required does not refer to the amount of time invested attending formal learning events. Instead it refers to the time that employees need on the job to learn; for example, time that is a part of everyday work to learn from reviews and receive feedback about projects and tasks from their immediate supervisor. Supervisors must provide coaching and development daily and create plans for future learning with employees.

As I mentioned in the last section, you must think about what you will stop doing so you can do a better job of what you will do. Just as our brains have patterns and mindsets that may need to be changed or shifted, our organizations also have organizational patterns and mindsets—"the way we do things around here." Changing the culture may require you to uncover some of these established organizational patterns and challenge them.

To be a true culture of learning, we must tolerate and celebrate creativity, risk, and failure. To transform itself, an organization must accept failure as part of the learning process—just as you try and learn and fail until you get it right. And like individual success, learning occurs when you reflect on what happened, what it means, and what you will do differently as a result.

All of these are elements in learning to learn. In the process of building a learning culture, you need to remember the importance of attending to a brain-friendly workplace and how motivation is changing.

Influencing the Brain-Friendly Workplace

Covering all the possibilities to align learning means you need to consider future workplace issues. A report by Bersin (2016) predicts that a revolution in corporate learning is continuing. Specifics include MOOCs; low-cost (often free) online courses; high-quality, low-cost video production; an increased passion for self-directed learning; and a changing audience.

Today's learners are mobile, short on time, and want to learn on their schedules. They are collaborative, distracted, impatient, and overwhelmed. The Center for Creative Leadership's 70-20-10 framework for learning has renewed interest, especially in the 70 percent (on the job learning) and the 20 percent (learning from others). All of these facts add up to a need to attend to a changing world.

In her book *The Brain-Friendly Workplace*, Erika Garms (2014) also identifies organizational challenges on the horizon. She suggests that we will need to identify and work toward improving a brain-friendly workplace to ensure increased creativity and productivity. Among the challenges she sees converging in the workplace are upheaval in management; continuous, overlapping, accelerated transition; and new and different employee motivators.

Motivation: It's a New Game

Raymond Wlodkowski (2003), a psychologist, researcher, and national consultant in adult and professional learning, surmises that four motivational conditions are essential in creating intrinsic motivation in an adult learning setting:

- **Establish inclusion.** Create a learning atmosphere in which learners and trainers feel respected.
- **Develop attitude.** Create a positive disposition toward the learning experience through personal relevance and choice.
- **Enhance meaning.** Create challenging, thoughtful learning experiences that include learners' perspectives and values.
- **Engender competence.** Create an understanding that learners are effective in learning something they value.

It is important to note that these conditions are established collaboratively by the trainer and the learners. Even though the workplace is experiencing a change in what motivates some employees, these are basic enough that I predict they will not change. Note also that these are all intrinsic motivators, even though we can influence all of them externally. Researchers at the Center for Creative Leadership say that external motivation is not bad, but "lack of internal motivation appears to be problematic. Managers who lack internal motivation are likely to have unfavorable job attitudes and may leave the organization" (Cullen-Lester 2016).

Other studies show that what motivates employees on the job has changed dramatically. *The Brain Friendly Workplace* suggests at least four key shifts to consider (Garms 2014):

- The definition of the employee contract has changed to be virtually unrecognizable and nonexistent.
- Personal satisfaction is driven by different factors.
- Managerial demographics have shifted to younger and less experienced.
- Increasing performance is almost entirely dependent on employee motivators.

Even though these all relate to on-the-job motivation, you should extract assumptions for motiving your learners.

Many studies conducted around motivation in learners have found that it is influenced by personality traits and openness to the experience. Motivation to learn can be enhanced by organizational and supervisory support: Adults have a higher motivation to learn when they see the training content is related to their jobs. Eduardo Salas and colleagues (2012) state that "motivation to learn matters, before, during and after training and it should be promoted throughout the learning process." Sounds like another dose of Malcolm Knowles to me and it's great to have confirmation.

Remember that self-determined motivation (whether a consequence of values or pure interest) leads to better long-term outcomes than controlled motivation (Davis and Middleton 2006). Data gathered from a report by the Corporate Learning Consortium asked, "What motivates you to learn online?" Respondents could select two options and the results were (Jennings, Overton, and Dixon 2016):

- 76 percent want to do their job faster and better.
- 75 percent learn for their own personal development.
- 60 percent want to increase their productivity.
- 47 percent want to keep up with new technology.
- 42 percent are motivated by working toward professional certification.

Each of these instances should be tempered by the fact that the world is changing, the workplace is changing, employees are changing, and motivation is in the process of evolving.

Based on my experience, the first step toward motivation is helping learners understand "what's in it for me." Jennifer Hofmann (2006) agrees in her e-book *101 Tips to Motivate the Online Learner*. She states: "In order for online learning to be successful, we need to create environments in which people can effectively learn. Motivation often comes down to answering the question, 'What's in it for me?'"

Attend to answering that question, "What's in it for me?" If there is nothing that will help learners solve a problem or make their work faster or better, you have a difficult task ahead of you. On the other hand, once you are over that hurdle (and perhaps there wasn't one) you can use all the other ideas presented in this book to maintain motivation: respect your learners, allow maximum participation, provide options, build community, create active learning, stretch through games, add a dose of novelty, individualize the learning, encourage learning through mistakes, and create an experience—not just a training session.

Cost of Not Training

Every organization steps back on occasion to explore whether it is doing the best job it can to develop the talent that is so critical for success. It is likely that a discussion about cutting back on training or even not providing any training may arise.

What is the cost of not training? Well let's start with my perspective: Training is not a cost. It's an investment. Does it matter what we pay for an investment? What's relevant is the ROI—what we get in return. One of the best ways to jeopardize an organization's future and increase the probability of difficulty is to look at training as a cost and pay the price of not training or providing substandard training.

"What's worse than training your workers and losing them? Not training them and keeping them."

—Zig Ziglar

Sometimes the argument is that once employees are trained, they will leave for a better paying job. Another excuse for not training is that there isn't enough time. Consider that if an employee takes a day to attend training and learns something that saves an hour per week, it takes only eight weeks to recoup the time. That means the ROI for that single training session approaches 600 percent for the year. Sometimes speaking in terms of the return on investment helps to make the case.

Lack of training can cause an increase in staff turnover and the costs associated with bringing in new employees, decreased morale and engagement, and lower profits and reduced productivity. Training and retaining employees is less expensive than hiring new employees. Trained employees work smarter. There are many ways to examine the cost of "not doing training," but I am sure you can see that one of the biggest drawbacks is having an organization of employees who have not reached their full potential. Organizations must invest in employees to be successful.

What We Know for Sure

Science tells us that we can rely on several proven facts:

- Learning must be aligned to the organization for success.
- Skilled employees are a strategic part of an organization's performance.
- Organizations whose learning strategy is aligned to organizational requirements are more agile and competitive (ATD 2016).
- Only 31 percent of organizations have well-developed learning cultures.
- Multiple changes in the future require attention to the brain-friendly workplace.
- Motivation requires four conditions created by the trainer and learners: inclusion, attitude, meaning, and engendered competence.
- Motivation expectations are changing with the youngest workforce.
- There is a cost to not training.

The Art Part

Your success will depend upon how well you adapt to the situation and your learners' needs. Tap into some of these ideas to help your learners grow, to develop yourself, and to add your personal creative touch.

Questions for learning. Help your employees make the switch to a more self-directed learning strategy. Suggest that they use three questions to begin their individual development plan:

- What do I need to support my success right now?
- What do I need to develop in my current role?
- What do I need to grow in my career?

Interview the C-suite. You may wish to interview the members of your C-suite, asking questions such as:

- What do you see changing in our future that may require changes in our processes?
- What does being in a culture of learning mean to you?
- How can we help you now? In the future?

Motivate online. Download *101 Tips to Motivate the Online Learner*. Challenge yourself to implement at least five new motivational strategies in your next online class.

Art and Science Questions You Might Ask

These questions provide potential challenges for your personal growth and development:

- What is the best way for your organization to start to link the learning strategy with your organization's requirements?
- Are you able to clearly articulate the critical priorities to which your company is committed over the next three years?
- Does your team know the key metrics of your business success?
- Can you articulate the capabilities required of your leaders over the next three years?
- How well do current courses align with strategic priorities?
- Can you measure the impact of learning activities against the strategic business goals?
- How well have you involved key stakeholders in developing and championing your development plans?

- How have you linked instructional design to the strategic priorities?
- What organizational "pattern" (the way we've always done it) do you need to challenge?
- How brain friendly is your organization? How do you address change?
- How can you learn more about what to expect in your workplace in the future?
- Intrinsic motivation seems to be the winner for success on the job and long-term results, so how can trainers influence it?
- Do you know what motivates your staff to learn?
- Do you know how you can better motivate your participants to learn?

How Do You Align Learning With Organizational Requirements?

Aligning learning with your organizational needs requires everyone to be on board. It is not an undertaking for the faint of heart. As you embark on this journey, remember to examine what you will start doing and what you will stop doing. Recognize that you will meet challenges along the way regarding "the way we've always done it around here." Pay attention to new workplace challenges and what's motivating to help guide your process. Also remember that nothing was ever learned that was easy. You will have stops, starts, restarts, and failures. Making changes in an organization mirrors some of the changes you go through as you learn.

Resources

ATD. 2016. *Building a Culture of Learning: The Foundation of a Successful Organization.* Alexandria, VA: ATD Press.

ASTD and PMI. 2014. *Managing the Learning Landscape.* Alexandria, VA: ASTD Press.

Bersin, J. 2016. *Predictions for 2016: A Bold New World of Talent, Learning, Leadership, and HR Technology Ahead.* New York: Deloitte Development.

Biech, E. 2010. *The ASTD Leadership Handbook*. Alexandria, VA: ASTD Press.

——. 2012. *Developing Talent for Organizational Results: Training Tools From the Best in the Field*. Hoboken, NJ: John Wiley & Sons.

——. 2014. *ASTD Handbook: The Definitive Reference for Training and Development*. 2nd ed. Alexandria, VA: ASTD Press.

Cullen-Lester, K., M. Ruderman, and B. Gentry. 2016. *Motivating Your Managers: What's the Right Strategy?* Greensboro, NC: Center for Creative Leadership.

Davis, K., A. Winsler, and M. Middleton. 2006. "Students' Perceptions of Rewards for Academic Performance by Parents and Teachers: Relations With Achievement and Motivation in College." *Journal of Genetic Psychology* 167(2):211-220.

Garms, E. 2014. *The Brain-Friendly Workplace: 5 Big Ideas From Neuroscience That Address Organizational Challenges*. Alexandria, VA: ASTD Press.

Hofmann, J. 2006. *101 Tips to Motivate the Online Learner*. East Lyme, CT: InSync Training.

IBM. 2014. "The Value of Training: Building Skills for a Smarter Planet." Somers, NY: IBM Corporation.

Jennings, C., L. Overton, and G. Dixon. 2016. "70+20+10=100: The Evidence Behind the Numbers." *Towards Maturity*, February 2. www.towards-maturity.org/article/2016/02/02/in-focus-702010-100-evidence-be-hind-numbers.

Robinson, D., and J. Robinson. 2008. *Performance Consulting: A Practical Guide for HR and Learning Professionals*. 2nd ed. San Francisco: Berrett-Koehler.

Robinson, D., J. Robinson, J. Phillips, P. Phillips, and D. Handshaw. 2015. *Performance Consulting: A Strategic Process to Improve, Measure, and Sustain Organizational Results*. 3rd ed. San Francisco: Berrett-Koehler.

Salas, E., S. Tannenbaum, K. Kraiger, and K. Smith-Jentsch. 2012. "The Science of Training and Development in Organizations: What Matters in Practice." *Psychological Science in the Public Interest* 13(2): 74-101.

Wlodkowski, R. 2003. "Fostering Motivation in Professional Development Programs." *New Directions for Adult and Continuing Education*, 2003(98):39-48.

Why Bother With Assessment and Evaluation?

Needs assessment? Analysis? Why bother? It seems like a lot of work. It takes too much time. I don't know how to design a needs assessment. Evaluation? Smile sheets? Reaction forms? Happy sheets? Whatever they are called. Aren't they under attack by the performance people? Who needs that trouble? I don't have time. My supervisor doesn't support evaluations. There are so many obstacles that get in the way of even the best intentions of evaluating training.

Whoa! Hold that thought. Let's look at assessment, evaluation, and the relationship between the two. Then we'll determine if we should bother or not.

What's a Needs Assessment?

A needs assessment usually starts the training cycle and planning to determine needs or gaps between the current and the desired condition. (Remember the discussion of the training cycle in chapter 1?) In a training setting it generally refers to a gap in employee performance. It does not necessarily mean that training is the solution. A needs assessment is an effective tool to clarify problems and even identify solutions.

Controversy arises when it is called a training needs assessment. Some believe that adding the word *training* diminishes the value of the needs assessment because it assumes a desired solution (Triner, Greenberry, and Watkins 1996). I don't know about you, but the artist in me refuses to get hung up on a word. If the assessment shows the gap can't be closed with training, then address the real problem.

The classical approach is to determine the discrepancy between the desired and actual knowledge, skills, and performance using a variety of methods, including interviews, observations, questionnaires, and tests. These methods involve gathering, analyzing, verifying, and reporting data. The discrepancy may translate into a training need or lead to something else. For example, a needs assessment in human performance improvement is used to discover needs related to performance issues, such as processes, resources, or organizational structures. A front-end needs assessment serves several purposes:

- It places the training need or request in the context of the organization's needs. Training adds value when it serves a business need.
- It validates or dispels the initial issues presented by a sponsor. Although sponsors and clients know the business, they don't always know the cause of or the remedy for issues that involve human performance.
- It ensures that the ultimate training design supports employee performance and thereby helps the organization meet its needs.
- It results in recommendations regarding nontraining issues that may be interfering with the achievement of desired organizational and employee goals.
- It establishes the foundation for back-end evaluation.

Needs assessment may occur at three levels: organizational, task, and individual.

- An organizational assessment evaluates the level of organizational performance. It may determine the skill, knowledge, and attitude needs of an organization. It also identifies what is required to alleviate an organization's problems and weaknesses, as well as enhance strengths and competencies. Organizational assessments consider factors such as changing demographics, political trends, technology, or the economy.

- A task assessment examines the skills, knowledge, and attitudes required for specific jobs and occupational groups. It identifies how and which occupational discrepancies or gaps exist, as well as examining new ways to do work that could fix those discrepancies or gaps.

- An individual assessment analyzes how well individual employees are doing a job and determines their capacity to do new or different work. It provides information on which employees need training and what kind.

PLAN YOUR NEEDS ASSESSMENT

Ask questions that will provide the best information. Determining what questions to ask is one of the most important considerations you have when conducting a needs assessment. Start with the end in mind—what do you want to accomplish. In doing so, think about results at the higher levels that are more costly and strategic, as well as what is of interest to the organization and management (Phillips and Phillips 2016). Consider these questions as you plan your needs assessment:
- Who is being trained? What are their job functions?
- Are they from the same department or from a variety of areas or locations in the organization?
- What are the deficiencies? Why has this occurred? What is it costing the organization or the department?
- What kind of data do you need?
- What are the backgrounds and educational profiles of the employees being studied?
- What do employees expect? Desire? What do managers expect? Desire?
- What are you trying to accomplish with the needs assessment?
- How will the results of the needs assessment benefit the organization?

> ## PLAN YOUR NEEDS ASSESSMENT (CONT.)
>
> - What are the expected outcomes? What effect will these outcomes have on which organizational levels?
> - Which data gathering method will work best: questionnaires, surveys, tests, interviews?
> - Who will administer the assessment—in-house or external consultants?
> - Will the analysis interrupt work processes? What effect will this have on the workforce and productivity?
> - What is the organizational climate?
> - Will there be a confidentiality policy for handling information?

There isn't much controversy about conducting needs assessments. You will of course want to ensure that your instrument is reliable and valid. And quite honestly, I don't spend too much time worrying about that unless I need the analytics for another comparison or use. Use common sense.

ADDIE: A to E

ADDIE, A to E, or is it? We typically think of the acronym to represent analysis, design, development, implement, evaluate. That puts evaluate at the end—the last thing we think about. Absolutely not!

Although evaluation is the final step in ADDIE, in actuality, it starts the design and delivery process. That's because it provides the details that allow you to establish goals and continuously improve the training session. Knowing how participants have been affected by the training program gives you the data necessary to determine what worked, what didn't, and what changes may be necessary to be more effective. Anyone will tell you that you need to establish goals so you can measure results. That means you'd better put it up front so you know the goal. I believe that "evaluate," the E, belongs in every step.

- **In analyze:** Clarify the goal; the business result requires evaluation.
- **In design:** Determine which questions will be useful to evaluate each level.
- **In development:** Validate and evaluate instructional plans.

- **In implement.** Evaluate at Level 1 and at times Level 2, along with ongoing evaluations.
- **In evaluate.**

What would a new model with this much emphasis on evaluation look like? $A_eD_eD_eI_eE$. Evaluation should be in your hip pocket ready to grab throughout the entire process.

The Evaluation Process

How clear is your organization about the value of evaluation? It certainly isn't due to a shortage of information or models. Books are published every year. Conferences always feature evaluation topics and niche conferences. Articles are written (and we presume read), classes are taken, and electronic resources are searched. What's the problem? Evaluation needs to become an integral part of the training cycle. The information must be seen as an important part of the process. No matter where your organization stands in the evaluation debate, as a trainer and facilitator you can do your part to disseminate information about its importance.

Your plan for evaluation should begin soon after the needs assessment is complete. Specifying evaluation criteria is straightforward; the primary training needs are used to identify both class objectives and training outcomes (Goldstein and Ford 2002).

The Beginning of Evaluation for Training

In November 1959, Don Kirkpatrick wrote and published articles about evaluation based on his PhD dissertation in the *ASTD Journal*. He described evaluation in four words, currently referred to as the Kirkpatrick Four Level Evaluation Model: Reaction, Learning, Behavior, and Results. He emphasized that all four levels are important, especially if the purpose of training is to get better results by changing behavior. In their book *Implementing the Four Levels*, Don and his son Jim write about the "importance of evaluating the four levels, or as many as you can" to "build a compelling chain of evidence of the value of learning to the bottom line." They emphasize the importance to present the value of training in a way to "maximize the meaningfulness to the hearts and minds of your internal stakeholders," (Kirkpatrick and Kirkpatrick 2006). A vast majority of organizations use the Kirkpatrick model today (Salas et al. 2012).

In the 1970s Jack Phillips wrote his original work on training evaluation. He called for the training community to move beyond Level 4 to include a financial accounting of program success, return on investment (ROI). ROI shows the monetary benefits of the impact measures compared to the cost of the program. The value is usually stated in terms of either a benefit-cost ratio (ROI is a percentage), or the time period for payback of the investment. One of the advantages of ROI is that it can more readily demonstrate how training supports and aligns with the organization's business needs.

The Value of Evaluation

Evaluation is important, it takes time, and it is essential. Professional trainers build in time to measure results to ensure everyone in the training program knows what needs improvement, what kinds of assistance participants may need after they return to their jobs, and what obstacles still exist that prevent transfer of training. So what are the four levels?

- **Level 1: Reaction**—Learner attitudes toward the training opportunity, such as a satisfaction with involvement or what was learned.
- **Level 2: Learning**—Knowledge and skills learned, such as being able to state best practices or having new skills for tasks on the job.
- **Level 3: Behavior**—Changes in execution and implementation of skills learned and practiced on the job.
- **Level 4: Results**—Quantifiable results that demonstrate the impact training has on the organization.

Expanding the Four Evaluation Levels

Don Kirkpatrick's original work has evolved into the New World Kirkpatrick Model, which Jim and Wendy Kirkpatrick (2016) published in *Kirkpatrick's*

Four Levels of Training Evaluation. The revised Kirkpatrick model incorporates a return on expectations and emphasizes identifying results (Level 4) up front, and underscores the need to focus on the collective efforts of the training department, supervisors, and senior leaders to accomplish return on stakeholder expectations. The process provides indicators of value through a holistic measurement of both qualitative and quantitative measures from a program or initiative, with formal training typically being the cornerstone.

To achieve return on expectations, learning professionals must ask questions to clarify and refine the expectations of key business stakeholders and convert those expectations into observable, measurable business or mission outcomes. Focusing on return on expectations is like turning the Kirkpatrick model on its head, because you need to ask questions and start with Level 4 first. These questions might include:

- What will success look like to you?
- What will participants do with what they learn?
- How will this training effort affect our customers?
- What impact will participant development have on our bottom line?
- How will you know we are achieving the goal?
- What is your goal?

In addition, the New World Kirkpatrick Model emphasizes the need to partner with supervisors and managers to encourage them to prepare participants for training and to play a key role after training by reinforcing the learned knowledge and skills. You also identify indicators that the training is achieving the objectives. It is understood from the beginning that if the leading indicator targets are met, the initiative will be viewed as a success. These steps are all completed during your design.

For example, if your company was providing training for sales staff, you might ask these questions:

- What skills do you want employees to perform?
- What desired outcomes should the company see due to these new skills?

- What indications will you have that the new skills will produce the results you desire?
- What will your customers experience based on these new skills?
- What data will you use for these measures?

These sample indicators could be used at each of the four levels.

Level 1: Reaction

At Level 1, you would determine whether:

- Participants are satisfied with the relevancy of the training.
- Participants believe the training program covers the required objectives.
- Participants agree the trainer encourages participation and questions.
- Participants want more opportunities to role play.

Level 2: Learning

At Level 2, you would determine whether:

- Participants are able to state the features and benefits of the company's top-selling products.
- Participants are able to use research results to reinforce benefits.
- Participants can demonstrate how to quickly bridge from their opener to the main topics of the sales call.
- Participants know the difference between fact questions and priority questions.

Level 3: Behavior or on-the-Job Application

At Level 3, you would determine whether participants can:

- Describe how a product meets a specific need.
- Establish rapport with customers during their sales calls.
- Plan their use of visuals prior to sales calls.
- Use more open questions than closed questions in their sales calls.

Level 4: Business Results

At Level 4, you would determine if:

- Participants have increase sales each week by at least 2 percent over a four-week period.
- Customers have reported increased satisfaction with the service received from representatives.
- Participants are making more sales calls than in previous weeks.
- Customer retention has increased by 10 percent over the prior year.

A thorough evaluation of your training program might involve all four levels. Each level of evaluation has value in its own right, but it is the combination of evidence that truly assesses how effective the training has been.

"Logic will get you from A to B. Imagination will take you everywhere."

—Albert Einstein

More About Evaluation

Is your training evaluation guided by what matters or by what is easiest to measure? As you examine the four levels of evaluation in more detail, think about what you should be measuring at each level.

Level 1: Reaction

The most common kind of training evaluation is Level 1. It is easy, fast, and inexpensive when compared to evaluation efforts at other levels. When your program has ended, you will naturally want to find out if the training met the participants' expectations. Try to obtain a picture of participants' reactions to the training program as a whole, as well as a sense of their response to the various parts. What questions might you ask?

- Rate the following on a 1-5 scale:
    a. I feel prepared to use what I learned.
    b. The program was relevant to what I need on the job.
    c. The training program has motivated me to implement what I learned.

    d.   The program achieved the stated objectives.

    e.   The trainer encouraged participation and questions.

- What did you find most useful in the program?
- What do you still need to be successful on the job?
- What suggestions do you have to improve this program?

Evaluate Yourself With the 4 Cs

Evaluating you and your results helps you determine whether you are doing your job (Silberman and Biech 2015). When evaluating learning and development opportunities, I believe you can use the 4 Cs to evaluate how well you are doing.:

- **Competence.** Do you deliver content in a way that ensures their competence?
- **Commitment.** Do you inspire commitment to return to the job and implement what was learned?
- **Confidence.** Do you instill confidence in them so they will be successful?
- **Customer Service.** Do you satisfy the learner and your client?

Translating the 4 Cs

The first one is easy and logical. We are supposed to improve our learners' knowledge, skills, and attitude. That's competence. But if we do not also increase learners' commitment to change and confidence that they can change, they will not implement the new skills, performance will not change, and everything will remain the same. You must provide enough influence that the participant will return to the job and put into practice the skills and knowledge that were delivered during the learning session. Do the following example questions evaluate the 4 Cs?

    a.   I feel prepared to use what I learned (competence and confidence).

    b.   The program was relevant to what I need on the job (customer satisfaction).

c. The training program has motivated me to implement what I learned (confidence and commitment).

d. The program achieved the stated objectives (customer satisfaction).

e. The trainer encouraged participation and questions (engenders confidence).

Think about the 4 Cs when you design your Level 1 evaluation process.

Level 2: Learning

Besides finding out how participants viewed the training program, you need to know what knowledge, skills, and attitudes (KSAs) they acquired. The most common way to measure learning is the use of tests. However, it's not easy to construct a test that is both reliable and valid: A reliable test is one that gets similar results time after time. A valid test measures what it purports to measure and not something else. So, take time to get feedback about your test items and pilot them before using them with your actual participants. With the objectives of active training programs in mind, be sure to go beyond testing factual recall. See if participants can state the information in their own words, give examples of it, and apply it in a variety of situations. Without this information, it is impossible to determine whether the training achieved real learning as opposed to memorization.

To further substantiate that test results prove that learning occurred, it is desirable (although not always practical) to test participants' KSAs before the training begins as well as after. This gives you a baseline that makes it easier to state the changes that occurred as a result of the training program.

In addition to testing, you can obtain evidence that learning has taken place by doing any of the following:

- Performance on job-relevant tasks at the end of the training program, usually involving in-basket exercises, games, or case studies.

- Interviewing participants to see how they would respond to job-related problems.

- Assignments that require participants to integrate what they learned.

Don't overlook the value of asking participants directly about what they learned and how it will be applied. Self-report does not constitute proof but it provides some indication that learning occurred. The simplest approach is to use a questionnaire or interview to ask participants questions such as:

- What tools, skills, or ideas do you now have that you did not have at the beginning of this program?
- What have you learned that you can put to immediate use?
- What have you already practiced outside the session?
- What intentions or plans do you have as a result of the program?
- What do you want to learn next?

Level 3: Behavior

The easiest way to assess whether your training led to on-the-job application is to survey or interview participants once they return to their jobs. Questions to consider include:

- How have you used the things you learned in the training program?
- How has the training program helped you perform better at work?
- What specific steps can you take to continue or improve the use of the skills and knowledge you learned from the training program?

Although self-reports of participants may have value, there is every reason to confirm that participants are actually doing what the training objectives were seeking. Post-training performance may be evaluated by observing their actual job performance or obtaining feedback from supervisors or other key people, such as customers. You can try a procedure that combines participant self-report and supervisory feedback. You might do this by asking participants to complete a follow-up form at the end of a program that contains statements about how they plan to implement the training. Then, in three to four weeks, send another follow-up form to participants and their supervisors for evaluation. Level 3 data can also be obtained by:

- performance appraisals of participants
- on-site observation of sample participants on the job

- checklists of key behaviors that are completed by unbiased observers
- interviewing supervisors.

Examples of Level 3 measures, listed by Barksdale and Lund (2004), include:

- process measures (for example, participants follow a new business process back on the job)
- productivity measures (for example, participants' errors are reduced)
- cost measures (for example, participants identify methods to reduce costs)
- revenue measures (for example, participants increase their referrals to other products)
- safety measures (for example, participants follow safety procedures).

One of the challenges of Level 3 evaluation is to provide evidence that the participant's behavioral changes were a result of the training program and not the results of other factors. This is difficult to "prove." However, if this is a requirement for you, consider the following questions in a Level 3 study:

- How many people were in the study? (The more people involved in the study, the more confidence in the results.)
- Was there a control group? (If people who were not involved in the training program also changed, the training program may not have been necessary.)
- How large was the performance improvement? (Small changes in behavior may not warrant the time and expense of the training program.)
- Was the improvement sustained? (Behavior occurring immediately after the training may not continue several months later.)

Level 4: Results

Assessing the business results of training may be the most difficult to do. Level 4 evaluation may require time-consuming activities, such as focus groups, strategic interviews, and observation. However, if you use the New World

Kirkpatrick Model, your stakeholder will tell you what "results" they expect. It could include things such as a reduction in turnover in a specific department, increase in sales, or decrease in absenteeism. In addition to asking for stakeholder expectations, data may already exist in your organization. Consider these sources of data:

- employee engagement surveys
- organizational and team morale scores
- number of customer complaints
- employee retention; lost time
- sales revenue
- cost per sale
- safety ratings
- customer service ratings
- work flow and efficiency data
- awards from outside sources
- operating costs
- compliance versus violations
- accuracy studies
- consistency
- product defects.

These data sources influence the organization's bottom line by increasing sales, profits, revenues, market share, and so forth, but also affect organizational effectiveness indicators such as employee morale. The danger of the bottom-line definition of impact is the tendency to reduce everything to financial terms, which may trivialize many nonfinancial but important measures.

Of course, evidence from these kinds of Level 4 data doesn't constitute proof that the training was responsible for organizational results. If you are using an ROI model you will also use control groups. Evaluation guru Jack Phillips recommends additional alternatives such as trend-line analysis; participant, supervisor, and expert estimation; or input from customers and subordinates (Phillips and Phillips 2016b). The more evidence you provide, the more clout your Level 4 or ROI claims will have.

Return on expectations emphasizes that formal training events by themselves do not deliver significant bottom-line outcomes. It does not emphasize using estimates, assumptions, or empirical financial formulas to try to isolate the effects of training. However, it does acknowledge that the results always come from a variety of factors, and if you do not measure and know which factors aided in the transfer of learning to behavior and subsequent results, you will not be able to take any credit for the success. The return on expectation method does not attempt to isolate outcomes related to training, but it does place an emphasis on validating that the transfer of learning to on-the-job behavior is related to training.

ROI

Typically ROI objectives set the acceptable level of monetary benefits versus costs of the program. They may be expressed as a return on investment percentage, a benefit-to-cost ratio, or a time for payback. Examples of ROI include (Phillips 2016):

- Achieve at least a 20 percent return on investment within the first year.
- Achieve a 2:1 benefit-cost ratio.
- Realize an investment payback within six months.

Finally, remember that for trainers, evaluation of a training program is not only about outcome but also about process. Evaluation efforts should address what is happening in a training program as much as whether that program is making any difference. Why is process evaluation so important? Quite simply, without good records of what happened during a training program, it is not always clear what needs to be changed if the evaluation outcome is disappointing. Try to keep a log of the events during the learning program, how participants responded, and your own reactions. Or invite others to observe the training session and make observations about the program as it is being experienced. By doing so, you will be an active participant in your program.

The Purpose of Evaluation

I listed several purposes of assessments earlier in this chapter; now let's examine potential purposes of evaluation. To increase the impact of training evaluation practices, clarify the purpose for evaluation and tailor subsequent decisions about what and how to evaluate the training (Salas et al. 2012). Identifying the purpose of the evaluation increases the likelihood that data will be accepted, eliminates wasted time, and increases the acceptance of training in the organization. The purpose of evaluation is likely to include several of these:

- Determine business impact, the cost-benefit ratio, and the ROI for the program: What was the shift in the identified business metric? What part of the shift was attributable to the learning experience? Was the benefit to the organization worth the total cost of providing the learning experience? What is the bottom-line value of the course's effect on the organization?

- Improve the design of the learning experience: Evaluation can help verify the needs assessment, learning objectives, instructional strategies, target audience, delivery method, and quality of delivery and course content.

- Determine whether the objectives of the learning experience were met and to what extent: The objectives are stated in measurable and specific terms. Evaluation determines whether each stated objective was met. Nevertheless, knowing only whether objectives were met isn't enough; a practitioner must know the extent to which objectives were met. This helps focus future efforts for content reinforcement and improvement.

- Determine the content's adequacy: How can the content be more job related? Was the content too advanced or not challenging enough? Does all of the content support the learning objectives?

- Assess the effectiveness and appropriateness of instructional strategies: Case studies, tests, exercises, and other instructional strategies must be relevant to the job and reinforce course content. Does the instructional strategy link to a course objective and the course content? Is it the right instructional strategy to drive the desired learning or practice? Does the strategy fit with the organization's culture? Instructional strategies, when used as part of evaluation, measure the KSAs the learning experience offers.
- Provide feedback to the facilitator: Did the facilitator know the content? Did the facilitator stay on topic? Did the facilitator provide added depth and value based on personal experience? Was the facilitator credible? Will the evaluation information be used to improve the facilitator's skills?
- Give participants feedback about what they are learning: Are they learning the course content? Which parts are they not learning? Was there a shift in knowledge and skills? To what extent can participants demonstrate the desired skills or behavior?
- Identify the KSAs being used on the job: What parts of the learning experience are being used on the job? To what extent are they being used?
- Assess the on-the-job environment to support learning: What environmental factors support or inhibit the use of the new knowledge, skills, attitudes, and behaviors on the job? These factors could be management support, tools and equipment, or recognition and reward.

Training Was a Success—or Was It?

Evaluation data provide a great deal of information, but can't tell you everything. For example data can tell you if participants learned the content, but cannot tell you whether they were encouraged to implement the content on the job.

Will Meets Level 1

Rumblings about the limitations of the smiley sheet have been making headlines for years. It appears that there are three specific concerns by those who are opposed to using Level 1 evaluations, which include:

- We don't measure the actual performance (Shrock and Coscarelli 2007).
- Level 1 evaluations are typically completed at the end of the class, when the Ebbinghaus forgetting curve is at its peak, suggesting that learners are at their peak performance. Certainly this is not where they will be after going home and on to work the next day. (See the sidebar on page 233.)
- Scientific research conducted by two separate teams in 1997 and 2008 showed that there is no correlation between the responses on Level 1 evaluations and learning results (Alliger et al. 1997; Sitzmann et al. 2008). Nor were Level 1 evaluations good predictors of future performance.

In his book, *Performance-Focused Smile Sheets: A Radical Rethinking of a Dangerous Art Form*, Will Thalheimer (2016) addresses smiley sheets head-on and declares all-out war on them. He is accurate in stating his observations. And I do agree I've seen some pretty bad Level 1 and Level 2 evaluations. But that's the designer's fault—not the fault of the model. Thalheimer also tries to make a case for what he calls a "Performance-Focused Smile Sheet."

However, it's important to recognize that Level 1 evaluations were never intended to measure or even predict performance. If they were, they would be called "Performance," but instead they are called "Reaction." Creating an evaluation step to predict performance is a great idea, but let's use Level 1 to evaluate exactly what it was intended to measure—learners' reactions.

Could Level 1 evaluation be improved? Yes, but let's not create something for which it was never intended to be used. Instead, perhaps another level should be added—Level 1.5?

THE FORGETTING CURVE

The problem is no surprise to you. Participants forget information they have been exposed to during your training experiences. This dilemma was hypothesized and studied by German psychologist Hermann Ebbinghaus in 1885. He discovered that information is exponentially forgotten from the time learners consume it. The graph shows how rapid this loss occurs (Ebbinghaus 1964; Loftus 1985).

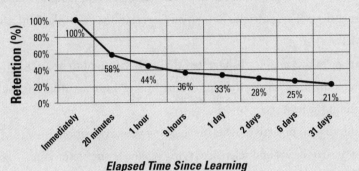

Elapsed Time Since Learning

Testing or Examining—What's the Difference?

In their book *Telling Ain't Training*, Harold Stolovitch and Erica Keeps (2011) discuss the difference between tests and exams in one of their chapters. Since this is closely related to Level 2 evaluation, here are a few highlights:

- The word *test* creates stress for both high and low performers. Try to avoid it and use *practice check* or *game* instead.
- Testing is a natural part of training because learners want to try out new skills.
- To make testing most successful, deliver feedback with the results.
- Frequent testing or verification is best. It increases attention, engages the learner, and consolidates learning.
- Start with the performance objective for any test item.
- Use written or oral tests for declarative knowledge; use performance tests for procedural knowledge.

Tests, or shall I say practice checks, are a great way to learn.

The Art of Using Evaluation Results

Evaluating what you do is critical, but it doesn't always happen. As a professional, you have a responsibility to build evaluation into every training event. You need to measure results at every point and design evaluation at the beginning. Pair evaluation measures during design and development using both quantitative measures (Kirkpatrick's Four Levels or Phillips's ROI) and qualitative measures (Kirkpatrick's Return on Expectations or Brinkerhoff's Success Case Method).

Earlier in this chapter I suggested that ADDIE ought to be $A_eD_eD_eI_eE$. You can model the need for continuous evaluation by implementing some of these throughout the process:

Refer to your objectives when developing your evaluation.

- Learn the art and science of tying results to the bottom line.
- Share results with your clients and your participants.
- Use a flipchart for a quick evaluation at the end of a short session— draw a large T-grid with the words *works well* on one side and *need to improve* on the other side. Then ask for ideas from your participants.
- Allow for anonymity to get the most honest answers.
- Keep a copy of your evaluations. Use the ideas and suggestions they contain to improve your future performance and program designs.
- Pilot all tests prior to using them with participants.
- Meet with supervisors following the training to determine how much of the learning was transferred to the workplace.
- Work with key leaders to identify how training affects the bottom line.
- Consider conducting a focus group with key supervisors if a training session will be repeated. It can tell you what skills seem to be transferring to the workplace and which ones are not.

Investment in training is assumed to have positive returns. The evaluation of training is inherently a good thing, but how can you be certain that the investment of training dollars is a wise decision? Can you clearly define the return on investment? Actually, you can't. Allocating funds for training in comparison to other investments is often done on quasi-faith. Yes of course, employees must be developed. They must learn new skills and improve performance. But when tight budgets are at stake, the lack of an exact science makes it difficult to invest money in training and development. One study states that research and analysis regarding the cost analysis for training is effectively absent (Fletcher and Chatham 2010).

Tying It Together

I started this chapter with a discussion of assessment. Assessment and training evaluation should be tied together. A critical purpose in evaluation is to determine whether learning objectives (based on the assessment) were achieved. Even more important is to determine whether accomplishing the objectives resulted in enhanced performance on the job. Since learning is usually multidimensional, including KSAs, determining whether objectives were achieved usually requires different types of measures (Kraiger 2002; Kraiger et al. 1993).

As I suggested earlier in this chapter, an effective design is one that considers the role of evaluation in every ADDIE step. Following a needs assessment, identify both training objectives and evaluation criteria (Goldstein and Ford 2002).

One final word: When designing your evaluation, use precise affective, cognitive, and behavioral measures that reflect the intended learning outcomes (Salas et al. 2012). Coming full circle, these should be based on the objectives as a result of your needs assessment.

What We Know for Sure

Science tells us that we can rely on several proven facts:

- Kirkpatrick's Four Levels of Evaluation is the model that is used more often than any other.
- Needs assessments and evaluation processes should be linked.
- The four levels each evaluate a different set of expectations.

- Start with Level 4 to measure return on expectation and get buy-in from stakeholders.
- Tests are a good way to learn and remember content.
- Controversy over evaluation will most likely always exist.
- Identifying the purpose of the evaluation increases the likelihood that data will be accepted, eliminates wasted time, and increases support of training in organizations.
- The best results occur when you use needs assessment data to develop both objectives and evaluation criteria that are related.
- Success is more likely if your evaluations are written using precise, cognitive, and behavioral measures that reflect the training objectives.

The Art Part

Your success will depend upon how well you adapt to the situation and your learners' needs. Tap into some of these ideas to help your learners grow, to develop yourself, and to add your personal creative touch.

Survey monkey. Consider asking participants to download an evaluation while in the session and email it to you. Keep in mind, however, that there are two drawbacks to doing so. Emailing responses decreases anonymity. And waiting until after the session will dramatically decrease the number of responses you receive—often by more than half—unless there is a reward for completing it. ATD holds participants' certificates until after the evaluation has been completed. If you prepare ahead of time you could email everyone in the session a link to a provider such as SurveyMonkey, which eliminates the issue of anonymity.

Obtain feedback along the way. You may not want to wait until the end of your session to learn about your participants' needs and satisfaction. Design your training program to obtain feedback and data on an ongoing basis so you can make adjustments before it is too late. Even observing participants' behavior gives you clues about their satisfaction. Do they smile? Do they seem alert? Involved? Do they ask questions?

Behavioral barometers. Behavioral cues are often good evaluation barometers; however, they give you incomplete feedback. You could fill in the gaps by guessing how the participants think and feel, but although these guesses might be accurate, they may be influenced by your fears (if you are anxious) or your ego (if you are too confident). Verifying your impressions is the only way to obtain accurate and detailed feedback.

Add the range. The next time you average scores on your Level 1 evaluations, be sure to add the range to show the high and the low spread of numbers.

Art and Science Questions You Might Ask

These questions provide potential challenges for your personal growth and development:

- Are your training evaluation results linked closely to business results?
- How well are you meeting your customers' expectations?
- How informed are your senior level managers about the results your department achieves?
- When doing a needs assessment, identify the advantages and disadvantages for conducting it in-house or using a consultant from the outside.
- How well do your evaluations measure what your organization requires?
- What data do you have that measures your value to the organization?
- How many of the questions on your Level 1 evaluation will be used to make decisions?
- What can you measure to demonstrate that learning has occurred?
- What kinds of measurement will show that behaviors have changed on the job?
- What kinds of information will your stakeholders want to see that demonstrates the effectiveness of training?

Why Bother With Assessment and Evaluation?

When done right, the planning for a needs assessment and evaluation begin about the same time. The evaluation systems currently used are constantly under fire. Despite developments in evaluation theory and practice, many models still rely on judgments. Both needs assessments and evaluation are viewed as less objective and not as value-free as we would like (McNamara, Joyce, and O'Hara 2010). Why bother? Well, until a better solution comes along, the system can still address our needs:

- Level 1, Reaction as an immediate customer satisfaction. There is plenty of research that says we need to motivate, build relations, and meet the learners' needs. That deserves reaction time.
- Level 2, Learning to ensure that knowledge and skills were gained. Remember that you need to go beyond delivering competencies. You need to deliver a heathy dose of commitment and confidence too.
- Level 3, Behavior that shows there was a performance change. We are concerned that the learners are making changes on the job after the session ends.
- Level 4, Results demonstrating a business impact. This is the information your stakeholders care about.
- ROI for those few times when you are measuring a key or long-term project and you need to have more exact numbers—a return on the investment.

It's up to you to ask the right questions.

Perhaps we do need a new process. As I was expanding what I already knew about evaluation, I came across a new 10-step model. Just what this fast-paced, complex, uncertain world needs—more complexity and more to do! Perhaps you will create a new system. And if you do, I challenge you to keep it practical, useful, simple, and functional.

Resources

Alliger, G., S. Tannenbaum, W. Bennett, H. Traver, and A. Shotland. 1997. "A Meta-Analysis of the Relations Among Training Criteria." *Personnel Psychology* 50:341-358.

Barksdale, S., and E. Lund. 2004. "How to Differentiate Between Evaluation Levels 3 and 4." In *Training and Performance Sourcebook,* edited by M. Silberman. Princeton, NJ: Active Training.

Biech, E. 2008. *ASTD Handbook for Workplace Performance.* Alexandria, VA: ASTD Press.

———. 2014. *ASTD Handbook: The Definitive Reference for Training and Development.* 2nd ed. Alexandria, VA: ASTD Press.

Brinkerhoff, R. 2003. *The Success Case Method.* San Francisco: Berrett-Koehler.

———. 2006. *Telling Training's Story.* San Francisco: Berrett-Koehler.

Ebbinghaus, H. 1964. *Memory: A Contribution to Experimental Psychology.* New York: Dover (Originally published, 1885).

Fletcher, J.D., and R.E. Chatham. 2010. "Measuring Return on Investment in Military Training and Human Performance." In *Human Performance Enhancements in High-Risk Environments,* edited by J. Cohn and P. O'Connor, 106-128. Santa Barbara, CA: Praeger/ABC-CLIO.

Goldstein, I., and J. Ford. 2002. *Training in Organizations: Needs Assessment, Development, and Evaluation.* 4th ed. Belmont, CA: Wadsworth.

Kirkpatrick, D., and J. Kirkpatrick. 2006. *Evaluating Training Programs: The Four Levels.* 3rd ed. San Francisco: Berrett-Koehler.

Kirkpatrick, J., and W. Kirkpatrick. 2016. *Kirkpatrick's Four Levels of Training Evaluation.* Alexandria, VA: ATD Press.

Kraiger, K. 2002. "Decision-Based Evaluation." In *Creating, Implementing, and Managing Effective Training and Development: State-of-the-Art Lessons for Practice,* edited by K. Kraiger, 331-375. San Francisco: Jossey-Bass.

Kraiger, K., J. Ford, and E. Salas. 1993. "Integration of Cognitive, Skill-Based, and Affective Theories of Learning Outcomes to New Methods of Training Evaluation." *Journal of Applied Psychology* 78:311-328.

Loftus, G.R. 1985. "Evaluating Forgetting Curves." *Journal of Experimental Psychology: Learning, Memory, and Cognition* 11(2):397406. doi:10.1037/0278-7393.11.2.397.

Mager, R.F., and P. Pipe. 1997. *Analyzing Performance Problems.* 3rd ed. Atlanta: Center for Effective Performance.

McNamara, G., P. Joyce, and J. O'Hara. 2010. "Evaluation of Adult Education and Training Programs." In *International Encyclopedia of Education*, edited by P. Peterson, E. Baker, and B. McGraw. Duzel, E. 2006. "Novelty Aids Learning." www.physorg.com/ news73834337.html. Dublin City University.

Phillips, J., and P. Phillips. 2016. *Real World Training Evaluation: Navigating Common Constraints for Exceptional Results.* Alexandria, VA: ATD Press.

Phillips, P. 2010. *ASTD Handbook of Measuring and Evaluating Training.* Alexandria, VA: ASTD Press.

———. 2016b. *Handbook of Training Evaluation and Measurement Methods.* 4th ed. New York: Routledge.

Pollock, R., A. Jefferson, and C. Wick. 2014. *The Field Guide to the 6Ds: How to Use the Six Disciplines to Transform Learning Into Business Results.* San Francisco: John Wiley & Sons.

Salas, E., S. Tannenbaum, K. Kraiger, and K. Smith-Jentsch. 2012. "The Science of Training and Development in Organizations: What Matters in Practice." Psychological Science in the Public Interest 13(2): 74-101.

Schacter, D.L., D. Gilbert, and D. Wegner. 2011. *Psychology.* 2nd ed. New York: Worth Publishers.

Shrock, S., and W. Coscarelli. 2007. *Criterion-Referenced Test Development: Technical and Legal Guidelines for Corporate Training.* 3rd ed. San Francisco: Wiley & Sons.

Silberman, M., and E. Biech. 2015. *Active Training: A Handbook of Techniques, Designs, Case Examples, and Tips.* Hoboken, NJ: John Wiley & Sons.

Sitzmann, T., K. Brown, W. Casper, K. Ely, and R. Zimmerman. 2008. "A Review and Meta-Analysis of the Nomological Network of Trainee Reactions." *Journal of Applied Psychology* 93(2):280-295.

Stolovitch, H., and E. Keeps. 2011. *Telling Ain't Training*. Alexandria, VA: ASTD Press.

Thalheimer, W. 2016. *Performance-Focused Smile Sheets: A Radical Rethinking of a Dangerous Art Form*. Minneapolis: Work-Learning Press.

Triner, D., A. Greenberry, and R. Watkins. 1996. "Training Needs Assessment: A Contradiction in Terms." *Educational Technology* 36(6):51-55.

Watkins, R., M. Meiers, and Y. Visser. 2012. "A Guide to Assessing Needs: Tools for Collecting Information, Making Decisions, and Achieving Development Results." Washington, DC: World Bank.

Science or Art? How Do You Ensure You Are the Best?

Earlier in this book I mentioned that you need to instill competence, confidence, and commitment in your learners. You read that training usually focuses on competence, but without commitment and confidence it is less likely that behaviors will transfer to the workplace. Well here is part two: You *also* need to exude these three. This chapter will help you review your actions and offer suggestions for your professional development.

Individuals are taking more responsibility for their development; this is a trend in our field that is expanding. What could you do to give your competence, confidence, and commitment a boost? How can you develop professionally to ensure that you are the best? This chapter provides ideas and guidance:

- Are you competent in all areas of design and delivery of training? Do you deliver content in a way that ensures their competence? Do your learners trust that you are capable?
- Are you committed to your learners? Are you committed to being the best that you can be in all your training sessions? Do you inspire commitment in your learners so that they want to return to the job

and implement what was learned? Do your learners see that you are conscientious?

- Are you confident in your own skills? Do you instill confidence in your learners so they will be successful? Can you convince your learners about their ability to use skills and knowledge to improve their own performance?

This chapter is much less about science and more about the art of your personal development. It's about addressing how you can cope with the VUCA world we've discussed in this book.

Are You Competent, Committed, and Confident?

What sets average trainers apart from experts? Behaviors, skills, and actions that you might not expect. Being an expert—a consummate professional trainer—goes way beyond writing a perfect objective, designing a motivating activity, or delivering flawless content. Although I can't provide a formula for how to model excellence, light fires in others, or make it safe to confide in you, I can offer you some ideas for what you need to know and do to begin your journey.

This chapter will move you well on your way to being considered an expert facilitator, with suggestions for how to improve your competencies, how to build your confidence, and how to demonstrate commitment.

Improve Your Competence

Do you conduct the ultimate learning experience every time? We all want to but for many reasons it doesn't work out that way. May I challenge you to boost your competence as a designer or trainer? Consider some of these suggestions.

Let the ATD Competency Model Be Your Guide

Dig into The ATD Competency Model, which provides a strategic model for the profession and is a good place to start. The Model enables individuals to align their work with organizational priorities, and provides a comprehensive view of the profession by defining various areas of expertise.

Having a defined set of competencies is a hallmark of any profession. In simple terms, this is what those in the profession collectively need to know and do to be successful. The Model, shaped like a pentagon is composed of two layers of competencies: foundational competencies and areas of expertise.

Figure 12-1: The ATD Competency Model

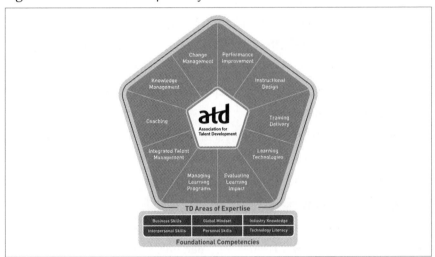

Foundational Competencies

Foundational competencies underlie the successful completion of many tasks, and are, therefore, found at the base of The Model. The Model defines each of the 19 foundational competencies, provides examples of key actions that are included in each, and groups them into six clusters (ATD website 2013):

- **Business skills:** The training profession continues to strengthen its role in the boardroom. With that role comes an expectation of business skills. The Model includes six business competencies: analyze needs and propose solutions; apply business skills; drive results; plan and implement assignments; think strategically; innovate.

- **Global mindset:** The training profession must adapt to the increased globalization of businesses. This includes six competencies:

accommodate cultural differences; convey respect for different perspectives; expand own awareness; adapt behavior to accommodate others; champion diversity; leverage diverse contributions.

- **Industry knowledge:** The training profession often must know other industries or industry sectors. This includes three competencies: maintain own professional knowledge; keep abreast of industry changes and trends; and build industry sector knowledge.

- **Interpersonal skills:** The Model identifies five interpersonal competencies: building trust; communicating effectively; influencing stakeholders; networking and partnering; and demonstrating emotional intelligence.

- **Personal skills:** The Model identifies two personal competencies: demonstrating adaptability and modeling personal development. These two should not come as a surprise, given the emphasis of both throughout this book.

- **Technology literacy.** The Model identifies two overarching technology literacy competency: demonstrating awareness of technologies and using technology effectively.

As a training professional you will want to create learning opportunities to upgrade your own knowledge and skills. You must also be in a continuous learning mode for two reasons: first to serve as a role model; second because training and development must stay ahead of and on top of new developments in the training profession and the industries we serve.

Areas of Expertise

Areas of expertise are the specific technical and professional knowledge and skills required for success in the training and development field. They comprise areas of specialization for the field. Although some professionals are highly specialized and involved in one or two areas, many people aspire to be generalists who can demonstrate deep expertise in more than one area. The ATD Competency Model identifies 10 areas of expertise:

- change management
- coaching
- evaluating learning impact
- instructional design
- integrated talent management
- knowledge management
- learning technologies
- managing learning programs
- performance improvement
- training delivery.

The foundational competencies and areas of expertise provide a model for understanding the requirements of the profession. Among other things, The ATD Competency Model can be used to guide your career planning decisions. You can use The Model as a guide to evaluate your areas of expertise and determine what areas to focus on for your professional development. Step back and take stock of where you are and where you want to be. Determine some measure of success, drive a stake in the ground, and head for it. You can establish measures that include both knowledge and skills. Next, identify a developmental plan for continued growth—even consider certification.

Learn More About How We Learn

There's a huge surge in cognitive science, sometimes erroneously called neuroscience. I've incorporated several of the terms and concepts throughout this book, but there is still much more to learn. You can start by becoming comfortable with the language and how our brain works. With 50 to 100 billion neurons, our brain is fascinating. Learn about the parts of the brain such as the cerebellum, hypothalamus, and amygdala; or the chemicals that affect our brains, such as dopamine, cortisol, or serotonin; or even the brain's processes, such as encoding or retrieval. It is even more valuable for you to know how you can use cognitive science to improve your training efforts. Start with these quick examples (Jensen 2008; Medina 2008):

- Chunk content to prevent information overload.
- Space content over time to improve long-term memory and overcome the forgetting curve.
- Test to spark retrieval and increase memory and what is to be remembered.
- Writing helps learners organize and remember more of the important things.
- Move to stimulate the brain.
- Novelty catches your learners' attention.
- Stimulate all the senses, especially visual, to encourage learning.
- Challenge learners around difficult concepts to enhance learning.
- Practice to remember.
- Mix it up is a relatively new concept (add it to your watch list) called "interleaving"; mix topics up instead of mastering one skill at a time.

Tap Into Theories and Models of the Profession

This book touches upon some of the foundational concepts of the training profession, such as understanding the theories and what they tell us about the rationale for best practices. There are many, but the sidebar offers several for you to start with.

Practice to Be a Consummate Facilitator

As a trainer, you will encounter every kind of mind-set in your training session. Some participants will view training as punishment for some unknown offense; others will already "know" everything and defy you to teach them. Some will bring the baggage of a bad junior high experience, as if that bad report card arrived yesterday. Still others will bring daily burdens with them, both personal and work related.

When you prepare to help these folks, remember that your role as a trainer goes much further and deeper than just getting through the content for the day. You have an opportunity to make a difference—a big difference—in their lives. On the days that you make a difference to just one person, you will feel the magic and the power of training. Those are the days that are the most rewarding. A consummate facilitator creates an atmosphere that addresses everyone's needs.

THEORIES AND MODELS THAT UNDERPIN BEST PRACTICES

This chapter is presented to help you take personal responsibility for your professional development. One important step you can take is to learn more about the theories and models that form the foundation of our profession. This knowledge gives you a leg up to better understand the science, and provides you with a rationale to apply your art to the design and delivery of learning:

- Bruner's Scaffolding
- Vygotsky's Zone of Proximal Development
- Bandura's Social Learning Theory
- Keller's ARCS Model of Motivational Design
- Maslow's Hierarchy of Needs
- Elaboration Theory
- Kolb's Experiential Learning
- Dick and Carey Model
- Kemp's Instructional Design Model
- Merrill's First Principles of Instruction.

Make It Safe to Learn

Creating a safe haven for learning begins with you. One of the key reasons that you invest so much time in preparation is so you can be certain that the various training elements are aligned and working in concert as best they can. That frees you up to attend to your participants and address their needs. Chapters 2 and 6 present some ideas, and here are a few more:

- Touch base with participants prior to the session, stating the purpose and objectives of the training session.
- Greet participants as they arrive, learn their names, welcome them to the session, and find out something about them.
- Inform participants about what's in it for them.

- Respect each and every participant—even the difficult ones.
- Use names and sincere reinforcement.
- Ensure confidentiality about what is discussed and what occurs in the training session.
- Let them in on who you are—not just your credentials, but who you are as a person.

Create an Engaging Learning Environment

An engaging learning environment is one in which learners want to participate and get involved. Here are a few things you can do to create an engaging learning environment:

- Allow the group to contribute ideas about the direction of the session. This participant-driven technique allows participants to take ownership of the session. Yes, you still need to teach the things that are required, but you can usually do that within the expectations of the group. Chances are they will identify topic areas that match the objectives. If not, a bit of subtle direction from you can reshape the expectations. And if it is a single participant's need, such as a problem with a boss, you can always offer to discuss the topic at a break or after the session.
- Identify novel ways to get and keep a group involved. I assume that you already have a training design that is customized for the group, activity-oriented, experiential, creative, fun, fast-paced, varied, and participative. You can always have a couple of quick ideas up your sleeve that boost motivation.
- Encourage learners to ask questions at any time and use a "parking lot" faithfully for questions that need to be answered later.
- Watch behavior and behavior changes during the session. If an active participant becomes withdrawn, you need to check it out. Never hesitate to pull people aside and ask if you said or did something that upset them. Chances are that you have not. It may be a personal

issue, a headache, or a boss who continues to text emergency messages. But you will make an impression with the person that you care, which is key to creating an environment that is conducive to learning. And in the off chance that you did actually say something that was misconstrued and upset the person, your actions provide an opportunity for you to right the wrong.

Participant engagement and involvement is key to successful training. A huge part of this is the trainer's facilitation skills and the creation of a safe and engaging learning environment.

Exude Enthusiasm

Your enthusiasm will take you a long way. Love what you do. Love the participants. Love the materials. And if you don't love it all, you need to look like you do! Your enthusiasm is the secret sauce to training success. It will be the launching pad for your participants to want to listen, learn, participate, and make the desired changes based on the training you deliver. You should inspire hope, energy, and excitement about the future. However, never confuse enthusiasm with entertainment, funny stories, jokes, or silliness. Enthusiasm is passion for what you do, commitment to whom you do it for, and confidence in how you do it.

I am passionate about learning and development. And yes, some days I have more enthusiasm than others. I'll bet you have days like that too. Even so, you owe it to your participants to give every session everything you have. Self-talk works well for me: "This will be the best darn training these participants have ever experienced!" Here are a few other ways that help me rejuvenate myself when I need it:

- Even though the topic is not new to you, it is new to the participants. Remembering that they may be hearing the information for the first time is exciting. Think about how exciting it will be for them to experience this topic. Determine how to have more participant involvement.

- Do something that is out of the ordinary: if you are showing a video, serve popcorn; ask participants to use crayons for a particular activity; hold the discussion outside on a nice day; turn the facilitation over to a participant in a virtual setting.
- A day before the session, examine the part of the program you dislike the most. Chances are it never was right for you. Rework that part so that it eliminates why you don't like it. In my case it would be identifying a way to increase participation.
- Download the free ATD Trainers' Tool Kit App for new ideas. It offers more than 50 free traditional classroom and virtual training activities you can use in your sessions.
- Experiment with activities you have not used before, such as funneling, an in-basket, or a relay.
- Try a new presentation technique or media; for example, use a related TEDTalk or conduct a debate.
- Invite a guest speaker to conduct the part of the workshop that is most energy draining for you.
- Find cartoons or quotes that relate to the session and introduce them after breaks or as energizers.
- The night before the session pull out your smile file, which is filled with thank-you cards, fabulous evaluations, special notes, cartoons that make you laugh, clippings, or articles about you. Spend 20 minutes looking through it. What? You don't have a smile file? Better start one today!

Go the Extra Mile

Go the extra mile? Gosh! Isn't conducting a great training session, creating a safe and engaging environment, and exuding enthusiasm enough? Well, being good at what is in your job description is only the beginning. You still need to search for ways to improve your learners' experience and your organization's results. There will be times when your participants ask questions that can't be answered during the training session due to either a lack of time or because you don't have the necessary resources. This is a great opportunity for you to go the extra mile. Here are three ways to support your participant following the training session:

- Find an article, highlight the pages that answer the participant's question, and deliver it in person with a verbal explanation.
- Find a video that answers the question, share the URL with the participant, and relate the information to his situation.
- Introduce the participant to a subject matter expert who can provide an explanation and additional resources.

Take time and continue to learn. If you don't devote time to improve your skills, who will?

"You have brains in your head,
You have feet in your shoes.
You can steer yourself
Any direction you choose."

—Dr. Seuss

Build Confidence

Confident people have an aura about them that makes others want to be part of what they are doing. They are admired by and inspire confidence in others. According to the Mayo Clinic, low self-esteem affects almost every aspect of our lives (Neff, Ya-Ping, and Dejitterat 2005). I am certainly no confidence expert, but I find a few things to be helpful. Think of self-confidence as something you can develop if you practice every day. It starts with knowing everything there is about your profession. Nothing builds confidence like knowing your stuff, having a positive mindset, and being prepared and ahead of change. I addressed improving competencies already, so let's begin by examining mindsets.

Mind Your Mindset

Your learners are the foundation to a successful mindset. The most important thing to remember is to put learners first. Of course you will need to ensure that the design and delivery is what is best for them. But this mindset goes beyond your learners, to the attitude you have toward your job, your organization, and the changes occurring around you. Your professional mindset must include the outlook you have about the rest of the world. Face each day with a positive attitude, make and keep commitments, be authentic and approachable, and look out for your colleagues. This mindset brings out the best in you and your learners. Your expertise will shine through if you have a positive mindset that reflects the importance of what you do.

"Optimism is the faith that leads to achievement. Nothing can be done without hope and confidence."

—Helen Keller

Stay Ahead of Change

One of the best ways to boost your confidence is to have a plan about the future. Develop your skills and knowledge to maintain your place on the cutting edge. By doing so, you are providing the kind of developmental opportunities your employer and participants expect and deserve. Staying in touch with the changes and the excitement of the profession will keep you enthusiastic and passionate about what you do. For example, are you prepared for learning in the future? Try imagining learning where:

- the classroom goes to the learner
- learning is there when you need it
- you have personally curated content
- all learning is individually customized and on-demand
- each element of learning is life-long focused
- learning occurs in an "augmented reality"

- smartphones move to a heads-up display and then to the "chipped" person
- interaction occurs in holographic rooms
- you introduce *Star Trek*'s holodeck and transporter.

We live in exciting times in this profession. Changes are happening rapidly that force us to stay ahead of them. It makes our jobs challenging and thrilling. What can you do now to prepare for the future?

- Recognize that your development is your responsibility.
- Create an individual development plan (IDP) that is linked to your organization's strategy.
- Build a professional learning network (PLN) using social networks such as LinkedIn, Facebook, and Twitter.
- Participate in MOOCs or other events to get experience.
- Take an active role in an online community, perhaps become a community manager.
- Invest time to reflect on the work you do and what you are learning.
- Model good social work behaviors for the rest of your department or organization.
- Help others in your organization develop their individual development plans.

Have confidence in your ability to support your learners now and in the future. If you don't believe in you, who will?

Demonstrate Commitment

Commitment is a pledge that binds you to completing an action or reaching a goal. Whether in your professional or personal life it is a fundamental principle of success. Total commitment can be difficult, but think of one commitment you've made. It can go way beyond this chapter, but to get started, I'd like to suggest that you begin with commitment to your organization, your profession, and to your own lifelong learning.

Lead Your Organization

What does your organization need and how can you support it? Right now your organization probably needs help in answering the many questions about talent development. How can we increase the quality of informal leaning? How can learning analytics help me? How can we best use mobile learning technology for our employees? What are we going to do about developing our leaders? Your commitment starts with taking the lead to find out what's most important to your organization and how you can help.

Start by obtaining a copy of your organization's strategic plan and business plan. Read through them and tie what you do to them. Identify your contribution to the organization's success. Go the extra mile and get copies for your training colleagues and start a discussion at your next staff meeting about how your department could do more to contribute to the organization's success.

Help your colleagues see that the emphasis is moving from classroom and e-learning training to blended, social, and collaborative learning. Think of your own job as more of an internal consultant than a trainer.

Review chapter 10 and follow up with some of the resources included there. Learn how you can help align learning to your organization's requirements. Take a leading role to ensure your relevance, too.

Give Back to the Profession

Training is a profession that gives a great deal to its members. Think about how you can give back to the profession, your community, and individuals. Throughout your career you have most likely received support from others. Now it is time to give back; here are some ideas to get you started:

- Volunteer your services to a government, civic, or non-profit organization.
- Volunteer to serve on a committee for your professional association.
- Speak at a local ATD chapter meeting.
- Write an article for a training journal.
- Mentor someone new to training.

- Volunteer to speak to your local school or community college.
- Send a thank-you card to someone who has contributed to the profession.
- Start a scholarship fund.

Giving back to the profession is good for the soul. Find a way to commit today.

Be a Lifelong Learner

This chapter is intended to move you toward being an expert trainer. Take a moment to think about your expertise. Who will evaluate whether you are an expert trainer? Your supervisor will rate your performance, certainly. But the true evaluators are your learners. How they see you is critical to how much they learn and what they put into action upon returning to the workplace.

Becoming a lifelong learner isn't new to our profession—in fact, we invented the idea. Have you ever thought about all the skills in which you need to be proficient? I sometimes get exhausted just thinking about everything I need to do my job. This is what makes the job so exciting, but it is also what necessitates us to become lifelong learners.

I once read that most people achieve only a third of their potential. Successful professionals in any position achieve much more than a third of their potential because they continue to learn and grow. What do lifelong learners do?

- They assess where they are compared with where they want to be and determine a plan to get there.
- They improve their processes continuously by identifying new ways that are better and more efficient, and implementing them.
- They are on the cutting edge of their industry trends. They are aware of the state-of-the-art practice and the fads of the day; have knowledge of the training gurus and their philosophies; interact with professional organizations; and read the journals and newsletters that help them stay abreast of the field.

- They understand the basics of the job and how to implement them in today's world. They are steeped in the history, research, and models that provide the foundation of our work.
- They are in the know about their customers (internal and external). They keep up-to-date about all the things that are important to their customers.

Ask yourself how you stack up against these five qualities of lifelong learners. Remember this is an investment in you. If you won't invest in you, who will?

Yes, it takes a great deal to be your best: competencies, confidence, commitment. But, you can do it! Be all the things that you are capable of being.

"If we did all the things we are capable of, we would literally astound ourselves."
—Thomas Edison

Go ahead. What's stopping you? Astound yourself. Find the passion in your life. Trainers need to have a spark because we light fires for so many others. Love what you do and do what you love.

What We Know for Sure

Science tells us that we can rely on several proven facts.

- Mentoring works to help you become your best.
- ATD can provide information to improve your knowledge and skills.
- Networking with other trainers is an important social learning activity (20 percent) based on the 70-20-10 framework.
- Co-facilitating and providing feedback to one another is a way to learn from experience on the job (70 percent) based on the 70-20-10 framework.
- Reading this book and attending a train-the-trainer or facilitation workshop are ways to learn formally (10 percent) based on the 70-20-10 framework.

- The world will continue to change; you need to change with it.
- "Your job" isn't "yours"; it will change. Be prepared.
- You are responsible for your own continuous learning and development to remain marketable.

The Art Part

Your success will depend upon how well you adapt to the situation and your learners' needs. Tap into some of these ideas to help your learners grow, to develop yourself, and to add your personal creative touch.

Kid's dream. Think back to your childhood. What did you want to be? Have you achieved your goal? It's never too late. Make a list of all the things you would like to learn—professionally and personally. And then start learning them!

Go virtual. Attend virtual learning events. Hundreds of virtual learning opportunities are available—both those you can pay for and those that are free. Try one out. You will probably learn something that will help your next customer.

CPLP me. Look into getting your CPLP certification from ATD.

Attend the ATD International Conference & Exposition. All trainers should do this at least once. You will learn a great deal and meet many people to create a valuable network.

Expand your network. Network with other trainers inside and outside your organization. You'll be able to call on them when you have a question.

Mentor me. Find a mentor—today.

Take a class. Enroll in a train-the-trainer course, preferably one in which you are videotaped so you can obtain feedback on your training style.

Try it out. Experiment with activities you've never tried before, perhaps something from one of Thiagi or Mel Silberman's books or the hundreds of other activity books available.

ELA expert. Learn how to conduct a true experiential learning activity.

What's new? Register for monthly or weekly newsletters. Two that I like are produced by Zenger Folkman and the Center for Creative Leadership. There is always at least one idea in every one that makes me a better facilitator.

Maintain enthusiasm. Make a list of everything that inspires and rejuvenates you. Put it where you will see it every day.

Art and Science Questions You Might Ask

These questions provide potential challenges for your personal growth and development:

- How can you evaluate the skills and knowledge you have and compare them to what you still need?
- How might you invest in you—your skills, your knowledge, and your mindset—to better address your important role for your company or your client?
- How can you identify the skills required for building a partnership with the managers and supervisors in your organization?
- How can you do a better job of paying attention to what the participants tell you on the evaluations?
- Be aware of your customers' changing needs. How can you adapt the material and activities to meet their needs?
- Create your professional development plan. It should include short-term objectives, long-term objectives, a specific timeline, and the resources you will need to support you.
- What are you doing to expand informal, social, and on-the-job experiences into your participants' development routine?
- What do you need to do to be a life-long learner?

Science or Art? How Do You Make Sure You Are the Best?

Making sure you are at your best is your job. In the next chapter you will read a prediction from a future-thinker who believes that development will be an individual responsibility. I've always believed that. It's your life. It's your profession. Only *you* can ensure that you grow and develop in a way that is exciting for you and at the same time marketable to a changing world. You must remain:

- Viable
- Upbeat
- Competent
- Agile

You probably recognize the initial letters—VUCA—the volatile, uncertain, complex, ambiguous world we live in. This can be your personal VUCA antidote to ensure that you are the best you can be.

Resources

ATD. 2015. *Learners of the Future: Taking Action Today to Prevent Tomorrow's Talent Crisis.* Alexandria, VA: ATD Press.

Bersin, J. 2016. "Predictions for 2016: A Bold New World of Talent, Learning, Leadership, and HR Technology Ahead." New York: Deloitte Development.

Biech, E. 2009. *10 Steps to Successful Training.* Alexandria, VA: ASTD Press.

———. 2014. *ASTD Handbook: The Definitive Reference for Training and Development.* 2nd ed. Alexandria, VA: ASTD Press.

———. 2016a. *101 Ways to Make Learning Active Beyond the Classroom.* Hoboken, NJ: Wiley & Sons.

———. 2016b. *Training and Development for Dummies.* Hoboken, NJ: Wiley &Son.

Jensen, E. 2008. *Brain-Based Learning.* Thousand Oaks, CA: Corwin Press.

Knowles, M.S. III, E. Holton, and R. Swanson. 2015. *The Adult Learner: The Definitive Classic in Adult Education and Human Resource Development.* 8th ed. Burlington, MA: Elsevier/Butterworth-Heinemann.

Kouzes, J., B. Posner, and E. Biech. 2010. *Coach's Guide to Developing Exemplary Leaders.* Hoboken, NJ: John Wiley & Sons.

Levin, H. 1996. *Innovations in Learning: New Environments for Education.* Mahwah, NJ: Lawrence Erlbaum Associates.

Medina, J. 2008. *Brain Rules: 12 Principles for Surviving and Thriving at Work, Home, and School.* Seattle: Pear Press.

Neff, K.D., H. Ya-Ping, and K. Dejitterat. 2005. "Self-Compassion, Achievement Goals and Coping With Academic Failure." *Self & Identity* 4(3):263-287. doi: 10.1080/13576500444000317.

Rothwell, W., J. Arneson, and J. Naughton. 2013. *ASTD Competency Study: The Training and Development Profession.* Alexandria, VA: ASTD Press.

How Can Training Be Relevant in the Future?

I f I didn't answer your question about either the art or the science of training, it isn't because there isn't enough information. There is so much research available! It would be impossible to read all of it in five years, even if you did nothing else—and by then some of it will have changed, some of the "facts" will have been debunked by another scientist, and technology will have taken us in another direction where it just doesn't matter anymore.

What I tried to do was to present you with the most practical information I could find that was supported by science. And because we deal in change every day, with people who are unique, and in organizations that are changing, I presented options—the art. The artful alternatives are helpful during those times when the science just won't work. People are different, and facilitators need alternatives to ensure that they meet all participants' needs. Remember: It's all about the learner.

The huge number of myths that surround our work often hinder what we learn (DeBruyckere and Kirschner 2015). Myths such as "we are multitaskers" or "we only use 10 percent of our brains" have been with us for a long time. Unfortunately, many of these myths have persisted, and they prevent us from moving ahead. That said, I hope I've provided you with enough "science" to create a solid foundation of facts, and enough "art" to spur you on to do what you need to do for your learners.

"It isn't what we don't know that gives us trouble, it's what we know that ain't so."

—Will Rogers

The Art and Science of Training is a combination of what we know, what we don't know, and what we know that ain't so! It's about recognizing the "right" way and still jogging left when we must. We have the most exciting job in the world. And a part of that excitement occurs because we work with people who are often unpredictable and sometimes difficult. They keep us on our toes professionally.

Up to this point, this book has been about the science of yesterday that brought us to today. But what about tomorrow? What does the future hold for training? Can we stay relevant?

Predictions for the Future

By now most of you are familiar with *VUCA*—the term used to describe the volatile, uncertain, complex, and ambiguous world we are living in today (Johansen 2012). But have you placed yourself in the VUCA world and thought about what it means for you, your work, your department, and your organization?

So where is training heading in the future? We know that the label *training* has become obsolete, even though it was used in the title of this book. The term *talent development* more closely defines what we do today. I certainly do not have a crystal ball, but would like to share some predictions from fellow talent developers.

Nick Petrie (2014), a senior faculty member with the Center for Creative Leadership, cites four things that will change around leadership development:

- More focus on vertical development for how we develop. Horizontal development, or a focus on competencies, has been the focus to date.

The future will be on vertical development stages. The big difference is that horizontal development can be transmitted from an expert, but vertical development is dependent upon yourself. We've focused on the "what" of leadership; we need to shift to the "how" of development.

- Responsibility for development will shift to the individual—people develop fastest when they feel responsible for their own progress.
- A greater focus on collective rather than individual leadership will lead to determining how we spread leadership capacity throughout organizations and democratize leadership.
- A greater focus on innovation in leadership development methods that will not specify a model or a program. We will be experimenting with innovative approaches supported by technology.

In his one-year quest to answer the question, "what will the future of leadership development look like?" Petrie came away with the realization that there is no solution—yet. And it is in this word, *yet*, that he finds an exciting challenge for the future and the exhilarating thought that he is here to help create that solution.

Josh Bersin (2016), a leading provider of research-based HR information, describes the modern learner as distracted, impatient, and overwhelmed. Yet the availability of learning is one of the biggest factors in employee retention and engagement. He envisions that trainers need to begin focusing more on experience and less on design:

- Although formal learning will not end, we need to consider the life today's learners lead and provide learning where it is accessible, when the learner can access it.
- We will need to find untethered, collaborative, and available on-demand delivery mechanisms.
- There is a need for mobile, highly interactive, curated, and recommendation-based approaches to learning.
- "Instructional designers" must become "learning experience designers" who are creating highly engaging end-to-end experiences.

Bersin believes that learning and development needs to build its credibility on deep business expertise and a willingness to own business problems. That actually aligns with the message our profession has been hearing for several years. He also sees the responsibility for the ROI of learning shifting to your organization's people analytics team, which might consist of employees who ensure that data coming into the system is accurate and sanitary; employees who create a taxonomy that organizes the data for analysis; or employees who create sophisticated algorithms and models to predict customer behavior, pricing strategy, or profitable markets.

How Can Training Be Different?

The Bureau of Labor Statistics (2016) reported that the number of people in the United States who are self-employed reached 15.2 million in 2015. By 2020, it is expected that "more than 40 percent of the American workforce, or 60 million people, will be independent workers—freelancers, contractors, and temporary employees" (Fast Company). Increasingly, contractor positions are being held by the best and brightest. *Harvard Business Review* (2012) called this phenomenon "The Rise of the Supertemp."

The January 2016 issue of *TD* included a Gartner Infographic that predicted that by 2018 3 million workers around the world will be supervised by a nonhuman boss and 45 percent of the fastest growing companies will have fewer employees than smart machines. The world is changing as we watch. Think about what you do and the changes occurring today. How do you think the work you do might be different in the near future?

Wearables

Rather than going to the Internet or an app, the information may soon flow directly to your learners. Will technology provide instant skills and knowledge using AI and templates so that learners can be self-taught? YouTube and Siri already provide instant skills and knowledge. Will we even need trainers?

Augmented Reality and Virtual Reality

Virtual reality is an artificial, computer-generated simulation or re-creation of a real-life environment or situation. It immerses the user and trains them by creating a simulation of reality in which people can practice, for example, flight simulators. Augmented reality is a technology that layers computer-generated enhancements on an existing reality to make learning more meaningful through interaction, such as the recent Pokemon Go explosion. How can you use these technologies today? How can you prepare to use them in the future?

Augmented Intelligence

Keep this on your radar. It's different from artificial intelligence in that a computer system supplements and supports human thinking, analysis, and planning. It maintains the human intentionality by focusing on the interaction of humans and computers, rather than on computers alone. Technology can leverage computing power to tackle more information and tasks faster and simultaneously, saving time. But, will it reduce the need for employees? What are the limitations? How could you support this technology?

Independent Contractors

As mentioned, data from *Fast Company* states that by 2020 more than 40 percent of U.S. employees will be consultants, temporary employees, and contractors (2015). If work teams are made up of short-term employees on short-term assignments, what team skills are required? Will the skills be "transportable" (Haskins 2015)? Will team building become part of the past?

Mindfulness

Whether it is the latest long-lasting fad, or something to embrace long term, mindfulness has become a solution to our always-on world. As an example, Aetna estimates that since instituting its mindfulness program it has saved about $2,000 per employee annually in healthcare and gained about $3,000 per employee in productivity. The company now helps other companies implement their own mindfulness campaigns (Gelles 2015). What role do you see mindfulness playing in your organization? What will your role be in that arena?

Resiliency

Agility and resiliency are touted as the keys to successful leadership of the future. Do you know how to practice resiliency? Can you help others? What are you doing to grow your skills and knowledge in this area?

> "In the agricultural era, schools mirrored a garden. In the industrial era, classes mirrored the factory, with an assembly line of learners. In the digital-information era, how will learning look?"
>
> —Lucy Dinwiddie

New Roles

What will we call ourselves? Yes, we will have new roles—some that may only be in the workforce for a short period of time. While we can't predict them specifically, we can have fun imagining what some might be called: talent systems optimizer, experience designer, innovation implementer, corporate coach, engagement planner, opportunity optimist, corporate curator, analytics engineer, or how about a MOOC Master?

We know change is on the horizon. The report *Learners of the Future: Taking Action Today to Prevent Tomorrow's Talent Crisis* recommends that you begin by establishing a baseline assessment of the learning and development function's operational capabilities.

What We Know for Sure

Science tells us that we can rely on one thing for sure:

- The world is changing rapidly and will continue to do so.

The Art Part

Your success will depend upon how well you adapt to the situation and your learners' needs. Tap into some of these ideas to help your learners grow, to develop yourself, and to add your personal creative touch.

Mindfulness. Go online and find resources about mindfulness. Learn all you can about it. How could it fit into your organization?

On my own. Spend time thinking about the adjustment you would need to make if you found yourself in the ranks of the 60 million people who will be working as independents by 2020. What changes will you need to make? What are the pros and cons for this shift in employment?

My future. At your next department meeting discuss the direction your company is moving. Then have everyone make up a title for themselves.

Imagine. Take some time with colleagues or the participants in your next class to brainstorm at least 15 ways learning will occur in 2020.

Art and Science Questions You Might Ask

These questions provide potential challenges for your personal growth and development:

- What is your dream for the future of your organization? For your department? For you?
- What current approaches does your organization use that are the most effective for developing employees?
- What do you think your department should do more of to develop employees?
- What do you think your department should do less of to develop employees?
- How does the concept of a culture of learning, which was discussed in chapter 10, fit with the rest of the discussion in this chapter?
- What new skills is your learning function building in preparation for the future?
- Can you see why the term *employee* could soon be obsolete?

How Can Training Be Relevant in the Future?

It's certain that training will be different in the future. There will not be as much of an emphasis on "programs"; instead "experiences" will be designed for employees. It will be important to help employees learn how to learn, so preparing them to take responsibility for their own development will be necessary. Trainers need to be experts in the essentials that cognitive science has uncovered, such as chunking, spacing, testing, and other techniques that ensure learners learn quickly and retain information longer.

Learners of the Future: Taking Action Today to Prevent Tomorrow's Talent Crisis states that only 38 percent of learning functions are ready for 2020. Is your function ready?

"The Arts and Sciences, essential to the prosperity of the State and to the ornament of human life, have a primary claim to the encouragement of every lover of his country and mankind."

—George Washington

Resources

ATD. 2015. *Learners of the Future: Taking Action Today to Prevent Tomorrow's Talent Crisis.* Alexandria, VA: ATD Press.

Bersin, J. 2016. *Predictions for 2016: A Bold New World of Talent, Learning, Leadership, and HR Technology Ahead.* New York: Deloitte Development.

Biech, E. 2014. *ASTD Handbook: The Definitive Reference for Training and Development.* 2nd ed. Alexandria, VA: ASTD Press.

———. 2016. *101 Ways to Make Learning Active Beyond the Classroom.* Hoboken, NJ: Wiley & Sons.

DeBruyckere, P., and P. Kirschner. 2015. *Urban Myths About Learning and Education.* London: Academic Press.

Gelles, D. 2015. "At Aetna, A CEO's Management by Mantra." New York: *New York Times*, February 27. http://nytimes.com/2015/03/01/business/at-aetna-a-ceos-management-by-mantra.html?_r=0

Greenstone Miller, J., and M. Miller. 2012. "The Rise of the Supertemp." *Harvard Business Review*, May.

Haskins, S. 2015. "Got Transportable Skills and Wanderlust? 5 Locales to Consider." *Wall Street Journal*, July 7. http://blogs.wsj.com/expat/2015/07/07/got-transportable-skills-and-wanderlust-5-locales-to-consider.

Huggett, C. 2013. *The Virtual Training Guidebook: How to Design, Deliver, and Implement Live Online Learning*. Alexandria, VA: ASTD Press.

Johansen, B. 2012. *Leaders Make the Future: Ten New Leadership Skills for an Uncertain World*. San Francisco: Berrett-Koehler.

Kouzes, J., B. Posner, and E. Biech. 2010. *A Coach's Guide to Developing Exemplary Leaders*. Hoboken, NJ: John Wiley & Sons.

Petrie, N. 2014. *Future Trends in Leadership Development*. Greensboro, NC: Center for Creative Leadership.

———. 2015. *The How-To of Vertical Leadership Development—Part 2*. Greensboro, NC: Center for Creative Leadership.

Schrader, B. 2015. "Here's Why the Freelancer Economy Is on the Rise." *Fast Company*. August. www.fastcompany.com/3049532/the-future-of-work/heres-why-the-freelancer-economy-is-on-the-rise.

About the Author

 **Elaine Biech**, president of ebb associates inc, a strategic implementation, leadership development, and experiential learning consulting firm, has been in the field for more than 30 years helping organizations work through large-scale change. She has presented at dozens of national and international conferences and has been featured in publications such as the *Wall Street Journal, Harvard Management Update, Investor's Business Daily*, and *Fortune*. She is the author and editor of more than 60 books, receiving national awards for two of them.

Among her extensive body of published work are many ATD titles, including the flagship publication, *The ASTD Handbook: The Definitive Reference for Training and Development* (2014). Other ATD titles include *Change Management Training* (2016), *New Supervisor Training* (2015), *The Book of Road-Tested Activities* (co-published with Pfeiffer, 2011), *ASTD Leadership Handbook* (2010), *ASTD's Ultimate Train the Trainer* (2009), *10 Steps to Successful Training* (2009), *ASTD Handbook for Workplace Learning Professionals* (2008), and *Thriving Through Change: A Leader's Practical Guide to Change Mastery* (2007).

Elaine specializes in helping leaders maximize their effectiveness. Customizing all of her work for individual clients, she conducts strategic planning sessions and implements corporate-wide systems, such as quality improvement, change management, reengineering of business processes, and mentoring programs. Elaine is a consummate training professional, facilitating training on a wide range of workplace and business topics. She is particularly adept at turning dysfunctional teams into productive ones. As a management consultant, trainer, and designer, she provides services globally to public and private sector organizations to prepare them for current challenges.

A long-time volunteer for ATD, she has served on the association's national board of directors, was the recipient of the 1992 ASTD Torch Award, the 2004 ASTD Volunteer Staff Partnership Award, the 2006 Gordon Bliss Memorial Award. In 2012, she was the inaugural CPLP Fellow Program Honoree from the ASTD Certification Institute. Elaine was instrumental in compiling and revising the CPLP study guides and has designed five ATD certificate programs. She was the 1995 Wisconsin Women Entrepreneur's Mentor Award recipient, has served on the Independent Consultants Association's Advisory Committee, and on the Instructional Systems Association board of directors. Elaine is currently a member of the Center for Creative Leadership's Board of Governors and is Berrett-Koehler's curator for Advances in Leadership and Management library.

Index

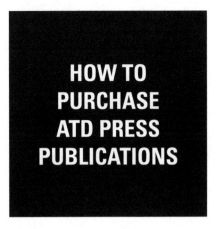

HOW TO PURCHASE ATD PRESS PUBLICATIONS

ATD Press publications are available worldwide in print and electronic format.

To place an order, please visit our online store: www.td.org/books.

Our publications are also available at select online and brick-and-mortar retailers.

Outside the United States, English-language ATD Press titles may be purchased through the following distributors:

United Kingdom, Continental Europe, the Middle East, North Africa, Central Asia, Australia, New Zealand, and Latin America
Eurospan Group
Phone: 44.1767.604.972
Fax: 44.1767.601.640
Email: eurospan@turpin-distribution.com
Website: www.eurospanbookstore.com

Asia
Cengage Learning Asia Pte. Ltd.
Phone: (65)6410-1200
Email: asia.info@cengage.com
Website: www.cengageasia.com

Nigeria
Paradise Bookshops
Phone: 08033075133
Email: paradisebookshops@gmail.com
Website: www.paradisebookshops.com

South Africa
Knowledge Resources
Phone: +27 (11) 706.6009
Fax: +27 (11) 706.1127
Email: sharon@knowres.co.za
Web: www.kr.co.za

For all other territories, customers may place their orders at the ATD online store: **www.td.org/books**.